A'level E

D1756437

This book is due for return on or before

ЅATIRE

What is satire? How can we define it? Is it a weapon for radical change or fundamentally conservative? Is satire funny or cruel? Does it always need a target or victim? Combining thematic, theoretical and historical approaches, John T. Gilmore introduces and investigates the tradition of satire from classical models through to the present day. In a lucid and engaging style, Gilmore explores:

- the moral politics of satire
- whether satire is universal, historically or geographically limited
- how satire translates across genres and media
- the boundaries of free speech and legitimacy.

Using examples from ancient Egypt to *Charlie Hebdo*, from European traditions of formal verse satire to imaginary voyages and alternative universes, newspaper cartoons and YouTube clips, from the Caribbean to China, this comprehensive volume should be of interest to students and scholars of literature, media and cultural studies as well as politics and philosophy.

John T. Gilmore is an Associate Professor in the Department of English and Comparative Literary Studies at the University of Warwick. He teaches, researches and has published on eighteenth-century literature written in English and Latin, the literature and history of the Caribbean, and Translation Studies.

Dixons Allerton Academy

101800

THE NEW CRITICAL IDIOM

SERIES EDITOR: JOHN DRAKAKIS, UNIVERSITY OF STIRLING

The New Critical Idiom is an invaluable series of introductory guides to today's critical terminology. Each book:

- provides a handy, explanatory guide to the use (and abuse) of the term;
- offers an original and distinctive overview by a leading literary and cultural critic;
- relates the term to the larger field of cultural representation.

With a strong emphasis on clarity, lively debate and the widest possible breadth of examples, *The New Critical Idiom* is an indispensable approach to key topics in literary studies.

https://www.routledge.com/literature/series/SE0155

SATIRE

John T. Gilmore

Routledge
Taylor & Francis Group

LONDON AND NEW YORK

First published 2018
by Routledge
2 Park Square, Milton Park, Abingdon, Oxon OX14 4RN

and by Routledge
711 Third Avenue, New York, NY 10017

*Routledge is an imprint of the Taylor & Francis Group,
an informa business*

© 2018 John T. Gilmore

The right of John T. Gilmore to be identified as author of this
work has been asserted by him in accordance with sections 77
and 78 of the Copyright, Designs and Patents Act 1988.

All rights reserved. No part of this book may be reprinted
or reproduced or utilised in any form or by any electronic,
mechanical, or other means, now known or hereafter invented,
including photocopying and recording, or in any information
storage or retrieval system, without permission in writing from
the publishers.

Trademark notice: Product or corporate names may be
trademarks or registered trademarks, and are used only for
identification and explanation without intent to infringe.

British Library Cataloguing-in-Publication Data
A catalogue record for this book is available from the
British Library

Library of Congress Cataloging-in-Publication Data
A catalog record for this title has been requested

ISBN: 978-0-415-48081-9 (hbk)
ISBN: 978-0-415-48082-6 (pbk)
ISBN: 978-0-203-38342-1 (ebk)

Typeset in Times New Roman PS
by Deanta Global Publishing Services, Chennai, India

To the memory of my parents,

Terence James Gilmore
(1916–1998)

and

Kathleen May Gilmore,
née Rowley
(1923–2011)

without whose commitment to my education
this book would not have been possible.

CONTENTS

SERIES EDITOR'S PREFACE

The New Critical Idiom is a series of introductory books which seeks to extend the lexicon of literary terms, in order to address the radical changes which have taken place in the study of literature during the last decades of the twentieth century. The aim is to provide clear, well-illustrated accounts of the full range of terminology currently in use, and to evolve histories of its changing usage.

The current state of the discipline of literary studies is one where there is considerable debate concerning basic questions of terminology. This involves, among other things, the boundaries which distinguish the literary from the non-literary; the position of literature within the larger sphere of culture; the relationship between literatures of different cultures; and questions concerning the relation of literary to other cultural forms within the context of interdisciplinary studies.

It is clear that the field of literary criticism and theory is a dynamic and heterogeneous one. The present need is for individual volumes on terms which combine clarity of exposition with an adventurousness of perspective and a breadth of application. Each volume will contain as part of its apparatus some indication of the direction in which the definition of particular terms is likely to move, as well as expanding the disciplinary boundaries within which some of these terms have been traditionally contained. This will involve some re-situation of terms within the larger field of cultural representation, and will introduce examples from the area of film and the modern media in addition to examples from a variety of literary texts.

PREFACE

This book has been far longer in the making than originally anticipated, and I am especially grateful to John Drakakis, a very prince of editors, and to Polly Dodson at Routledge, for their exceptional patience and understanding.

Susan Bassnett originally suggested that I should undertake the task, and I am grateful to her and to other colleagues, past and present, in both the Department of English and Comparative Literary Studies and the former Centre for Translation and Comparative Cultural Studies at the University of Warwick, for their support and encouragement. Simon Swain's support for a period of study leave was of significant benefit in keeping the project going, and the hospitality of Hamish Adam and Christina Bruce in Dubai enabled me to make real progress with one of the chapters.

John Drakakis made many helpful suggestions during the writing, as did Iman Sheeha شيحا إيمان, who read the entire manuscript. For particular ideas, points of information, or general support, I am indebted to Paul Botley, Wanyu Chung 鐘琬瑜, Maria Cohut, David Dabydeen, Lynn Guyver, Piotr Kuhiwczak, Lynne Long, Maria Petrone, Madeleine Scherer, Christian Smith, Jane Stevenson, David Taylor, Michael Tsang and Chantal Zabus. My wife Marita and our children Alex, Annabelle and Giselle, continue to put up with the peculiar demands of being an academic's family, and Alex in particular has endeavoured to make me more aware of contemporary culture. Another debt is acknowledged in the dedication.

Unless otherwise stated, quotations from the Bible are from the King James Version, and references to Shakespeare are to *The Riverside Shakespeare* (Evans, 1974). Where no particular edition or translation is mentioned, references to classical authors are given in a conventional format which should make them accessible in any standard edition. All unattributed translations are by myself.

Coventry,
May 2017

1

INTRODUCTION

In 1682, Louis XIV (king of France, 1643–1715) granted his official patronage to the leading Jesuit educational establishment in his country, and the Jesuits removed the old name, "Collegium Claromontanum societatis Jesu", from the façade and replaced it with "Collège de Louis-le-Grand". Soon afterwards, it was found that someone had attached a Latin couplet to the main gate:

> Sustulit hinc Jesum posuitque insignia regis,
> > Impia gens, alium non colit illa Deum.

> [Where once the name of Jesus was proclaim'd
> > We see the arms and titles of the king,
> A change by which an impious race is sham'd –
> > 'Tis not another God whose praise they sing.]

As Sigmund Freud pointed out in *Jokes and their Relation to the Unconscious*, a bare statement of facts, however striking or incongruous, does not make a joke. One does not have to accept Freud's sometimes laboured attempts to distinguish between jokes, the comic and humour to agree with his argument that what is needed is what he calls the joke-work, something in the manner in which the joke is expressed which makes it striking and entertaining to listeners or read-ers (Freud, 2001). In other words, the medium is the message. In the same way, a straightforward statement that the Jesuits, in their haste to show their appreciation of royal favour, had acted rather oddly in giv-ing prominence to the king at the expense of the name of the Saviour to whom they owed their own name and ultimate allegiance, would not of itself be satirical. It is made so, however, by being expressed in a strictly regulated verse form which the author has used to good effect: the name of Jesus is emphasised by being placed at the end of the first half of the first line, immediately before the caesura, and is at the same time opposed to the reference to the king at the end of the line, while the subject of the verb in the opening line is postponed until the next, where the phrase *impia gens* ("impious race", ironically referring to the Society of Jesus) is given added emphasis by its appearing at the beginning of the line, and contrasted with *Deum* ("God") at the end. The conclusion manages not only to criticise the Society of Jesus, but also to suggest that Louis XIV had far too high an opinion of himself. The fact that the epigram is in Latin gives a further twist to the knife, as Jesuit colleges generally, and the Collège de Louis-le-Grand in particu-lar, placed great emphasis on training their pupils to write Latin verses. One such pupil indeed turned out to be the author of the epigram, or at least got the blame for it, and was imprisoned in the Bastille as a result. The scandal reached as far as the Netherlands, where the exiled French philosopher Pierre Bayle learnt of the couplet and wanted to know more of the circumstances (Vissac, 1862: 187, 211–212).

This epigram and the circumstances surrounding it bring together a number of points which need to be discussed in any analysis of the nature of satire. In the first place, it raises the issue of the importance of form in relation to satire. Secondly, it shows how satire is dependent, not only on having a target, but also on having an audience. Freud says the same thing about what he calls "tendentious jokes" (that is, jokes which one person tells about another in order to entertain a third person), and draws atten-tion to a passage in Shakespeare which is equally applicable to satire:

> A jest's prosperity lies in the ear
> Of him that hears it, never in the tongue
> Of him that makes it ...
>
> (*Love's Labour's Lost*, V, 2; Freud, 2001: 100, 144)

Satire is only effective if it is perceived by persons other than its author to be such, and responses can change depending on factors such as time and circumstances. The author of the epigram may well have not anticipated the consequences which befell him, which raises a third point about the capacity of satire to provoke strong reactions: the best known recent examples of this are the international controversy which arose in 2005 following the publication in the Danish newspaper *Jyllands-Posten* of a group of cartoons of the Prophet Muhammad which were widely viewed as blaspheming Islam, and the 2015 attack on the offices of the French satirical newspaper *Charlie Hebdo*, which left 12 people dead and another 11 injured. Is anything a suitable topic for satire, or are there limits? To what extent do such limits differ with time and place?

If satire depends on audience response, so too do questions of definition. When, in the first century CE, the Roman teacher of rhetoric Quintilian (Marcus Fabius Quintilianus) claimed that satire was something entirely Roman, that it was the one literary genre for which the Romans owed nothing to the Greeks, he was able to do so because he and his contemporary readers thought of satire as a particular literary form, that is, poems of some length offering social criticism in Latin hexameter verse. This excluded aspects of Roman literature which we might now consider to be satirical, such as many of the epigrams of Martial (Marcus Valerius Martialis, c. 40 – c. 103 CE) and, of course, much else in terms of both earlier and later forms. Nevertheless, as we shall see, Roman views of satire had a significant effect in later periods, and the idea that satire meant formal verse satire was particularly influential in English literature in the seventeenth and eighteenth centuries. As late as 1970, when Arthur Pollard published his volume on *Satire* in the old Critical Idiom series, he could discuss his subject purely in literary terms (or, to be more precise, purely in terms of written literature) and place a major emphasis on authors of the traditional canon such as John Dryden (1631–1700), Jonathan Swift (1667–1745) and Alexander Pope (1688–1744). These are elements which still have to be very much part of the picture, but a modern survey necessarily has to be wider in scope. As Pollard himself put it (22), satire is "a chameleon adapting itself to its environment". For each of us, our ideas of satire are likely to include – but are certainly not limited to – not only satirical verse, but novels, plays, cartoons, cinema films, television programmes and material found online in formats such as social media and YouTube clips. We can make a connection between, say, the eighth satire of the Roman poet Juvenal (Decimus Iunius Iuvenalis), written in Latin verse around the end of the first or the beginning of the second century CE, which ridicules the pretensions of those who vaunt their noble descent while behaving in an ignoble manner, and a YouTube clip of the animated music video of Weird Al Yancovic's song "Weasel Stomping Day" (2006), which uses an imaginary public holiday to satirise the belief that anything can be justified by saying, "It's tradition, that makes it OK". But while we may be willing to accept that both of these are examples of satire, possibly in very different ways, it is harder to define what they have in common, to identify some sort of Platonic idea of satire, an irreducible core which we feel has to be present at the heart of every one of its very different incarnations.

A useful example is the American singer-songwriter Tom Lehrer's "National Brotherhood Week" (Lehrer, 2000). Lehrer was inspired to comment on National Brotherhood Week, an annual event in the United States of America organised by what was then called the National Conference of Christians and Jews, by the fact that the African-American human rights activist Malcolm X had been assassinated on the first day of the Week in 1965. Lehrer's comments that different groups in American society hated each other were, unfortunately, little more than statements of fact, while his suggestion that the attempts to alleviate this situation through something like National Brotherhood Week were simply hypocritical could be viewed as an expression of personal opinion. Several things transform the piece and turn it into something we can recognise as satire. The first is its presentation as a jaunty, upbeat song with piano accompaniment, in a style which deliberately contrasts with the seriousness of the content, while the use of rhyme helps to connect the rapid train of images and thoughts. Second is Lehrer's use of exaggeration and his creation of incongruous and impossible scenarios: while we can accept the idea of at least some people managing to display false cordiality to those they consider their inferiors, as long as it is only for a week, the thought of Lena Horne, the African-American singer and Civil Rights activist, and Jim Clark, the sheriff of Dallas County, Alabama, responsible for violent assaults on protestors during the 1965 Selma to Montgomery marches, "dancing cheek to cheek", clearly belongs only to fantasy – or to satire. Thirdly, there is an element of self-deprecation, also found in different ways in some of Lehrer's other performances, and this helps to draw in the audience, albeit in the manner of a fish being drawn in on a hook. The catalogue of religious groups who hate their traditional opposites ends with Lehrer (himself Jewish, though he once said in an interview that his family's Jewishness was more the Jewishness of the delicatessen than of the synagogue) emphasising that "everybody hates the Jews". The audience applause which can be heard in recordings of Lehrer's performance is perhaps mingled with squirms of uncomfortable self-recognition as he skewers the complacent pieties of would-be liberals:

> Be nice to people who
> Are inferior to you.
> It's only for a week, so have no fear,
> Be grateful that it doesn't last all year.

It is a strategy which does not work in all circumstances: as the character Borat in the 2006 film of the same name, the British comedian Sacha Baron Cohen displays outrageous anti-Semitism. The international Jewish organisation, the Anti-Defamation League, noted in a press release that while Baron Cohen was "himself proudly Jewish", and used humour in the film "to unmask the absurd and irrational side of anti-Semitism and other phobias born of ignorance and fear", they were concerned "that the audience may not always be sophisticated enough to get the joke, and that some may even find it reinforcing their bigotry" (Ynetnews, 2006).

Lehrer's song raises other questions which might come into a more general discussion of satire. On one level, it is very much of its time and place, and the United States of America of the early twenty-first century is a very different place from the USA of the 1960s. Current events often seem to invite satirical treatment, but even extremely successful topical satires can fail to last as the situations which gave rise to them fade from public consciousness. A case in point is provided by the work of John Wolcot (1738–1819), whose verse satires written under the name "Peter Pindar" were enormously popular in the late eighteenth and early nineteenth centuries but which have become virtually unreadable, as even specialists on the period struggle to identify his allusions to contemporary personalities and events. While Lehrer has not performed in public since 1972, audio and video recordings are widely available online and in other formats, and these, together with performances and adaptations of his work by others, have helped to maintain and extend a following. It is the nature of the work itself, however, as much as Lehrer's abilities as a performer, which has ensured its survival. The United States of America has moved on since the Civil Rights era, and National Brotherhood Week itself has not been observed since the 1980s, but racial and religious prejudices are still with us. Nor, of course, are they exclusive to the United States of America: Lehrer's song was adapted for a British television performance in 1974 by Marty Feldman and Derek Griffiths who suggested that, for a British version of National Brotherhood Week, Enoch Powell, the standard bearer of opposition to non-white immigration, would "work the buses blacked up as a Sikh". If we accept that human nature, at least in some respects, is fairly constant, then some manifestations of satire are likely to have an enduring appeal beyond the circumstances of their original creation. Lena Horne and Sheriff Clark are important in the song as types rather than as particular historical individuals, and not that much is lost if the present-day listener is no longer sure of exactly who they were. Lehrer himself replaced them in at least one recorded performance with the famous boxer Cassius Clay (the later Muhammad Ali) and Mrs Wallace (alluding to the wife of Alabama's segregationist governor George Wallace), while the British adaptation of the song by Feldman and Griffiths substituted political opponents Edward Heath and Michael Foot, the then prime minister and leader of the opposition, respectively.

This leads to the issue of whether satire is about individuals or types of human behaviour. This is a question which has been debated since classical antiquity when the Roman poet Horace (Quintus Horatius Flaccus, 65–68 BCE), for example, discussed in his own satires how far and under what circumstances it was legitimate for the satirist to refer to specific persons. For example, he imagines (*Sat.* II, i) a conversation between himself and a well-known lawyer called Trebatius, who reminds him that the Romans had what we would now call a law of libel:

> Si mala conderit in quem quis carmina, ius est
> ludiciumque.
>
> (II. 82–83)

[If anyone writes wicked poems about someone else, there is a law and a court for that.]

Horace had previously claimed that he would not attack anyone in personal terms unless he had been provoked by them:

> at ille,
> Qui me commorit, (melius non tangere, clamo),
> Flebit, et insignis tota cantabitur urbe.
> (ll. 44–46)

[But he who provokes me (it is better to leave me alone, I exclaim) shall weep, and he will be notorious and sung about all over the city.]

How the end of the poem is divided between the two speakers depends on punctuation, which is a matter of modern editorial conjecture, but the point of the conclusion is clear. If the satirist attacks someone who truly deserves it, any lawsuit will be thrown out of court:

> Si quis
> Opprobriis dignum latraverit, integer ipse,
> Solventur risu tabulae; tu missus abibis.
> (ll. 84–86)

[If someone who is himself blameless shall have barked at one who is deserving of reproaches, the case will be laughed out of court, and you will go away dismissed.]

The boundary between satire and invective or personal abuse can be difficult to define, though the attempts of the poet, critic and lexicographer Samuel Johnson (1709–1784) are instructive. In his *Dictionary*, he gives the straightforward statement that satire is "A poem in which wickedness or folly is censured". For modern readers, the insistence on satire as something which takes poetic form is too restrictive, but the idea of censuring folly or wickedness looks as though it has something, at least the kernel of a possible definition of the genre. Johnson does not stop there, however. He elaborates by saying that "Proper *satire* is distinguished, by the generality of the reflections, from a *lampoon*, which is aimed against a particular person [...]" This seems clear enough, but if we turn to the entry for "lampoon", he tells us that this is "A personal satire; abuse; censure written not to reform but to vex". This introduces a new concept, that "proper satire" aims to reform, to bring about change in human behaviour, while a lampoon, or "personal satire", seeks only to annoy its chosen target. Yet if we return to Johnson's original definition, after making the distinction between satire and lampoon, he says "but they are too frequently con-founded" (Johnson, 1755–1756, s.v. "satire", "lampoon"). Not only is it the case that it is hard to draw a definite line between what Johnson here terms "personal satire" and "proper satire", the idea that satire seeks "to reform", while appealing, is open to question. There does not seem to be an enormous difference in this respect between, for example, the poem *On King Charles* by John Wilmot, Second Earl of Rochester (1647–1680), and the same author's *A Satyr against Mankind* (Ellis, 1994, 30, 72–77). The first is certainly a "personal satire" which attacks Charles II for his willingness to allow pleasure, especially sexual pleasure, to distract him from affairs of state, and which does so in obscene detail:

> Nor are his high desires above his strength,
> His sceptre and his prick are of a length;
> And she that plays with one may sway the other
> And make him little wiser than his brother.
> [...]
> Restless he rolls about from whore to whore,
> A merry monarch, scandalous and poor.

Rochester's *Satyr against Mankind*, by contrast, engages in more of a "generality of reflections" on human folly, specifically, the ten-dency to overrate human reason which "makes a mite/Think he's the image of the infinite", and the self-seeking hypocrisy of courtiers and clergymen at the court of King Charles. Even when we allow for the possibility (Ellis, 1994, 358) that the speaker of the poem is actually the "Satyr" of the title, a mythological creature, part man, part goat, who is sometimes associated with the origin of the term "satire" (see Chapter 3), but who is not to be identified with Rochester himself, it seems clear that the poet does not expect his lines to produce any general reformation of human manners, any change in the behaviour of "that vain animal/Who is so proud of being rational". The well-attested story that Rochester only put *On King Charles* into the hands of its subject as a result of mistaking it for another poem when he was drunk, and that he fled the court as a result, suggests that he had no more expectation of changing the behaviour of the individual human animal who was the king. In the same way, readers may well feel that Swift wrote *Gulliver's Travels* (first published in 1726), not because he hoped to change human nature, but because he despaired of it.

Examples of what appears at first to be purely "personal satire" often turn out to be more generally applicable. This is the case with one of the earliest identifiable authors of something which we might now categorise as satire, the ancient Greek poet Archilochus of Paros (seventh century BCE), whose work now survives only in fragments. There is a story which was well known in antiquity, and is referred to in passing by the Roman poet Ovid (Publius Ovidius Naso, 43 BCE–17 or 18 CE), among others, that a certain Lycambes promised one of his daughters to Archilochus in marriage, but then reneged on his promise. Archilochus composed a poem about this, which is said to have attacked Lycambes so savagely that he and his entire family hanged themselves. This makes Archilochus sound like an ancient version of the internet troll, but a modern critic (Carey, 1986) argues that, whatever we may decide about the historicity of the alleged suicides, the surviving fragments can be read as suggesting that Archilochus was using Lycambes as an example to make a more general point about the sanctity of oaths and the inevitability of divine punishment for unjust behaviour. As the Barbadian proverb puts it, it was a case of "God don't like ugly".

Something similar may be happening in the work of the contemporary British cartoonist Steve Bell, whose cartoons of David Cameron (prime minister, 2010–2016) always showed him with a condom over his head, the teat end on top clearly identifying it for what it is. Bell had used consistent visual references for his targets before, such as the way he drew John Major (prime minister 1990–1997) with his underpants outside his trousers, "like a reverse Superman". He has claimed more than once that the condom is simply a reference to the smoothness of Cameron's complexion, but online comments suggest that readers interpreted it as Bell clearly suggesting that he thought of Cameron as a dick, a vulgar term literally referring to the penis, but also expressing contempt for the person referred to (Bell 2013; Slattery 2010). This seems like little more than personal abuse, but Bell can do more subtle things with it. One of his cartoons, for example, shows the then prime minister as Karl Marx, his face almost disguised by the heavy dark moustache and full white beard, but the exaggeratedly high forehead and the fact that the receding line of white hair starts just behind the teat of the condom allow for immediate identification of the subject as another of Bell's representations of Cameron. A speech bubble parodies Marx's famous summary of the ideal to be realised in a higher stage of a communist society ("From each according to his ability, to each according to his needs") by having the Cameron/Marx figure say "From each according to their vulnerability, to each according to their greed" (Bell 2011). As a summary of left-wing criticism of the social policies of the Conservative-Liberal Democrat coalition government led by Cameron, this is pithy and effective, while the visual imagery offers further layers of implied meaning. As a pseudo-Marx, Cameron (and the government he leads) may wish to appear caring, and the cartoon is based on one of the most frequently reproduced photographs of Marx, in which his heavily bearded features could be seen as suggesting a kindly Victorian uncle. Nevertheless, Cameron's being disguised in such a manner suggests the idea of the wolf in sheep's clothing, while the repetition of the condom image offers a cruder and more violent suggestion as to what Bell thinks Cameron is really doing to the more deprived members of British society.

The same use of recurrent imagery to identify the targets of satirical cartoons can be found in other contexts. In 2006, the South African cartoonist Zapiro (Jonathan Shapiro) began to draw the politician Jacob Zuma with a shower on his head, in reference to a much-publicised statement in which Zuma appeared to claim that showering after sex was an adequate precaution against the transmission of HIV (Blair, 2009). Zapiro has continued to deploy this image, even after Zuma became president of South Africa in 2009, in spite of threats of lawsuits. Again, this could be seen as personal abuse, but taken in combination with the fact that South Africa has possibly the highest rate of HIV infection in the world and that there was a history of the government downplaying the seriousness of the problem, it could also be read as symbolising a more general questioning of Zuma's fitness to lead the country.

If some kind of artistic technique, something akin to Freud's joke-work, is needed to turn a statement of fact or expression of opinion into satire, it has to be said that technique of itself is not enough. This is true of caricature, for example, in which one distinguishing feature of the subject is exaggerated to the point of absurdity. This might include cartoonists focusing on the height of former French president Charles de Gaulle (1890–1970), or the allegedly small hands of Donald Trump, or, in literature, a work like Dryden's poem *Mac Flecknoe* (first published 1682), which hammered away at what Dryden claimed was the unrelenting dullness of the work of his contemporary, the poet Thomas Shadwell (c. 1642–1692). As discussed further below with reference to the visual arts (Chapter 8), caricature may be used for satirical purposes, but is not satirical in itself. Similarly, while Bell makes adroit use of parody in the cartoon discussed above, parody is not necessarily satirical. To take a once popular example, the poem *The Splendid Shilling* (1701), by John Philips (1676–1709), is a parody of the style of *Paradise Lost*, by John Milton (1608–1674), which was first published in 1664 and had achieved canonical status by the beginning of the eighteenth century. Philips's poem worked, however, simply because contemporary readers found amusement in the contrast between the deliberately grand style, full of pseudo-Miltonic inversions, Latinised place-names and mythological allusions, and the bathos of this being used to describe the misery of the impoverished poet in his garret, reluctant to venture out for fear of being arrested for debt. There is no sign of any satirical target, and the poem appears to take it for granted that the inconveniences and humiliations attendant on poverty are simply facts of life:

> [...] when Nocturnal Shades
> This World envelop, and th'inclement Air
> Persuades Men to repel benumming [sic] Frosts
> With pleasant Wines, and crackling Blaze of Wood;
> Me lonely sitting, nor the glimmering Light
> Of Make-weight Candle, nor the joyous Talk
> Of loving Friend delights, distress'd, forlorn,
> Amidst the Horrors of the tedious Night,

> Darkling I sigh, and feed with dismal Thoughts
> My anxious Mind; or sometimes mournful Verse
> Indite [...]
>
> (Philips, 1720, 25)

This is in sharp contrast to, say, the way in which Charles Dickens (1812–1870) satirises nineteenth-century British society's relationship to money and the iniquity of imprisonment for debt in *Little Dorrit* (1855–1857) and suggests that poverty is a problem which society needs to deal with. In the same way, not all comic songs – not even all comic songs by Tom Lehrer – are satirical in nature, and not every poem in Latin hexameters or every eighteenth-century English poem in heroic couplets is a satire. Humour itself is not necessarily satirical, and while many satires make use of humour, this is often a kind of shock technique, where the effect is produced by making us question why we are laughing. Why, for example, do we laugh at Lehrer's "We will all go together when we go", a song about nuclear annihilation? The only possible answer is that given by George Gordon Byron, sixth Baron Byron (1788–1824), in his mock epic *Don Juan* (1819–1824, at IV, iv): "And if I laugh at any mortal thing,/'Tis that I may not weep ... " (McGann, 2008, 519). Satire can employ techniques such as exaggeration, the use of obscenity, scatological humour, the creation of imaginary societies or imaginary universes, alternative versions of history and beast fables, but none of these are necessarily satirical in themselves. For example, role reversal, with masters changing places with their slaves or servants, was a feature of the ancient Roman Saturnalia and later carnivals, but whatever satirical adjuncts may have gone with this (such as the long tradition of political and social commentary in Caribbean calypso), the disruption of the established order was purely temporary, and, by functioning as a sort of safety valve, may have actively helped to secure its continuance. Role reversal shapes the story of *Vice Versa*, a novel by F. Anstey (pseudonym of Thomas Anstey Guthrie, 1856–1934), first published in 1882 and still in print, in which a magic charm causes a father and son to find themselves in each other's bodies, with the father obliged to experience the realities of life at his son's boarding school (Anstey, 1954). (A similar theme, with a mother/daughter exchange, appears in Mary Rodgers's *Freaky Friday*, first published in 1972 and the basis of three film adaptations.) While Anstey's novel is subtitled "A Lesson to Fathers", and considerable humour is milked from the situation in which the unfortunate Mr. Bultitude finds himself, the comedy does not appear to be satirical: at the end of the novel, father and son resume their accustomed bodies and social positions, and while Mr. Bultitude promises to be nicer to his son in future and to move him to a different school, there is no real criticism of either Victorian parenting or educational practices. Other role reversal fictions provide a contrast, however. The early nineteenth-century Chinese novel by Li Ruzhen (c. 1763–1830), which is known in English as *Flowers in the Mirror*, is a fantasy which includes a voyage to the Country of Women, where women rule and it is the men who have bound feet and are confined to the household, in a role reversal which offers sharp criticism of gender relations in the China of the Qing Dynasty (Li, 1985). Another example among many which could be cited is the series of novels for young adults by the contemporary author Malorie Blackman which began with *Noughts & Crosses* (Blackman, 2001). In this, an alternative history, in which black people are the oppressors and white people are the oppressed, satirises racism.

The one thing which the different sorts of technique would appear to have in common is that they are simply tools which the satirist uses to persuade an audience to take a particular view of the target. But is this relationship necessarily a three-cornered one, as Freud suggested was the case with the "tendentious joke"? With Lehrer's "National Brotherhood Week", it might appear that the satirist is inviting liberals to laugh at racists. After all, out-and-out racists are likely to reject or ignore Lehrer's message. It is also the case, however, that the song is, in part, aimed at the sort of person who is not quite as free of racism as they would like to think, and who is being invited to consider this uncomfortable fact. But if the audience is also the target, the fact that satire depends on audience response can lead to unintended results. Caryl Churchill's play *Serious Money* (1987) satirised the get-rich-quick culture of the 1980s but had an extended run in London's West End because it was enjoyed by the very people in financial industries that it was attacking. Satirists who know that their targets also constitute their audience may keep their work relatively mild, as seems to be the case with the "Alex" cartoons by Charles Petrie and Russell Taylor, which first appeared in the *London Daily News* in 1987 and which have continued in the *Daily Telegraph* since 1992. The satire of "Megabank" and the financial institutions of the City of London is that of the in-joke: the cartoon appears in the business section, and even during an international recession could hardly have been said to be calling for the overthrow of capitalism. There can be other unexpected consequences when satire is, or seems to be, in the eye of the beholder. History is full of examples of what was intended as satire being taken literally. In *The Shortest Way with the Dissenters* (1702), by Daniel Defoe (c. 1660–1731), the suggestion made by the persona which the writer adopted, that Christians who did not belong to the established Church of England should be violently persecuted, was so close to the actual opinions of some Church of England partisans that many readers were unable to tell the difference. The uproar which followed led to Defoe's being arrested and imprisoned, fined and made to stand in the pillory. More recently, the American satirical website The Onion named the North Korean leader Kim Jong-un as its "Sexiest Man Alive" for 2012, only for this to be reported as straight fact by the online edition of the *People's Daily*, the official mouthpiece of the Communist Party of China. As one critic said of this and similar instances, this kind of reaction "revealed something about the literalists' own belief system" (BBC, 2012; Schneider, 2014). The reverse can also happen, as with the poem *Ver-Vert* (1734), by Jean-Baptiste Gresset (1709–1777), about a parrot owned by a convent, where the author was profoundly embarrassed to find a humorous *jeu d'esprit* taken as a satirical attack on the religious life (Gilmore, 2006).

In some cases, the adaptation of the relationship between author, audience and target seems to be taken a stage further, as when Freud tells the story of the Jew in the railway carriage (Freud, 2001, 80–81, 112). The Jew is described as a Galician, which implies he is dressed in a traditional manner which would have made it easy for others to identify him as a Jew. He takes his feet off the seat in the carriage when "a gentleman in modern dress" comes into the compartment, but puts them back again when the gentleman's enquiry about the date of the Day of Atonement reveals him to be a fellow Jew. Freud, the secularised and assimilated Jew who published his book on jokes in 1905, long before he was forced to leave Vienna to escape the Nazis, says that he includes this joke "as evidence of something being demonstrated by a detail". Like some of the other Jewish jokes which Freud included, however, it seems to belong to a wider category in which the joker (or satirist), the audience and the target are sometimes the same. With the Jamaican proverb "Money mek cocobay man shake gubna hand" ("If he has money, even a leper can shake the governor's hand"), the target is the speaker's fatalistic acceptance of his own poverty, not the hypothetical rich leper. The same idea is behind Ashanti proverbs such as "Even the crab, which lives where the gold dust is, eats palm nuts" (traditionally stigmatised as the food of poor people), or "When you are suffering from poverty and happen to fall into cold water, it scalds you" (Rattray, 1916, 67, 158), or the English popular song *She was poor but she was honest*, which laments the fate of the innocent country girl seduced and abandoned by the squire (see Chapter 7). Freud's joke about the Jew in the railway carriage depends on the idea that a Jew in modern dress is still a Jew, that is, a member of an oppressed minority, and in the same way the creators of proverbs and folk songs can offer profound insights into their own situation, but it is not a situation they expect to be able to change. The satirical impulse, some of the time, appears to be a defence mechanism of the helpless, offering comfort, however meagre, in an otherwise unbearable existence.

On other occasions, satire appears to be socially conservative, mocking those who are thought to be getting above themselves, for example, as in the Barbadian proverb "The pint pots are down and the gill pots are up", or *The Diary of a Nobody* (1892), by the Victorian English writers George Grossmith (1847–1912) and his brother Weedon Grossmith (1854–1919), a comic novel which mocked the social pretensions of the irredeemably lower-middle-class Mr. Pooter. The depressingly long line of misogynistic and homophobic satires from antiquity to the present similarly uses satire in defence of a patriarchal heteronormativity. These have a clear kinship with Freud's "tendentious joke", in that the (usually male) writer invites his audience to share his view of third parties.

The different kinds of satire, and the examples mentioned so far, which I have deliberately chosen for variety of geographical origin, raise two final questions. Part of Jacob Zuma's reaction to Zapiro's cartoons was to suggest that satire had no place in South Africa, as an import from Western societies which was opposed to African traditions of respect for elders (Blair, 2009). To what extent is satire universal, or are the examples we think of as satire simply manifestations of a specifically Western tradition? Secondly, what effect does satire actually have? As the cases of the Jesuit schoolboy and of Defoe indicate, satire can sometimes recoil on the satirist, and the story of Lycambes suggests that at least "personal satire" can have an effect on its targets. Socially conservative satire obviously does not want things to change, but does satire actually produce change at all? As Robert Darnton asked, "Do books cause revolutions?" (Darnton, 1997). Did the scurrilous and often highly inventive pamphlets about sexual activities of the court of Versailles contribute to the events of 1789, or did they merely reflect social and economic changes which would have brought about a revolution whether or not any particular satirist had set pen to paper? It is certainly the case that satirists themselves sometimes despair of their metier: as Lehrer once put it, "Political satire became obsolete when Henry Kissinger was awarded the Nobel peace prize" in 1973 (Purdom, 2000), since Kissinger was a particularly hawkish member of administrations which presided over US foreign policy during the period of the war in Vietnam. More recently, during the 2016 presidential election campaign in the United States of America, Matt Groening, creator of *The Simpsons*, noted that he had made Donald Trump president in a 2000 episode of the enormously popular and internationally distributed animated sitcom, because Trump's was "of course the most absurd placeholder joke name that we could think of at the time", adding "that's still true. It's beyond satire" (Marlton, 2016). After the election result, Groening's comments, which had originally appeared in an interview with the Australian cartoonist First Dog on the Moon (pseudonym of Andrew Marlton), were widely reproduced, with the British tabloid paper *The Sun*, for example, using them as the basis of a story which started on the front page (10 November 2016) with images of Homer Simpson, whose characteristic "D'oh!" provided the main headline, and Trump as he had appeared in the *Simpsons* episode "Bart to the Future" in 2000. For some readers, of course, this juxtaposition in itself constituted satirical comment on the election result.

The Australian–British novelist Kathy Lette observed that "Satires are like sausages – you really don't want to know what goes into making them" (Lette, 2014). The idea appears to be that, like Shelley's remark about casting "a violet into a crucible that you might discover the formal principles of its colour and odour" (*Defence of Poetry*, 1821), too-close analysis will spoil the effect. This book, however, does seek to find out something about the making of satires and how they function. In keeping with the general focus of the New Critical Idiom series, it concentrates mainly on the Western literary tradition, and mainly on literature in English. However, extensive reference will be made to other literatures, particularly those of classical Greece and Rome, which have been influential in the development of satire in English. Some use will also be made, for comparative purposes, of satire in other traditions, and attention will also be paid to oral forms of satire, such as proverbs and popular song, and to satire in the visual arts, from print caricatures to television, film and the internet. Any attempt to produce a chronological history of satire would need to be encyclopaedic in scope, nor does it appear viable in a book of this length to try and include every satirist of note. The chapters which follow are intended as a series of studies which combine thematic, theoretical and historical approaches to ask questions about the nature of satire, without necessarily claiming that definitive answers are possible.

2

BEAST FABLES FROM AESOP TO *ANIMAL FARM*

Whether directed at individuals or human types, satire often overlaps with other literary forms which are not necessarily satirical in themselves. These include fables, short stories with a moral purpose, often featuring animals or inanimate objects, and allegories, in which a story or description is intended to be read on at least two different levels, with the surface meaning suggesting another. In *The Republic*, by the ancient Greek philosopher Plato (c. 427–347 BCE), the limitations of human understanding are discussed by imagining a group of prisoners in a cave whose knowledge of the outside world is limited to the shadows they can see on the wall of the cave. Should one of them get out, he will at first be blinded by the sunlight, but will gradually attain a knowledge of the reality behind the shadows. If he returns to the cave, on the other hand, he will have become unaccustomed to the darkness, and because he now appears to see worse than the others, they will refuse to believe the truth of his reports of the real world outside the cave. As a result, the one who had ventured outside might well prefer to remain there. Plato used the allegory to argue that, in an ideal state, those who had achieved a higher degree of knowledge should be compelled, if necessary, to return among those who were still ignorant, and to improve their condition by governing them. Those who did not want to do this were, Plato claimed, precisely those who ought to be rulers, since those who wanted to rule should not be allowed to do so because they would only be seeking advantages for themselves. While this offers both a general argument about the human condition and a suggestion for its improvement, this sort of allegory would not normally be classed as satire.

Texts which were not originally allegories sometimes have an allegorical reading imposed upon them by later readers, a famous example being the way in which the Old Testament book of *The Song of Songs* in the Bible, apparently written in praise of human erotic love, came to be interpreted as an allegory of Christ's love for His Church. By contrast, the novel *Animal Farm* (1945), by George Orwell (the pen name of Eric Blair, 1903–1950), although subtitled by its author as "A Fairy Story" and drawing on a very long tradition of telling stories about animals, is much more than a story about animals rising up against human domination on an English country farm, as it invites an allegorical reading which turns it into a satirical comment on the tendency of popular revolutions to end in the creation of a dictatorship that simply replaces one set of rulers with another whose outlook differs little. Why exactly most readers would consider *Animal Farm* to be satire, but would not think the same way about Plato's cave, is not an easy question to answer. The history of the beast fable may offer some suggestions.

The urge to anthropomorphise animal behaviour, and to use animals as a point of comparison with humans, has been around long before the Roman writer Plautus (Titus Maccius Plautus, c. 254–184 BCE) introduced into one of his plays (*Asinaria*, l. 495) a version of the proverb "Homo homini lupus" ("Man is a wolf to his fellow man"), later used by Thomas Hobbes and Sigmund Freud, among others. In this phenomenon, we may be able to find some hints, at least, towards an answer to the ultimately insoluble question of the origins of satire. Stories about animals, on their own or in interaction with humans, can be found in many different cultures and historical periods. Their prominence in animated cartoons, from the earliest days of Winsor McCay's *Gertie the Dinosaur* (1914) to Disney's *The Princess and the Frog* (2009) and *Zootopia* (2016), ensures that they remain a staple of popular entertainment. While many examples aim only to amuse an audience, some do have a didactic or satirical purpose. In the Japanese film *Spirited Away* (director Hayao Miyazaki; Studio Ghibli, 2001), for example, the parents of the main character, Chihiro, are turned into pigs after overindulging themselves on the food which appears to be freely available in abandoned restaurants in the magical world they have stumbled into, and this can be seen as a satire on the excesses of consumerism.

However, stories about animals are not necessarily beast fables, which can perhaps be defined as stories which feature animal as well as human characters, or animals alone, but which are told for some purpose outside of the story itself, that is, to comment on some aspect of human behaviour. Anna Sewell's *Black Beauty* (1877) is told from the point of view of the horse who is the title character, and who can understand and report on what is said by humans. The book urges kindness to animals, horses in particular, and offers criticism of humans who are cruel to them, but like Henry Williamson's novel *Tarka the Otter* (1927), with its naturalistic descriptions of wildlife and its criticism of hunting, it is not concerned with other aspects of human behaviour. Works of fiction with animal characters or featuring animal-like toys such as A. A. Milne's *Winnie-the-Pooh* (1926) or Kenneth Grahame's *The Wind in the Willows* (1908) seem like straightforward entertainment, even if the nostalgia for an idealised vision of childhood or rural life which they offer is sometimes used for satirical purposes in other genres. Animal characters continue to be a standard feature of much literature produced for younger children. The anthropomorphism is often unquestioning, as is the case with Cyndy Szekeres' *Little Puppy Cleans His Room* (1994), a work whose overt moral purpose is sufficiently indicated by the title. A contrast is offered by Rob Lewis in *Tidy Up, Trevor* (1994), a much more subversive work which could be read as a satire of the kind of book which, like *Little Puppy*, makes heavy-handed attempts to influence children's behaviour: while young Trevor the turtle obeys the instructions of adult turtles and tidies up, he creates absolute chaos in the process.

Beast fables comment on human behaviour more generally. In Europe, at least, they begin with Aesop, who may have been a historical person from the sixth century BCE, a slave who was commonly believed to have been a Phrygian (that is, from Asia Minor), but who was perhaps from Thrace on the Greek mainland. By the time of Plato, Aesop had already become a legendary figure whose name was applied to a collection of fables with no definite boundaries, and which included material which was almost certainly not by Aesop, some of which was not even Greek in origin. Even in antiquity, some of the stories in "Aesop" were referred to as Libyan or Egyptian tales, and parallels can be found in other cultures. Particularly influential was the *Pañcatantra*, an Indian collection of stories which were carefully interlinked to form a treatise on government, probably dating from around 300 CE. Numerous translations in many languages extended the influence of these stories into Arabic and European folk traditions and literatures, and they were used by La Fontaine as a basis for some of his own fables (Olivelle, 1997). Most of these stories are designed to inculcate some sort of moral about human life. For example, in Aesop's "The Dog Who Carried the Meat" (Temple and Temple, 1998, 137), a dog who has stolen a piece of meat (a bone in a well-known later adaptation) sees his reflection in the water when he is crossing a river. In attempting to grab the piece of meat in the reflection, he drops and loses the piece he was actually holding in his mouth. In the first story in the *Pañcatantra*, "The Monkey That Pulled the Wedge", a carpenter goes off for his lunch, leaving a log of wood half split with a wedge holding it apart. An inquisitive monkey comes along and pulls out the wedge, without stopping to realise that he has left some delicate portions of his anatomy dangling in the slit (Olivelle, 1997, 8). Both of these could equally well be given the moral "Consider all circumstances before taking action". The same is true of mediaeval bestiaries, where anecdotes about the real or imaginary characteristics of animals are used to inculcate moral lessons of an often explicitly Christianised form. Allegedly, for example, the testicles of a beaver were excellent medicine, so a beaver would bite off its own testicles when pursued by hunters, who would stop to pick them up, leaving the beaver to escape. This can be found in Aesop, but it was a mediaeval commentary that added the suggestion that from this the pious reader was meant to learn that he should cut off all his own vices and throw them in the devil's face (Barber, 1992, 43–44). Similar moralising occurs in other forms at much later dates. The fables in Latin verse of the French Jesuit, Petrus Justus Sautel (1613–1662), were long popular as school texts, and were explicitly described as "elegiae oblectandis animis, et moribus informandis accommodatae" ("elegiac verses designed to delight minds and shape morals"). One of his best known was that on the fly drowned in a bowl of milk, which, in a rather long-winded manner, stressed the importance of resisting temptation (Sautel, 1728, 5–10). The same theme was treated in a more light-hearted vein by Thomas Gray (1716–1771) in his *Ode on the Death of a Favourite Cat Drowned in a Bowl of Goldfishes* (1747):

> [...]
> The slipp'ry verge her feet beguil'd,
>   She tumbled headlong in.
> [...]
> From hence, ye Beauties, undeceiv'd,
> Know, one false step is ne'er retriev'd,
>   And be with caution bold.
> Not all that tempts your wand'ring eyes
> And heedless hearts, is lawful prize;
>   Nor all, that glisters, gold.
>
> (Starr and Hendrickson, 1972, 6)

Gray's cat, Selima, is identified as female, and the reference to "ye Beauties" indicates the poem's dependence on stereotyped notions of feminine curiosity and cupidity.

None of this, however, is satire as we usually understand it. Matters are complicated by the fact that modern commentators cannot agree on the purposes of some of the traditional collections. It is disputed, for example, whether or not the *Pañcatantra* offers a Machiavellian view of how the ruler should govern. In addition, some of the later versions of Aesop bear only the most limited resemblance to the original collection. Robert Temple suggests that some of the "Aesop" stories, such as the one about "The Lion and the Wild Ass", were intended as satirical (Temple and Temple, 1998, xix–xx), but they seem rather general and lacking in a specific target to the modern reader. Nevertheless, we should note Temple's summary of the general tone:

> The underlying ethos of the world of Aesop is "you're on your own, and if you meet people who are unfortunate, kick them

while they are down". The law of the jungle seemed to prevail in the world of men as well as of animals for Aesop. Perhaps that is why animal stories were so appropriate.

(Temple and Temple, 1998, xvii)

At the same time, we can see how stories like these can become satirical by the way they are used in different contexts, just as Temple suggests that one of the ways in which the collection we know as "Aesop" was used in ancient times was as a source of useful anecdotes which Greek lawyers could apply to opponents in debate. In other words, a collection of fables might originally be no more than raw material, available to be worked up in different ways. How a fable can be turned into something more obviously satirical can be seen in the well-known story of the town mouse and the country mouse. This can be found in "Aesop" (Temple and Temple, 1998, 178–179), where, although the original is in Greek verse, the story is told in a brief and straightforward manner. Having been invited to dinner in the country by his friend, the town mouse returns the invitation, assuring the country mouse that there is greater plenty and variety of food to be had in town. This proves to be the case, but their enjoyment of the meal is spoilt when they are interrupted by humans, causing a fright which induces the country mouse to return home. The moral, that it is better to live a simple life in safety than a luxurious one in constant danger, is explicitly stated. The same story is told by Horace (*Satires*, II, vi, 79–117), who develops it at greater length and in a more deliberately literary style. We are given more detail, and the tone inclines towards the mock heroic. The country mouse lives "paupere cavo" ("in a poor hole") but is referred to as "pater ipse domus" ("the master of the house himself"). In "Aesop", the mice have "only barley and corn to eat" in the country (Temple and Temple, 1998, 178), but Horace's country mouse offers his guest chickpeas and oats which he has hoarded, as well as raisins and half-nibbled bits of bacon. The town mouse disdains such humble fare, barely touching it "dente superbo" ("with his proud tooth"). Nevertheless, the country mouse eats only spelt and darnel, "dapis meliora relinquens" ("leaving the better things of the feast") to his guest. The use of "dapis", a word normally meaning something like "feast" or "banquet", neatly sums up the contrast between the host's view of life and the expectations of his more sophisticated guest. When the two mice arrive at a house in the town, we are told "iamque tenebat/nox medium caeli spatium" ("and now the night was holding the middle space of Heaven"), which parodies the elaborate circumlocutions used to indicate time in epic poetry such as the *Aeneid* of Horace's contemporary Virgil (Publius Vergilius Maro, 70–19 BCE). The mice are being set up as epic heroes, and while in "Aesop" there is no description of the house and its contents other than the presence of a rather wider range of food, if still of a rather humble type, than was to be had in the country mouse's hole, in Horace it is clear that in the town the two mice get into what is a very grand house indeed. It has ivory couches draped in scarlet cloth of the sort on which very rich Romans reclined to eat, and many courses left over from a "magna cena" (a "great" or "truly impressive" dinner) are heaped in baskets nearby. The town mouse proceeds to play the host, but he is not only "succinctus" (girded up), like a domestic slave, but described by Horace as acting "verniliter", which suggests not just that he is behaving in an obsequious manner, but specifically that he is doing so like a slave born in the household. The setting doesn't just reek of money, it reeks of old money. The country mouse, meanwhile, is stretched out on one of the couches, enjoying himself like a Roman plutocrat. Suddenly, however, there is an "ingens/valvarum strepitus" ("a mighty clang of double doors"), and both the double doors, and the Molossian hounds whose barking leaves the mice frightened out of their wits in a decidedly unheroic manner, are things which would only be found in very rich households. The country mouse tells his friend he has no need of this and takes off, saying "me silva cavusque/tutus ab insidiis tenui solabitur ervo" ("the woodland and a hole safe from ambushes will console me with a bit of vetch"), the term vetch suggesting broad beans or some similar food of a very humble nature in comparison with the urban feast. The basic meaning, that modest comfort in peace and quiet is preferable to dangerous luxury, is the same as in "Aesop", but Horace adds other layers of meaning. The town mouse is described as urging the country mouse to come to the city with him by pointing out that life is short, and that one should enjoy it while one can:

> [...] quo, bone, circa,
> dum licet, in rebus iucundis vive beatus;
> vive memor, quam sis aevi brevis.

[And so, my good fellow, live a happy life in pleasant circumstances; live mindful of the fact that you are a short-lived
creature.]

What the town mouse gives here is a good summary of the philosophy
of the Greek thinker Epicurus (341–270 BCE), which enjoyed considerable popularity in the Rome of Horace's time. Horace's treatment
of the fable shows the town mouse achieving precisely the opposite
of what he aimed at. This offers several layers of irony. In the first
place, Horace identified himself as a follower of this philosophy, calling himself in another poem (*Epistles*, I. iv, 16) "Epicuri de grege por-
cum" ("a pig from Epicurus's herd"). There may be an element here of
the slightly self-deprecating humour which many readers have found
in Horace's work. Then we should note that the fable comes at the end
of a poem in which Horace contrasts the advantages of a peaceful life
in the countryside with the hustle and bustle of life in Rome, where,
indeed, he enjoys the company of his friend and patron, the wealthy
and influential politician Maecenas (Gaius Cilnius Maecenas, 68–8
BCE), but has to put up with the envy this brings him, and constant
pestering from people who hope that he can secure them favours from
Maecenas. This seems to imply that the town mouse has got it wrong,
and that the fable, as Horace reworks it, is meant to remind us of the
true meaning of Epicurean philosophy, which was not, as it was viewed
by many in antiquity and later periods, an unqualified, hedonistic pursuit of material pleasure, but rather, as the country mouse discovers,
an appreciation of the inner peace to be found in modest comfort and
a lack of concern for worldly affairs. Finally, Horace's version of the
fable could be read as suggesting that the luxurious habits of upper-
class Romans of the first century BCE were excessive, and perhaps
even that those humans who enjoyed them for the moment did so in
as precarious a manner as the mice. While Horace is usually seen as a
supporter of the new regime, whereby the Emperor Augustus (reigned
27 BCE–14 CE) had brought peace and stability to the Roman world
by replacing the frequent upheavals of the old republican system with
what was, in effect, rule by one man, such a reading would suggest
an implied criticism that a peace in which the position of the traditional oligarchy was no longer secure had been bought at the cost of
accepting a dictatorship. Horace's version is clearly more elaborate

and sophisticated than that found in "Aesop", but while we may agree with the eighteenth-century editor who claimed that "This Satire is full of Morality and Instruction" (Watson and Patrick, 1760, II, 183), different readers are likely to find different things in it.

A much later example of such reworkings is the way in which the Aesopian fable of "The Dog Who Carried the Meat" was employed in the 1720s to satirise the greed of the speculators in the financial enterprise known as the South Sea Bubble, and, by extension, the prime minister of the day, Robert Walpole (Temple and Temple, 1998, 137; Dabydeen, 1985, 61–62). Other types of adaptation are represented by *The Pooh Perplex: A Student Casebook* (1963), in which Frederick Crews offered a series of parodic essays on *Winnie-the-Pooh* which satirised different schools of literary criticism, and Jan Needle's *Wild Wood* (1981), which rewrote *The Wind in the Willows* as a satire on Thatcherite Britain. Alexander Lenard's remarkably popular Latin translation of Pooh as *Winnie ille Pu* (1960) can be read as a self-parodying satire of a certain type of intellectualism, which perhaps reaches the heights of its accomplishment with the rendering of Pooh's ditty, "On Monday, when the sun is hot", in the style of the great mediaeval hymn, the *Dies Irae*.

In mediaeval Europe, the beast fable and the bestiary contributed to the extensive literary cycle of stories in various languages about Renard the Fox, which often included satirical elements directed against the aristocracy and the clergy, who, of course, formed most of the audience for the stories. Chaucer's *Nun's Priest's Tale*, with its story of Chauntecleer the cock, Pertelote the hen and how Chauntecleer is carried off by Russell the fox, parodies a number of elements of the Renard stories, and satirises the rhetorical and poetic practices of his own time (Benson, 1988).

Discussion of "Aesop" raises two important points of wider application. First of all, what text or version of "Aesop" are we actually talking about? Most people knew "Aesop" through later adaptations, such as those in Latin verse by the Roman ex-slave Phaedrus (first century CE), which John Henderson (2004) has shown to be, in many cases, satires of specific aspects of the Roman society of Phaedrus's time, or often very freely adapted vernacular translations such as those by Roger L'Estrange (1691, 1699) and Samuel Croxall (1722), both of which were coloured by the translators' views of the politics of their own day. The French adaptations of Aesop by Jean de La Fontaine (final versions collected by the author, 1692), who added fables of his own, were often allegories of the France of Louis XIV. The story of the frogs who asked Jupiter for a king, and got first a log, with whose inactivity they were displeased, and then a stork, which proceeded to eat them up, can be found in Aesop. Even though Aesop refers to the frogs as being "annoyed with the anarchy in which they lived" (Temple and Temple, 1998, 53), La Fontaine's version, in which the frogs are described as "se lassant/De l'état démocratique" ("tiring of the democratic state"), seems to refer to the anti-monarchist upheavals known as the Fronde in the early years of Louis XIV, and to be advocating acceptance of "the powers that be" (Darmon and Gruffat, 2002, 116–117). La Fontaine became, in turn, a source and an inspiration for many later translators, adaptors and original fabulists in different languages, such as the Russian Ivan Krylov (1768–1844). A fable such as "Peasant and Sheep" shows Krylov adapting the form to his own society, satirising both the stereotypical stupidity of the peasant and the rapacity of the governing class. In this narrative, a peasant takes the sheep to court, accused of having killed and eaten two fowls. The magistrate is a fox, whom one is left to assume may well have had something to do with the disappearance of the fowls, but who is quick both to accept the peasant's plea and condemn the sheep to death, making sure that the meat remains in court for his own use, while the peasant is left with the sheep's skin (Pares, 1942, 67–68).

Secondly, like all texts, these have contexts. A text (or group of texts) which exemplifies both of these issues is provided by the stories of the French writer Charles Perrault (1628–1703), who gave us the earliest literary versions of stories with which we all think we are familiar, such as Cinderella, Puss in Boots and Little Red Riding-Hood. We are so familiar with them that they readily lend themselves to parodic intertextuality, such as the appearance of Puss in Boots (voiced by Antonio Banderas) in *Shrek 2* (DreamWorks Animation, 2004), and the comment by Eddie Murphy, as Donkey, that "I'm sorry, the position of annoying talking animal is already taken!" It is the numerous later versions, however, with which we are really familiar. A reader encountering Perrault himself for the first time can be quite startled by the extent to which Perrault's stories differ from the later adaptations. Context is also revealed as important: when we discover that Perrault was an unsuccessful courtier, whose career was ruined by rivals at the court of Louis XIV, a story like Puss in Boots, in which the title character employs ingenious tricks and violence, or the threat of violence, to turn an impoverished miller's son into the Marquis de Carabas, begins to look much more like a satirical attack on the pretensions of the nobility, in spite of Perrault's dedication of his book to a member of the royal family.

Context shows itself as important in other examples as well. Rochester's "A Satyr against Mankind" makes vivid use of contrasts between the behaviour of other animals and man, "that vain animal/ Who is so proud of being rational". Without the extensive notes of a modern scholarly edition, the modern reader is likely to miss the allusions to Rochester's contemporaries at the court of Charles II, and see only a more generalised commentary on the less appealing aspects of human nature (Ellis, 1994). In a similar manner, Swift's *Gulliver's Travels* (1726) has become a children's book because few people reading it outside an academic course think of it as a satire on early eighteenth-century politics. Interestingly, it is perhaps the beast fable aspect which remains the freshest in episodes such as Swift's contrast between the noble, horse-like Houyhnhnms and the degraded, human-like Yahoos, and this is precisely the section which often gets left out of later adaptations. For example, the fantasy film *Gulliver's Travels* (dir. Rob Letterman; 20th Century Fox, 2010), starring Jack Black in the title role, offered only a version of Lilliput as a country of small people which bore little resemblance to that described in Swift's text.

A different sort of contextual change appears in the transformations of the Ashanti folk hero, Anansi. Sometimes a man, sometimes spider, sometimes both, Anansi is a trickster figure who will do anything he has to in order to provide for his family or to save his own skin, though if he has to choose between his family and his own comfort and safety, he always puts himself first. In their West African context, Anansi stories seem like commentaries on human nature generally (Rattray, 1930). Among the descendants of enslaved Africans in the Americas, however, Anansi survived and took on a different emphasis. In the English-speaking Caribbean, he remained the spider Anansi, or Nansi under various spellings, while he becomes Nanzi in the Papiamentu language of Curaçao. Elsewhere, he changes into a rabbit, perhaps influenced by the figure of a hare which is widespread in African folklore: he is Compère Lapin in St. Lucia, Tio Conejo in Venezuela and, of course, Br'er Rabbit in the southern United States of America, though here some influence from Native American traditions is also likely. The stories told about him in different places are often very similar, and Anansi's connection with his African origins remains clear, but in the Americas, Anansi stories became the folklore of the oppressed, sometimes showing an element of protective self-mockery, and often hinting at the extremes to which the desperate can be driven by the need to survive. Sometimes the nature of the trials that confront Anansi is made explicit. In the Curaçao stories, the character who is often Nanzi's opponent is called Shon Arey ("Massa King") in the Papiamentu language, with Shon being the title of the boss of a firm, or that of a master of slaves (Geerdink-Jesurun Pinto, 1952; 1972).

Just as the Black British poet John Agard (2000) shows the almost infinite adaptability of Anansi to comment on sex, race and a wide range of modern topics, the beast fable proves a versatile instrument in the hands of many twentieth-century satirists. To take one example, the poems of Trilussa (pen name of Carlo Alberto Salustri, 1871–1950), written in the Romanesco dialect but circulated all over Italy, often used animal references. In *All'Ombra* ("In the Shade"), published in 1932, when the speaker expresses satisfaction at being able to address a pig and a donkey by their right names without fear of imprisonment, it is suggested, without being openly stated, that this is because the animals will not be able to repeat his comments. The implied criticism of the fascist regime of the dictator Benito Mussolini (1883–1945), which was intolerant of any opposition and whose censorship policies extended to spying on the private conversations of ordinary Italians, would have been obvious (DuVal, 1990, 110–111).

The perspective of an animal lends itself to a satirical view of humans. An influential eighteenth-century example was Francis Coventry's *The History of Pompey the Little, or, The Life and Adventures of a Lap-Dog* (1751), in which a dog's passing through the hands of a succession of owners is used as a vehicle for a series of sharply drawn portraits of different social types, some of whom were recognised by contemporaries as particular individuals. A variation which replaced the animal with an inanimate object was Charles Johnstone's *Chrysal, Or, The Adventures of a Guinea* (1761–1765), which followed the coin's circulation through four volumes and several countries to provide "Curious and interesting Anecdotes of the most Noted persons in every Rank of Life, whose Hands it passed through". Both *Pompey* and *Chrysal* had many successors, including the story of "Tobermory" (1911) by Saki (pen name of H. H. Munro, 1870–1916), which sends up the hypocrisy of upper-class manners by describing what happens when a country house party learns that one of the guests has succeeded in teaching the cat to speak. Surprise turns to consternation at the thought of what he might reveal of what he saw and heard when he was merely a dumb animal and allowed to wander around the house unchecked in a manner which would never have been permitted to a human observer.

Animals can also be used to create alternative worlds and histories, sometimes of a distinctly dystopian variety. Much of the power of the novella *Metamorphosis* (1915) by Franz Kafka (1883–1924) depends on the multivalent possibilities created by Gregor Samsa's transformation into a "vermin". Although he may be best known to English readers as a "cockroach", and Kafka certainly had some sort of insect in mind, the German text is imprecise about his exact nature. While Kafka's story may have been little more than a bizarre fantasy to its initial readers, the events of the twentieth century have transformed Gregor's alienation from his family, rejection and death into a fable of the horrifying consequences of treating our fellow creatures as something other than ourselves (Kafka, 2007). Gregor's difference could, obviously, have been something more specific and realistic, involving issues such as race, sexual orientation, religion, politics or immigration status, for example, but this would have limited the story. His metamorphosis into an insect forces us to exercise our imaginative understanding, and turns his plight into that of an Everyman.

An interesting later example is the novel *Māo chéng jì* ("Records of Cat City") by Lao She (pen name of Shu Qingchun, 1899–1966), published in Chinese in 1932 and translated into English by William Lyell in 1970 as *Cat Country*. The narrator is a Chinese who emerges from a spacecraft wrecked on Mars to find himself in a country inhabited by cats, whose addiction to mind-altering substances, subservience to foreigners and foreign ideas, venality and disunity in the face of outside threats, all bear more than a passing resemblance to China in the period before the establishment of the People's Republic in 1949.

Lao She is often long winded, and the cat-people are essentially a non-realistic literary device, but the novel is good in parts, and in some ways, such as the passage on the nature of revolutions (268–269), anticipates Orwell.

Perhaps the outstanding modern version of the beast fable is Orwell's *Animal Farm* (1945), in which the liberation from human rule initially promises a sort of animal utopia but gradually descends into the domination of the pigs and the enforcement of the idea that "All animals are equal but some animals are more equal than others". One feature of the book is that, unlike Lao She, the animal characteristics are all carefully delineated: the pigs are convincingly pig-like, the sheep behave in a sheepish manner and so forth. This allows the story to be enjoyed on a superficial level as simply "A Fairy Story", to use Orwell's original subtitle, though many children will find it a little too gruesome to be pleasurable. It also benefits from being rooted in very specific circumstances of the early twentieth century, and the real-life equivalences which have been pointed out by many critics, such as the resemblance of Napoleon to Stalin and Snowball to Trotsky, among others, help to give it coherence. However, it also works very effectively, as Orwell stated he meant it to, as a satire about dictatorships generally, and the increasing authoritarianism of supposedly democratic governments has given it, along with *Nineteen Eighty-Four*, enduring topicality.

3

EARLY SATIRE, FROM THE BIBLE TO ANCIENT ROME

Satire in particular literary forms, as distinct from proverbs and fables, has a history so long that it is impossible to say exactly when it began. Modern critics have found satirical elements in ancient Egyptian and Babylonian literature, and there is evidence for political satire in the Bible. The biblical Old Testament Book of Esther, for example, is conventionally interpreted as a straightforward story of a conflict between good and evil. It is set at the court of Ahasuerus, who "reigned from India even unto Ethiopia, over an hundred and seven and twenty provinces", and who is usually identified with Xerxes I (King of Persia 486–465 BCE), who is mainly remembered in Western tradition for his unsuccessful invasion of Greece in 480 BCE. The king's evil minister, Haman, enraged by the refusal of Mordecai the Jew to bow to him, seeks the destruction of the Jewish people, but with the help of his uncle's daughter, Esther, who has become Ahasuerus's queen, Mordecai is able to reverse the situation. Haman is hanged on the gallows which he had ordered to be prepared for Mordecai, and it is the enemies of the Jews who are destroyed. As Ze'ev Weisman (1998) suggests, however, the narrative can be read as a satire on political power. The king's activities are limited to drinking and feasting, lust, and the imposition of taxes. Mordecai is not just any Jew, but one of the king's courtiers and someone who is shown to be an astute political operator: not only does he uncover a conspiracy against the king by two of his chamberlains, but he makes sure that this is recorded in writing. It is the written record which secures for Mordecai the position of "the man whom the king delighteth to honour", a position which Haman thought was his, and his alone. Esther secures Haman's downfall by persuading him that he is specially favoured, as he alone is invited to dine with her and the king at the banquet where they are plied with wine for two days, after which Esther denounces Haman as the enemy of her people, and Haman's attempt to beg Esther for his life is turned against him, in what may be intended as a ludicrous scene. Whether as a result of the wine he has taken, or in an attempt at supplication, "Haman was fallen upon the bed whereon Esther was", and when the king sees this and asks "Will he force the queen also before me in the house?", Haman's fate is sealed. Even though there are several references in the text to the idea that the law of the Medes and Persians is unalterable, the king reverses his earlier commands and gives the Jews authority "to destroy, to slay, and to cause to perish" all their enemies. Over 75,000 of these are killed, but the Jews refrain from exercising the right to plunder, which they had also been given. Throughout the kingdom, royal officials help them "because the fear of Mordecai fell upon them". At this point (Esther, ix, 3–4), Weisman notes (1998, 157), "Suddenly the description 'Jew' is dropped and the title 'the man' appears alone". If we read the narrative as suggesting that "this man Mordecai" is, like Haman, raised to power by the capriciousness of royal favour, the implication is that this is not a secure or lasting solution to the troubles of the exiled Jews. If Mordecai can replace Haman in this manner, so, too, might another Haman replace Mordecai. As Weisman says, despite the association of the Book of Esther with the Jewish festival of Purim, "a festival notable for its frivolity and almost pagan license" and "despite the comic and grotesque elements that accompany the fall of Haman, it is doubtful that the tale radiates optimism; after all, the 'Hamans' of the world have not disappeared with his demise" (1998, 140, 154).

The date of the Book of Esther is uncertain, with estimates ranging from sometime during the reign of Xerxes I down to the third century

BCE. This period also saw the development of what is known as Old Comedy in Greece, a genre associated mainly with the Athenian playwright Aristophanes (449 or 448–c. 385 BCE). Eleven plays of Aristophanes survive (out of a total of forty or so), and other writers of Old Comedy are known to us only through fragments or references to their work, so that he is our major source for the genre (Aristophanes, 2002). Old Comedy developed out of the specific circumstances of Athenian democracy, which allowed for much wider participation in politics than was usual in ancient societies, though this should not be overstated: only adult male citizens had democratic rights, while all women and the large numbers of slaves and resident foreigners in Athens were excluded. Audiences for Old Comedy, as for contemporary tragedy, were large, socially varied and not restricted to the citizen body: some resident foreigners attended, there were sometimes visitors from outside Athens and there are references to the presence of women. Formal conventions included restrictions on the number of actors (with men playing both male and female parts), the chorus and the use of masks and grotesque padding, often with oversized leather phalluses for male characters. Plays could verge on the slapstick, with plenty of sexual and scatological humour: as Aristophanes's *The Clouds* (first produced 423 BCE) shows us, the fart joke has a very long history. There was a tendency to rely on stereotyped humour: it was regularly suggested, for example, that politicians had been homosexual prostitutes in their youth. At the same time, plays also turned on topical themes, subjecting particular individuals or ideas to ridicule as a means of suggesting that they fell short of what the playwright felt his audience was likely to agree were socially acceptable norms. In the case of *The Clouds*, this involved satirising the growing popularity of Sophistic philosophy. This is represented in the play by the character of Socrates, and modern readings of the play are inevitably coloured by the knowledge that the real philosopher of that name was condemned to death in 399 BCE for corrupting the youth of Athens and not believing in the gods, accusations very similar to the way in which he is portrayed in the play. Nevertheless, as Sommerstein (Aristophanes, 2002, 67–68) suggests, we should not be in too much of a hurry to see cause and effect here, in view of the long interval between the play and the trial and the fact that Socrates could almost certainly have avoided the death penalty had he wished to do so. It is possible that Socrates was chosen as a representative Sophist in the play simply because he had what were considered to be particularly ugly features which could easily be given a stylised and exaggerated form in an actor's mask, creating a caricature still recognisable as intended for a comic version of Socrates himself. Old Comedy frequently portrayed other living contemporaries, usually in a negative manner.

The Clouds begins with an old man, Strepsiades, worrying about his debts, which are caused by the extravagant lifestyle of his son, Pheidippides. He decides to go to Socrates's "Thinkery" to learn how to use the "Wrongful Argument", so that he can worm his way out of paying his debts. He encounters Socrates, supposedly in the air, but in fact suspended from a crane in a parody of the way a god would have made his appearance in a contemporary Greek tragedy. Socrates invokes the cloud-goddesses who form the chorus of the play and whom he describes as almighty, while he explicitly denies the very existence of Zeus, the chief god of the Greek Pantheon. Strepsiades proves unable to follow Socrates's verbal gymnastics, and persuades Pheidippides to become his pupil instead. Pheidippides goes to the school, is taught by personifications of the Right and Wrong arguments and learns how to defeat his father's creditors by playing on words to demonstrate an alleged procedural irregularity. He has also learnt to use the same methods, however, to justify beating his father. The Chorus of Clouds, having at first appeared to favour Socrates and lead Strepsiades on, tells the latter that he has only got himself to blame for the mess he has got himself into. The Chorus reaffirms the rule of the Olympian gods, and points out to Strepsiades the moral that "it is right to fear the gods". The play ends with a disgusted Strepsiades destroying the Thinkery and driving away Socrates and his students as a punishment for their having wronged the gods.

While it is true that Socrates left no writings of his own, and our knowledge of him comes from the accounts of others, particularly those of his students Plato and Xenophon, it is clear that the representation of him in *The Clouds* (and, by extension, of sophistic philosophy more generally) is coloured by deliberate exaggeration and distortion, two important weapons in the armoury of satire. These satirical techniques, much used by later writers in many different circumstances, are aimed at all sorts of targets. Here, they seem intended to give humorous force to the not unreasonable criticism that the sophists appeared to question everything, but did not offer anything positive themselves. At the same time, while the character of Socrates in the play is allowed to mock the gods, belief in them is reaffirmed at the end so that the play has a teleological objective, and, as in many other works, despite what might be termed localised criticism, in *The Clouds* satire is ultimately enlisted for conservative purposes.

Greek comedy, and the means whereby it achieved some of its effects, inevitably changed over time. What is referred to as New Comedy is particularly associated with the work of Menander (c. 342/341–c. 290 BCE). In comparison with the Old Comedy, this is less satirical, in that it is less concerned with targeting particular individuals or ideas, and is more like modern situation comedy. Much of ancient Greek comedy has been lost, but Aristophanes was discovered by Western European readers in the Renaissance, and his influence has been seen in humour and satire from Rabelais (see Chapter 4) to the work of the British comedy group Monty Python (1969 onwards).

While the ancient Greeks wrote their comedies in verse, they were also responsible for the development of satire in prose, a genre associated with the name of Menippus of Gadara (third century BCE). The works of Menippus have been lost, but he was a significant influence on a number of authors writing in Latin as well as Greek in the period from the first century BCE to the second century CE, and, through them, on the later development of what came to be known as Menippean satire (see Chapter 5).

During the same period, however, another genre developed which was to prove particularly influential in later times. This was satire written by Roman writers in Latin verse. The first name associated with this is Ennius (Quintus Ennius, 239–169 BCE), who was best known for his *Annales*, the first epic poem in Latin, describing the history of Rome from its legendary origins to the poet's own time, but who also wrote what were referred to as *saturae*. The works of Ennius survive only in fragmentary form, and the fact that we have only thirty-one lines of his *saturae* makes it difficult to say much about them. To take an example, a single line such as "simia quam similis turpissima bestia nobis" ("How like ourselves is that most ugly beast the ape") shows clear evidence of literary craft. To begin with, it is a line of hexameter verse, a form which writers in Latin adopted from Greek models such as Homer. Unlike many traditional forms of verse in English, this did not depend on rhyme, but on the use of patterns of long and short syllables. For the hexameter, the basic requirement was that each line consisted of six metrical feet: each of the first four could be either a spondee (two long syllables, usually indicated as – – when "scanning" or annotating the meter) or a dactyl (a long syllable followed by two short syllables –‿‿). The fifth foot had to be a dactyl, while the sixth was usually a spondee, though in practice the final syllable could be either long or short. Detailed conventions governed which syllables counted as long and which as short. Many other metrical forms came to be used in Latin verse, but the hexameter was always the most common. Ennius's line scans like this, with | used to indicate where one foot ends and another begins:

sīmĭă | quām sĭmĭ | līs tūr | pīssĭmă | bēstĭă | nōbīs

There is heavy alliteration in the s sounds. Even though the vowel lengths are different, an important issue in Latin verse, the opening syllables of the words "similis" ("like") and "simia" ("ape") echo each other, and this helps to suggest the traditional characterisation of the ape as a creature given to imitation. Taken on its own, the line could be open to different interpretations, but it has come down to us quoted in a work by the Roman philosopher, lawyer and politician Cicero (Marcus Tullius Cicero, 106–143 BCE), where the context suggests that Ennius was understood to mean that while the resemblance between apes and humans was striking, it was purely superficial, and that the habits of the two species were different (Warmington, 1967, I, 390–391).

Ennius was followed by Gaius Lucilius (b. 180 or 168–167, d. 103–102 BCE), who was described by his successor Horace as the *inventor* (creator) of the genre (*Satires*, I, x. 48). Somewhat less than 1,500 lines of Lucilius's poems survive, but none of the poems are complete, and in view of their fragmentary nature, there is a limit to what can be said about them for certain. For example, the line "subicit huic fulcrum, fulmentas quattuor addit" ("under this he fixes a bedpost, and adds four supports") may possibly have come from a passage which contrasted rural simplicity with urban luxury and excess, but all we really know is that, several centuries after Lucilius, it was preserved by being quoted by a grammarian who noted it as an example of "fulmentas" being used in a grammatically feminine form, instead of the neuter which would have been more usual (Warmington, 1967, III, 48–49).

The later Roman teacher of rhetoric and literary critic Quintilian famously said "satura quidem tota nostra est", that is, satire is indeed entirely Roman, by which he meant as opposed to other genres which Roman writers had borrowed from their Greek predecessors. Nevertheless, there was no consensus about the origin of the word, and differing views about the nature of the genre. The grammarian Diomedes (fourth century CE) associated satire with the satyr plays of ancient Greek theatre, which featured the satyrs of mythology, wild men with pointed ears, and perhaps horns and tails, who were assimilated by later Roman writers to the Italian concept of the fauns as creatures who were half-man and half-goat. In the satyr plays, the satyrs were involved in a variety of burlesque situations, so that in the only surviving complete example, the *Cyclops* of Euripides (c. 480–c. 406 BCE), they are the drink-loving followers of Silenus, a mythological figure usually seen as the companion of the wine-god Dionysus (Green, 1957).

The connection between satire and satyrs has a certain appeal: as late as 1963, the satirical comedy duo of Michael Flanders and Donald Swann alluded to it in the introduction to their revue *At the Drop of Another Hat*, commenting on what was seen as the "satire boom" of the early 1960s in British theatre and television by saying that "satire squats, hoof in mouth, under every bush" (Flanders and Swann, 1991). Modern classical scholars reject it as implausible on etymological grounds, however. Other suggestions put forward by Diomedes were that the name came from the *lanx satura*, a dish filled with a variety of foodstuffs and offered to the gods on ritual occasions, or that the name had something to do with a type of sausage. A definitive answer may be impossible, but there seems to be something in the idea that satire as a literary genre was associated in some way with the idea of a mixture of different ingredients (Coffey, 1976, 11–23). For Roman writers, the most important of these were humour, invective directed against groups or individuals and verbal ingenuity, especially in the use of particular verse forms.

Lucilius wrote in different poetic metres, but the surviving evidence suggests that most of his satires were in one particular metre, the hexameter, the form used by Ennius in the line discussed above. This was the practice followed by later Roman writers of verse satire: Horace, Persius (Aulus Persius Flaccus, 34–62 CE) and Juvenal. Horace wrote in different genres, including his *Odes* in a variety of lyric metres, but his satires are in hexameters. He referred to them as *sermones*, a word which suggested not that they were "sermons" in the English sense of the word, but that they were like ordinary everyday speech (*sermo*) – as opposed, say, to the deliberately high style of Virgilian epic, which was also written in hexameters. This is true to the extent that Horace does employ a more colloquial vocabulary (e.g., the occasional obscenity) that will not be found in Virgil, but the mere fact that these poems are written in a strict metrical form differentiates them from ordinary speech. One of Horace's characters (the lawyer Trebatius, *Satires*, II, i, 17) refers to "sapiens Lucilius", "the wise Lucilius", but elsewhere Horace complains that Lucilius wrote too much, too easily – "in hora saepe ducentos ... versus dictabat stans pede in uno" ("he often dictated two hundred lines in an hour, standing on one foot", *Satires*, I, iv, 9–10) – thereby implying that his own compositions were more carefully polished. This is borne out by the poems themselves, which show the careful arrangement of words for effect, and the mock-modesty in the comparison with ordinary speech is clearly not to be taken too seriously. Although Persius has a short preface in a different metre, his six satires, and the sixteen of Juvenal, are entirely in hexameters.

Lucilius was well known for sharp criticism of his contemporaries, including prominent figures whom he identified in his poems by name. This led some to compare his work with the tradition of invective in Greek iambic verse exemplified by Archilochus, and, indeed, some of Lucilius's poems were written in iambics. Lucilius appears to have been able to get away with what verged on personal abuse because he was rich and well connected. Although Horace represents himself as arguing with Trebatius for the satirist's right to criticise named targets, he was the son of a former slave and his success as a writer depended very largely on the patronage of the great: Maecenas, one of the chief advisors of the Emperor Augustus, and the emperor himself. As a result, Horace is considerably more circumspect than Lucilius. His targets are generally types rather than individuals, and at least some of the names used are far from specific or are those of persons of little or no social consequence. Writing in the reign of the Emperor Nero (54–68 CE), Persius avoids political subject matter for obvious reasons, and when Juvenal singles out prominent examples for criticism, they are all historical figures who were safely out of the way at the time of writing, figures such as Sejanus (Lucius Aelius Sejanus, 20 BCE–31 CE), the minister of the Emperor Tiberius (reigned 14–37 CE). In Juvenal's Satire X, the career of Sejanus is treated as an example of the capriciousness of fortune and the inconstancy of popular adulation. Having risen to supreme power as a result of imperial favour, his downfall is inevitable when this is withdrawn as a result of Tiberius fearing that his minister was usurping his own authority. After Sejanus's condemnation and summary execution, his statues are pulled down and melted:

> ... et crepat ingens
> Sejanus; deinde ex facie toto orbe secunda
> fiunt urceoli, pelves, sartago, matellae.

> [And the mighty Sejanus crackles; then from the face which was once second in importance in the whole world are made pitchers, basins, frying-pans and chamber-pots.]

The corpse of Sejanus himself is dragged through the streets on a hook for all to see, and bystanders reassure each other, "nunquam ... amavi hunc hominem" ("I never liked the man"). A once mighty figure has fallen, and the literal reworking of his statues as banal household implements is a powerful metaphor for the eclipse of his reputation.

In general, then, Roman satire offers reflections on human life, sometimes given with ironic detachment, sometimes made the basis of explicit or implied suggestions as to how readers or listeners might improve their own lives by changing their conduct. The reader or listener is here cast in the role of bystander, but the appeal is to moral and ethical values that are shown to be deficient in the subject of the satire. Juvenal's Satire X can be distinguished from a work like the *Ibis* of Ovid, in which the poet hurls abuse at a real or imaginary enemy identified only by the pseudonym of the title. Ovid does not suggest that Ibis, or that the audience, change their ways; he merely wishes a variety of gruesome fates upon him.

Sometimes the satire is clearly like one of Freud's "tendentious jokes" (see Introduction), in that the satirist invites the reader to share feelings of amusement or moral superiority to those satirised. The victims, however, fall into two types for the most part: either historical figures who can safely be used as examples without fear of repercussions, or social types such as the bore, the bad host or the overbearing patron, who are identified by names which appear to be generic or fictitious. In some cases, the names may have been recognisable to contemporaries as those of actual individuals, but this does not seem to be the main point. Satirists name a number of bad poets, for example, but we know nothing of the "hoarse-voiced Codrus" mentioned at the beginning of Juvenal's first Satire as the author of an epic on Theseus, and he may be no more of a particular individual than the unnamed poets referred to in the next couple of lines that follow as the writers of plays and of elegiac verse:

> Semper ego auditor tantum? nunquamne reponam,
> vexatus toties rauci Theseïde Codri?
> Impune ergo mihi recitaverit ille togatas,
> hic elegos?
>
> (Juvenal, I, 1–4)

> [Shall I always be just a listener and never respond, annoyed so many times by the *Theseïd* of the hoarse-voiced Codrus? Shall that man have declaimed his plays to me unpunished, and this one his elegies?]

The principle seems to be "parcere personis, dicere de vitis" ("to spare individuals, and to talk about vices"). This quotation raises important issues, however, about both the generic boundaries of satire, and its scope. It does not come from Juvenal or one of the other satirists already mentioned, but from Martial, whose work consists of over 1,500 epigrams, the vast majority of which are not in hexameters but in elegiac couplets. This was a verse form in which a line of hexameter verse was followed by a pentameter line, which was shorter and scanned differently, as we can see in the following epigram of Martial (VI, lxxix):

Trīstĭs ĕs | ĕt fē|līx. Scĭăt | hōc Fōr|tūnă că|vētō:
īngrā|tūm dī|cēt || tē, Lŭpĕ, | sī scĭĕ|rĭt.

[You are sad, in spite of material prosperity. Take care that Fortune does not become aware of this: she will call you ungrateful, Lupus, if she should know.]

If, as some critics (e.g., Coffey) have argued, Roman satire (apart from the Menippean tradition) is that which is written in hexameters, then Martial is not a satirist. Nor is Phaedrus, whose adaptations in Latin verse of the fables originally composed in Greek prose and attributed to Aesop were written not in hexameters but in a different metrical form, iambic trimeter. It is true that in one of his epigrams (XII, xciv) Martial complains that whatever sort of writing he tries his hand at, he is always being copied by a certain Tucca. The general arrangement, and the use of the phrase "quid minus esse potest?" ("what could be less?"), suggest that the genres are being listed in what is intended as a descending order of importance: epic, drama (whether tragic or comic), lyric poetry, satire, elegy, epigram. This implies that epigram is something distinct from satire, and, indeed, less prestigious. As Coffey (1976, 328) puts it, "The joke depends in part on the tacit acceptance of a hierarchy of genres".

Martial's self-deprecation is not to be taken too seriously, however. The line about "parcere personis, dicere de vitis" (*Epigrams*, X, xxxiii, 10) would remind some readers of the passage in Virgil's *Aeneid* where Aeneas is visiting the underworld and his father's spirit prophesies to him of the future glories of Rome, finishing with the idea that the future *artes* (skills, employment) of Romans will be to rule other peoples, and "parcere subjectis et debellare superbos" (*Aeneid* VI, 853; "to spare the conquered and to overcome the proud in war"). The epigrammatist, and the satirist more generally, aim to conquer vice (however that is to be defined) in the same way that Rome imposed its ideas of civilisation on those it considered to be barbarians. It is not always a pleasant process, and sometimes we may be reminded of the bitter summary of Rome's civilising mission which the historian Tacitus (Cornelius Tacitus, first to second centuries CE) attributed to the Caledonian chieftain Calgacus, "ubi solitudinem faciunt, pacem appellant" (*Agricola*, c. 98; "where they create a wasteland, they call it peace").

In another epigram (X, iv), Martial asks what is the point of reading mythological stories:

> quid te vana iuvant miserae ludibria chartae?
>> hoc lege, quod possit dicere vita "meum est".
> non hic Centauros, non Gorgonas Harpyiasque
>> invenies: hominem pagina nostra sapit.

> ["What use are silly stories badly told? Read this, which life can claim as its own. Here you find no Centaurs or Gorgons or Harpies: I write about people".]

This turns on two potential meanings of the word "sapit". On the one hand, "our page savours of man", and we should note that the Latin word "homo" includes both genders, as in the playwright Terence's much-quoted "Homo sum, humani nihil a me alienum puto" (*Heautontimorumenos*, Act I: "I am a man, I think nothing which is human is strange to me"). On the other hand, "sapit" also suggests knowledge and understanding, so that Martial is not just saying that he writes about people rather than about mythological creatures; indeed, he is making a claim that his work offers insights into human nature and its foibles.

As a programmatic statement, this is applicable not just to the epigrammatist, but to satirists more generally. It is true that not all epigrams are satirical. Martial's work includes poems like the epitaph for a slave girl who died young (*Epigrams*, V, xxxiv), which appears to express genuine sympathy and regret, or the poems celebrating the games laid on by the Emperor Titus in 80 CE for the opening of the Colosseum. Definitions of genre should not be unduly reductive, however, and particular texts are not necessarily always what they may seem to be at first: Martial was notorious to later readers for his gross flattery of the Emperor Domitian (reigned 81–96 CE), but Fitzgerald (2007) has argued for a more nuanced reading, pointing out that an epigram which appears obsequious in isolation may have the capacity to seem more critical when viewed in the context of accompanying poems where the arrangement itself contributes to a coherent whole. Significant overlap in material and approach between satire written in hexameters and other texts suggests that boundaries should not be too rigidly defined. The story of the Town Mouse and the Country Mouse appears in the Greek stories attributed to Aesop, and in the Latin verse adaptations by Horace and Phaedrus. In each of these, the moral is the same: that it is better to enjoy modest comfort in security than to seek after luxuries which can only be obtained by risking danger. The same argument appears in one of Martial's most famous epigrams (X, xlvi), which has been claimed to be "perhaps the most frequently translated poem in English literature" (Sullivan and Boyle, 1996, xvii); this is the version by Sir Richard Fanshawe (1608–1666; Bohn 1860, 470):

> The things that make a life to please
> (Sweetest Martial), they are these:
> Estate inherited, not got:
> A thankful field, hearth always hot:
> City seldom, law-suits never:
> Equal friends agreeing ever:
> Health of body, peace of mind:
> Sleeps that till the morning bind:
> Wise simplicity, plain fare:
> Not drunken nights, yet loos'd from care:
> A sober, not a sullen spouse:
> Clean strength, not such as his that plows;
> Wish only what thou art, to be;
> Death neither wish, nor fear to see.

In a similar manner, Persius (*Satires*, VI) suggests that wealth should be enjoyed without either extravagance or undue scrimping for the benefit of an unappreciative heir.

This and other themes which recur in the writings of Roman satirists, such as the similar arguments about what is appropriate to ask of the gods in Persius (*Satires*, II) and Juvenal (*Satires*, X), might suggest, as is argued by Jenkinson (1980, 1) in relation to those of Persius, that "influenced as we are by modern presuppositions about the word 'satire', we might feel that 'Sermons' or 'Moral Essays' were titles more aptly descriptive of their main content". This depends on what the reader's idea of a sermon is, which might well exclude the sexual and scatological elements that are common in Roman satire. An example is Horace, *Satires*, I, viii, whose narrator is a statue of Priapus, the god of gardens and fertility. His ithyphallic image is often a source of crude humour, and this particular Priapus begins by telling us that he has been made from the wood of a fig tree (which would have been too brittle for most other purposes). The poem begins in what seems a straightforward manner: to scare away birds and thieves, Priapus has been set up in some new gardens on the Esquiline Hill in Rome, which have been a paupers' cemetery. He sees two women arrive at night who are called Canidia and Sagana, and whose names are used elsewhere by Horace but who appear here to be inventions, since the first suggests grey hair and old age (*canities*) and the second is based on *saga* (a witch). They have come to the gardens at night because the area's previous use as a cemetery makes it possible to find human bones and poisonous plants there, and also makes it a suitable place to perform witchcraft rituals. They begin by digging a hole in the ground and sacrificing a lamb in order to summon ghosts with its blood. The fact that they are described as digging with their nails, and tearing the sacrificial lamb apart with their teeth, signals, perhaps, that their activity is a little exaggerated. Nevertheless, summoning ghosts with the blood of a sacrificed animal was a well-known ritual (compare Homer, *Odyssey*, XI), and belief in witchcraft was widespread at the time. The description the Priapus gives of the two women going about their business of casting spells with the aid of two images, one of wool and one of wax; of their magic ingredients, which are the beard of a wolf and the tooth of a speckled snake; and of their invocations of Hecate, goddess of crossroads and magic, and Tisiphone, one of the Furies, is at first similar to other Roman literary texts (e.g., Tibullus, *Elegies* I, ii) in which witchcraft is treated as something real and powerful. Being only a statue, Priapus can only look on, but he is not to remain a "testis inultus" ("unavenged spectator"). The witches have lit a fire to assist them in casting their spells, and it is presumably very close to Priapus, because when they put the wax image in the fire, it blazes up and causes the fig wood to split. Priapus says unambiguously "pepedi/ diffissa nate" ("I farted from my cloven buttock"), and while in Latin verse singulars are commonly used for plurals, and vice versa, purely for metrical reasons, the singular here is possibly an additional comic touch suggesting that the statue was misshaped or damaged to start with, since "nates" ("buttocks") is normally used in the plural. The fig wood is said to have sounded like a burst bladder. The witches run off in a panic, Canidia loses her false teeth, Sagana her wig, and they drop their magic herbs and enchanted bracelets. The reader is assured that he or she would have had a good laugh at the sight. But whether this is a "short piece of entertainment without uplift" (Coffey, 1976: 78), a misogynistic attack on stereotyped old women or something we can recognise as a satire directed against superstition, it is certainly very different from the great didactic poem *De rerum natura* ("On the nature of things) in which Lucretius (Titus Lucretius Carus, c. 99–c. 55 BCE) attempted to convert his readers from conventional Roman religion to Epicurean philosophy by rational argument.

Another example is Persius's fourth satire, an imagined dialogue between the Greek philosopher Socrates and his interlocutor Alcibiades, which appears to be arguing that there is not much point in studying philosophy if one is going to lead a worldly life. While this may seem suitable matter for a sermon or moral essay, the modern reader may be startled to find a significant part of the poem (nine lines out of fifty-two) devoted to Socrates giving as an example of the worldliness of Alcibiades the fact that he removes the hair from his private parts, a process described in considerable detail. This sort of thing, however, is very much part of the *lanx satura*, the mixed dish of Roman satire, and the use of exaggeration, distortion, frank references to sexuality and scatological humour continues to be employed by later satirists, many of whom (as we will see) acknowledged the influence of their Roman predecessors.

It can be difficult to understand texts from a culture widely separated from our own in space and time, and some critics would of course argue that it is impossible to do so with any real certainty. It used to be conventional, for example, to treat Juvenal's satires as a reliable source of information about Roman social history, and further, to mine them for snippets which could be used to construct a speculative biography of the poet. When Juvenal talks (III, 268) about the "diversa pericula noctis" ("the various dangers of the night"), such as having roof tiles drop on your head, we know that modern archaeology has demonstrated that jerry-building was a serious problem in ancient Rome. Nevertheless, when Juvenal goes on to say that you would be foolish to go out for dinner without having made your will, we may suspect him of comic exaggeration for effect. The question of attributing purpose to the writer is also a minefield for the critic or cultural historian. Juvenal claimed (I, 79) that "indignatio facit versum", his indignation, or, as Coffey usefully suggests (1976, 124), "a clamorous anger", made him write. The question of the poetic persona is one that has to be raised: is Juvenal really a grumpy old man, a "laudator temporis acti" ("a praiser of times past") in the phrase coined much earlier by Horace (*Ars Poetica*, 173), someone who cannot stand the ways in which Roman society has changed, or is this simply a pose? Are the grossly misogynistic attitudes expressed in his sixth satire to be taken at face value, or are they actually the substance of what is being satirised? We don't know. On balance, however, Roman satire appears to be conservative, devoted to criticising deviations from a traditional social order: for example, frugality is praiseworthy, but not meanness; wealth has its place in society, but ostentatious displays by the *nouveaux riches* are a fit subject for mockery. The double standards of a heteronormative morality lead to condemnations of female agency and of some types of homosexual behaviour (see Chapter 7). Slaves and freedmen should be kept in their place, and the social climber, such as the boor who accosts Horace in the Forum (*Satires*, I, ix), is to be shunned. We may think there is a degree of hypocrisy here, since Horace was himself the son of an ex-slave, but he acknowledges that his success was due to his father's willingness to give him a good education, and to the patronage of Maecenas and Augustus, and he sees no contradiction in fobbing off the attempts of the boor to get the poet to introduce him to Maecenas. Those in power, on the other hand, are to be treated with caution, if at all. Those who claim to espouse traditional values but are exposed as hypocrites are fair game, such as a certain Labullus, who is accused in an epigram by Martial (*Epigrams*, XII, xxxvi) of making an ostentatious parade of what is in fact a very limited generosity, in comparison with the great ones of the past. The behaviour of social inferiors, and those who do not share the poet's outlook on life, such as Canidia and Sagana, can be, and are, freely mocked.

We know the names of some Roman satirists, such as Manilius Vopiscus, Silius and Turnus, whose work has not survived (Coffey, 1976: 119). What has come down to us, surviving the hazards of manuscript transmission in the Middle Ages, was sufficiently varied and substantial to provide models and inspiration for many poets of later periods. Horace, Juvenal and Martial, in particular, became influential in the Renaissance and after because they were widely used as school texts, albeit frequently in selections or expurgated editions. As a writer mainly of short poems, Martial was especially popular with translators, and Sullivan and Boyle (1996: xxiv–xxv) argue that the practice of translating Martial's epigrams, with their predominance of closed elegiac couplets, was a vital factor in developing the heroic couplet in English, and an important contribution to the development of the tradition of formal verse satire in English. Drawing on Horace and Juvenal (and, to a lesser extent, on Persius) as well, this was, as we shall see (Chapter 4), one of the major literary forms in English from the late seventeenth to the early nineteenth century.

4

VERSE SATIRE AFTER ANTIQUITY

The satirists of ancient Rome continued to be read in the Middle Ages, to the extent that a modern critic can describe Juvenal, for example, as "a favourite author" for twelfth-century poets (Walsh, 1997: 130). Nevertheless, mediaeval satire was wide ranging, extremely diverse and far from exclusively dependent on classical models. Twelfth-century epics like Joseph of Exeter's poem on the Trojan War and Walter of Châtillon's on Alexander the Great might have been written in Latin hexameters in conscious imitation of the grand style associated primarily with Virgil, but satirical poetry in Latin and the vernacular languages of Western Europe showed that it had other resources to draw on. *Propter Sion non tacebo* ("I will not be silent on account of Zion"; Walsh, 1997, 54–56, 125–131), one of several poems by Walter of Châtillon satirising the corruption and venality of the Papal Curia, contains the lines

> tunc securus fit viator,
> quia nudus, et cantator
>   it coram latronibus.

[Then the traveller will be safe, because he is naked, and he will go as a singer before thieves.]

This is clearly a paraphrase of a well-known line in Juvenal (X, 22): "cantabit vacuus coram latrone viator" ["The empty-handed traveller will sing in front of the thief"], which is also quoted some two centuries later by William Langland (c. 1330–c. 1386) in his *Piers Plowman* (Langland, 2000, 164, 321). Walter's poem contains other allusions to Juvenal's satires and other ancient Roman authors, and makes some use of classical mythology. The dangers the visitor faces in dealing with the papal Curia are compared to those of the mythical Scylla and Charybdis, to Syrtes (a classical Latin term for sandbanks, but originally a particular geographical reference) and to Sirens, which Christian writers had long taken from Homer (via Ovid's *Metamorphoses*) as apt symbols of the perilous appeal of sin. Many aspects of the poem which Walter uses to drive home his message that papal officials are smiling hypocrites who shamelessly fleece visitors obliged to make use of their services are not classical at all, however. He makes use of puns to a much greater extent than we would expect in a classical Latin author: two successive lines suggest, for example, that the "cardinales" ["cardinals"] are "di carnales" ["fleshly gods"]. Sound effects are combined with biblical allusion in passages such as the following:

> tales regunt Petri navem,
> tales habent eius clavem
>   ligandi potentiam;
> hi nos docent sed indocti,
> hi nos docent, et nox nocti
>   indicat scientiam.

[Such, i.e., the cardinals, steer the barque of Peter, such hold the key and the power to bind; such teach us, though they are unlearned; such teach us, and night shows knowledge unto night.]

The "barque" or ship of St. Peter was a stock symbol of the Catholic Church guided by the Pope, who as successor to Peter was believed to possess the keys of the Kingdom of Heaven and thus had the power of binding and loosing, given to Peter by Christ in a famous passage in the Bible (Matthew, xvi, 18–19). The word play on "docent"/"indocti" leads on to the rhyme with "nox nocti", and another biblical allusion (Psalm xviii, 3, in the Vulgate), where, as Walsh points out, Walter has distorted the original message of the Psalm, in which the line about "night shows knowledge unto night" is part of the argument that "The heavens show forth the glory of God", but in this context suggests that the cardinals are like the blind leading the blind. Walter's poem makes use of exaggeration and grim humour – the papal officials are compared to Scylla and Charybdis, where dangerous rocks and sea monsters lie in wait for the mariner, and are said to be more cruel than wild beasts, so that even the visitor who arrives with a bag full of money will leave "pauper ... et egenus" ["poor and needy" – another biblical allusion; cf. Job, xxiv, 14; also Psalms, xxxiv, 10; lxix, 6 in the Vulgate; xxxv, 10; lxx, 5 in the King James Version (KJV)]. Some of this is the sort of strategy which can be found in classical writers and other satires, but Walter's medium is also an important part of his message in another way. "Propter Sion" is written not in the classical hexameters Walter used for his epic on Alexander, but in rhymed and rhythmical verse like that used by many other mediaeval writers. This particular poem uses trochaic tetrameter, a metre frequently employed for hymns, so that the contrast between the expectations of liturgical solemnity aroused by the form and the grimness of the content give added point to the attack on the hypocrisy of the cardinals and other church officials who are "intus lupi, foris vero/sicut agni ovium" [wolves in sheep's clothing; literally "wolves within, and outside like lambs of the flock", using another biblical phrase – cf. Psalm cxiii, 4, 6 in the Vulgate; cxiv, 4, 6 in KJV].

Latin continued to be a popular medium for satirical songs for several centuries, but material in the vernacular became increasingly prominent. Wright's pioneering collection of "political songs of England" from the thirteenth and fourteenth centuries includes examples in Latin, Norman French and Middle English. Some of these, such as the Middle English song about the Battle of Courtrai between the French and the Flemings (1302), are purely descriptive, while others are clearly satirical. A "Song on the Venality of the Judges", dating from the early fourteenth century, attacks the administrators of

royal justice rather than officials of the papal curia, and it is in a lively
and varied rhythm unlike Walter of Châtillon's parody of liturgical
solemnity. The author deploys biblical allusion, as well as other satiric
techniques. He opens with

> Beati qui esuriunt
> Et sitiunt, et faciunt
>   justitiam [...]

[Blessed are they who hunger and thirst, and who do justice ...]

This is an adaptation of part of Christ's Sermon on the Mount in the
Vulgate: "Beati qui esuriunt et sitiunt justitiam" (Matthew, v, 6; KJV:
"Blessed are they which do hunger and thirst after righteousness"). He
goes on to amplify this in his own way:

> Et odiunt et fugiunt
>   injuriae nequitiam [...]

[And hate and flee from the wickedness of wrongdoing ...]

Taken in the context of the song as a whole, the effect of what at
first appears to be a slight change is not only to give the statement
a catchy rhythm but also to emphasise the idea that the poor may
do what is right, but that those who have become rich through the
exercise of power and influence, especially judicial power, can
hardly be expected to do so. Instead, they favour the great and exploit
and despise the poor. Like Walter, the writer mentions the seeming
friends who approach those who have business in court, but whose
only wish is to be bribed. Again, like Walter, and like many other
satirists in different periods, he makes his point by drawing a contrast
between things as they ought to be, and as they really are. Those who
should protect the poor and the helpless are only interested in exploiting them:

> Utraque manu capiunt,
> Et sic eos decipiunt
>   quorum sunt tutores.

[They take with both hands, and thus they deceive those whose protectors they are.]

(Wright, 1839, 224–230)

A similar use of biblical imagery can be found in an English song of the same period, which contrasted the humility of Christ with the ostentation of the rich in Edward II's reign:

> Whil God was on erthe
>> And wondrede wyde,
> What wes the resound .
>> Why he nolde ryde?
> For he nolde no grom
>> To go by ys syde [...]

[When God was on earth, and wandered about, what was the reason he did not wish to ride? Because he did not want any groom to accompany him.]

(Wright, 1839, 240)

This might seem a rather weak point to anyone who remembered Christ's Entry into Jerusalem, where the biblical narrative describes him riding a donkey and surrounded by crowds (e.g., Matthew xxi, 1–9), but it could presumably be argued that this was an exceptional event, and that in any case the donkey was enough of a contrast with the fine mounts of mediaeval nobles. Nevertheless, it looks like an example of how the force of satire can be blunted when satirists have failed to fully think through the possible implications of what they are writing.

Another early fourteenth-century example collected by Wright uses the beast fable to criticise the legal system. The Lion, the King of Beasts, allows the Fox to get away with stealing geese, and the Wolf with killing sheep, but the Ass's protest that all he does is eat grass is not enough to save him from severe punishment:

> Al his bonis ȝe to-draw,
>> Loke that ȝe noȝt lete;
> And that ic ȝive al for lawe
>> That his fleis be al i-frette.

[Do you pull all his bones apart – take care that you do not leave any alone; and that is the judgement I give to everyone, that his flesh should be utterly destroyed.]

The point is made more explicit immediately afterwards:

> The lafful man ssal be i-bund,
>   And i-do in strang pine,
> And i-hold in fast prisund,
>   Fort that he mak fine.

[The man who obeys the law shall be bound, and suffer severe punishment, and be held in a secure prison, to make him pay a fine.]

(Wright, 1839, 195–205)

Much more developed satire can be found in mediaeval writers who are more self-consciously literary than the anonymous composers of the songs collected by Wright. Guild dramas, "composed by the learned for popular audiences", have a "frequently satirical tone" (Yunck, 1988, 140), and satirical elements can also be found in the works of William Langland, John Gower (c. 1330–1408) and Geoffrey Chaucer (c. 1340–1400). Taken as a whole, Langland's *Piers Plowman* is an allegory of human existence and of the search for salvation. However, the emphasis on the principle of "redde quod debes" ("pay what you owe") which Langland quotes out of its biblical context (Matthew xviii, 28; KJV: "Pay me that thou owest") to make it into a more general statement about Christian justice, and the obligations of the rich to the poor in particular, implies a criticism of his own society for failing to meet these obligations. At the same time, he satirises the friars for using their religious vows of poverty to secure for themselves a life of idleness at the expense of others. This is a target he shares with his contemporaries: "The chief villains of the fourteenth-century satirists were the friars" (Yunck, 142).

The characters who people the great panorama of fourteenth-century society in Chaucer's most famous work, *The Canterbury Tales*, are not all targets of satire, though some of them certainly are: for example, the Prioress, whose elegant attire and fondness for good living are more than a little too much for someone supposedly vowed to a life of poverty. The complexity of Chaucer's approach to satire can be shown by looking at his representation of the Pardoner, an official entrusted with the task of raising money for the Church by the display of relics and the sale of indulgences (documents confirming the remission of punishment for sins). There are four parts to this: the description of the Pardoner in the General Prologue to the Tales, what the Pardoner says by way of prologue to his own tale, the Pardoner's Tale itself and, finally, the reaction of the audience (Benson, 1988, 34, 194–202).

The Pardoner begins his Tale with conventional denunciations of drunkenness, gluttony and swearing, supported by references to the Bible, the Roman philosopher Seneca (Seneca the Younger, c. 4 BCE–65 CE) and ancient history. He then tells a story of three young men in Flanders, who are drinking in a tavern when they see a funeral go by, which turns out to be that of an acquaintance. They resolve to go in search of Death, in order to kill him and so prevent him from killing any more of their friends. They meet an old man, who may or may not be Death himself, and who tells them to go and look in a grove that he points out to them. In view of what happens subsequently, there is some irony in his manner:

> Se ye that ook? Right there ye shall him finde.
> God save yow, that boghte agayn mankyde,
> And yow amende!

The young men find a heap of gold coins under the tree that has been indicated, but decide to wait until nightfall before carrying it home to divide among themselves. They draw lots, and one is sent to buy bread and wine while the other two watch the gold and await his return. The two watchers decide to kill their companion when he returns, so that the treasure can be divided between the two of them. The third, however, hopes to get it all for himself, and buys poison to put in the wine he takes back to the other two. They kill him as planned, and then die of the poison, so that all three of them do indeed find Death under the tree, as the mysterious old man had foretold. The Pardoner concludes his tale by warning his listeners once more to beware of the very sin of avarice of which he himself is guilty.

It is the sort of story which illustrated many a mediaeval sermon, and it is certainly not original to Chaucer. Versions are found in many different cultures, and at different times; indeed, it forms the basic plot of the 1948 film, *The Treasure of the Sierra Madre*, directed by John Holt and starring Humphrey Bogart. There is the occasional satirical touch, such as the exaggeration with which the Pardoner denounces gluttony:

> Allas, the shorte throte, the tendre mouth,
> Maketh that est and west and north and south,
> In erthe, in eir, in water, men to swynke
> To gete a glotoun deyntee mete and drynke!

Nevertheless, the Pardoner tells the story straight. It is only when we see his Tale in conjunction with the other elements that the total effect becomes more complex. In the General Prologue, he is described in a manner that was likely to prejudice a mediaeval reader against him. He has staring eyes and long, lank fair hair. He is sexually ambiguous: he has a high voice, and it is suggested he is a eunuch or a homosexual. Above all, he is a deceiver and a hypocrite who exploits the poor. He carries fake relics, such as a pillowcase he claims to be the veil of the Blessed Virgin:

> But with thise relikes, when that he fond
> A povre person dwellynge upon lond,
> Upon a day he gat him moore moneye
> Than that the person gat in monthes tweye;
> And thus, with feyned flatterye and japes,
> He made the person and the peple his apes.

In the Prologue to his Tale, the Pardoner tells the assembled pilgrims on their way to Canterbury that he always preaches on the same topic:

> My theme is alwey oon, and evere was –
> *Radix malorum est Cupiditas.*

His Latin phrase is an adaptation of a biblical quotation (I Timothy vi, 10: "Radix enim omnium malorum est cupiditas" in the Vulgate, or

"For the root of all evils is greed"; KJV: "For the love of money is the root of all evil"). He goes on to describe how he uses his fake relics to get money out of the ignorant church congregations he visits, and unblushingly declares "I preche of no thing but for coveitsye". He is perfectly aware that he is not following biblical teaching, and that by taking from them the little that they have, he increases the poverty of his listeners:

> I wol noon of the apostles countrefete;
> I wol have moneie, wolle, chese and whete,
> Al were it yeven of the povereste page,
> Or of the povereste wydwe in a village,
> Al sholde hir children sterve for famyne.

These admissions could hardly be in stronger contrast to the overt moral message of the tale itself. The contrast appears to heighten Chaucer's satire on the way that some functionaries of the mediaeval church exploited their congregations.

Chaucer does not quite leave it there, however. As soon as he has finished his Tale, the Pardoner offers his relics to the listening Pilgrims, and suggests that they give him money in exchange for his pardons. His behaviour is so brazen that some critics have drawn attention to the fact that the Pardoner has "dronke a draughte of corny ale" while delivering his Prologue, and suggested that his candid admissions about his being " a ful vicious man" are the result of his being drunk. Be that as it may, the Host loses his temper with the Pardoner, abuses him in vulgar terms and threatens to castrate him and display his testicles as relics, thus reminding us of the suggestion in the General Prologue that the Pardoner may already be a eunuch. The group laughs, and the "worthy Knight" urges the Host and the Pardoner to kiss and make up, which they do. Is Chaucer suggesting that some things are beyond the potentially corrective power of satire, or that satire cannot actually change anything and that we must simply accept human nature, including its vices and follies, for what it is?

Satire in English and Scots continued to be produced in various forms and styles in the fifteenth and early sixteenth centuries. Well-known examples of writers in Scots include Robert Henryson (fl. c. 1460–1500) and William Dunbar (b. c. 1460, d. after 1513).

Henryson reworked a number of Aesop's fables, such as the Town Mouse and Country Mouse, which became "The Uplandis Mous and the Burges Mous" (Wood, 1958, 8–16). It is not only the language which is different: numerous details make the setting a specifically Scottish one, and the larder in which the Burges Mous feasts her cousin is clearly northern European and not Mediterranean:

> Baith Cheis and Butter upon their skelfis hie,
> And flesche and fische aneuch, baith fresche and salt,
> And sekkis full of meill and eik of malt.

There are also additions to the story. The mice are twice disturbed, the first time by the spenser or steward, after which the Uplandis Mous describes her fright in a manner which suggests Lenten abstinence in a Catholic country:

> I may not eit, sa sair I am agast;
> I had lever thir fourty dayis fast,
> With watter caill, and to gnaw benies or peis,
> Than all your feist in this dreid and diseis.

On the second occasion, the Uplandis Mous is actually caught by a cat and has a narrow escape. The moral of contentment with one's lot, "Blissed be sempill lyfe withouten dreid", is essentially the same as in Aesop, Horace and Phaedrus, but is made explicit over four eight-line stanzas and reinforced with a biblical reference.

Dunbar's works (Kinsley, 1969) include conventional satire on the friars, as evidenced in *How Dunbar was desired to be a Friar*. He also has a series of what his modern editor James Kinsley calls "Moralities", such as the powerful meditation on death as the end of all human life in *Timor Mortis Conturbat Me*, a poem in Scots with a Latin refrain which can be viewed as part of the tradition of satire as generalised reflection on human existence:

> Our plesance heir is all vane glory,
> This fals warld is bot transitory,
> The flesch is brukle, the Fend is sle:
> Timor mortis conturbat me.

[Our pleasure here is all vainglory, this false world is only transitory, the flesh is frail, the enemy (i.e., the Devil) is cunning, the fear of death frightens me.]

Dunbar also wrote *The Flyting of Dunbar and Kennedy*, an exchange of invective between himself and his contemporary, Walter Kennedy. While this ritualised combat of insults in Scottish verse may, as Kinsley suggests, have its origin in the practice of Gaelic-speaking bards, it is also reminiscent of classical models such as Archilochus (see Chapter 1) and Ovid's *Ibis* (see Chapter 2). A parallel can be seen in the practice of picong, the extempore exchange of ritual insults in song and rhyming verse between a pair of Caribbean calypsonians, such as that between the Mighty Sparrow (stage name of Slinger Francisco, b. 1935) and Lord Melody (stage name of Fitzroy Alexander, 1926–1988) recorded in 1957 (Francisco, 1957). While virtually a thing of the past, as few modern calypsonians are accustomed to extempore composition, picong was popular in the first half of the twentieth century. In view of the strong Scottish influence on Caribbean history, it may have Scottish as well as West African roots.

Dunbar's English near-contemporary John Skelton (c. 1463–1529) composed a wide range of poetry, experimenting with different metres, including the use of short lines with repeated rhymes on the same sound in a manner which has come to be identified as "Skeltonic" (de Sola Pinto, 1950, 2). Skelton himself referred to this as "ragged/Tattered and jagged", though he insisted "It hath in it some pyth" ("Collyn Clout", Kinsman, 1969, 97). Some critics have dismissed it as doggerel, though its vigour has been more appreciated in the nineteenth century by writers such as Elizabeth Barrett Browning and in the twentieth century by Robert Graves. This style certainly works effectively in a poem like *The Tunnyng of Elynour Rummyng*, with its vivid images of a tavern kept by an old hag of an ale-wife and the customers who come swarming when she has freshly brewed beer for them to buy. Eleanor Rumming was an easy target, but Skelton attacked more dangerous targets in poems like *Collyn Clout* and *Why come ye not to court?*, which satirised the corruption of the higher clergy and Cardinal Wolsey himself, who was at the time the all-powerful minister of King Henry VIII, something which according to one tradition forced Skelton to take sanctuary from the cardinal's intended vengeance in the precincts of Westminster Abbey. Lines like these from "Why come ye not to court?" show Skelton's verse could indeed have "pyth":

> Set up a wretch on high
> In a throne triumphantly,
> Make him a great estate,
> And he will play checkmate
> With royal majesty,
> Count himself as good as he,
> A prelate potential
> To rule under Belial,
> As fierce and as cruel
> As the field of hell.
>
> (de Sola Pinto, 1950, 108)

The accusation that Wolsey's arrogant manner and the pomp with which he surrounded himself showed that he did indeed "Count himself as good as he", that is, the king, could hardly have been more forcefully expressed. Nevertheless, it was not Skelton's satire, or even the fact that the same behaviour it attacked had made Wolsey many enemies, that brought about Wolsey's disgrace in 1529, but rather his failure to secure the king a divorce from Catherine of Aragon.

Another of Skelton's satires on Wolsey, "Speke Parott", may perhaps be satirising the "New Learning" of the Renaissance which led to new methods of teaching Latin and an interest in Greek and other learned tongues which was being promoted by Wolsey among others (Purdie, 2006, 44–45). After all, if a parrot can speak them, are they really of value in themselves?

> Yn Latyn, in Ebrue and in Caldee,
> In Greke tong Parott can both speke and seye.

The "New Learning", however, was far from a passing fad. While ancient authors had always retained some readers in the Middle Ages, there was now a renewed emphasis on their systematic study as a major part of education at school as well as university level. The revival of Greek learning in Western Europe had an effect on the development of prose satires, as the writings of Lucian of Samosata (second century CE) became popular as school texts (Chapter 5). The Roman satirists also benefited from a much wider readership, and increased familiarity with them was to have a profound effect on literary satire for some three centuries. One aspect of this was the popularity of the composition of satire in Latin verse, and two of the British writers best known in continental Europe were the Scot, George Buchanan (1506–1582), and the Welshman, John Owen (c. 1564–1622), both authors whose Latin poetry was often reprinted well into the eighteenth century. Buchanan produced Latin satirical poems against the Franciscan friars, in one instance loosely adapted from a poem in Scots by Dunbar, as well as epigrams directed against popes and bishops, and other targets, such as a mock encomium of a bawd, which shows his extensive knowledge of classical Latin authors (Buchanan, 1687; Ford, 1982, 47–62). While Buchanan employed a variety of Latin metres, Owen's numerous epigrams are almost all in Latin elegiac couplets modelled on those of Martial, and Owen himself was hailed as "the British Martial" (Owen, 1633). As with Martial himself, by no means all of Owen's epigrams were satirical in nature, but many certainly came into that category, and the number he directed at specifically Catholic targets both helped his popularity in Protestant Europe and ensured that his work was placed on the Catholic Church's *Index*, or official list of prohibited books.

A new departure in verse satire in English was marked by the work of Joseph Hall (1574–1656). In 1597–1598 he published *Virgidemiarum Six Books*, also known as *Virgidemiae* ("Harvests of Rods"). In the prologue, he made a bold claim:

> I first adventure, with fool-hardie might
> To tread the steps of perilous despight:
> I first adventure: follow me who list,
> And be the second English Satyrist.
> (Prologue, ll. 1–4; Davenport, 1949, 11)

This makes sense only if heavily qualified. As we have seen, there were certainly earlier satirists writing in English. Nevertheless, Hall is arguably the first to produce a substantial body of verse satires in English which are deliberately modelled on ancient Roman satirists, though he also refers to English predecessors such as Chaucer and Skelton. Like Martial, Hall said that he had no wish to repeat idle tales for his readers' amusement. It was, rather, his intention to reform his society:

> Nor Ladies wanton loue, nor wandring knight,
> Legend I out in rymes all richly dight.
> [...]
> Rather had I albee in careless rymes,
> Check the misordred world, and lawlesse times.
>
> (Davenport, 1949, 12)

Some of his targets were traditional: bad poets, besotted lovers unable to see the faults of their beloveds, unscrupulous lawyers, physicians who cared only for wealthy patients. Hall's satire (IV, iii), on those who boast of their distinguished ancestry but fail to live up to it, owes more than a little to Juvenal's eighth satire. Other satires may revisit standard themes, but still address more specifically sixteenth-century concerns. Horace may have complained about social climbers, but one of Hall's satires (IV, ii) tells of the farmer who "drudges all he can/ To make his eldest sonne a Gentleman" by giving him an expensive education. The son and his descendants repay him after his death by ignoring his memory to create a spurious noble ancestry for themselves, while at the same time maintaining the extravagant lifestyle to which they have become accustomed by extorting increased rents from their tenants and enclosing common lands. Hall complains of those who are dissatisfied with their lot and who cause social upheaval by refusing to remain in their station in life, such as the ploughman who sells his team and goes off to seek his fortune as a soldier. He points out that this sort of change can end unhappily:

> O warre to them that neuer tryde thee sweete!
> When his dead mate fals groueling at his feete,
> And angry bullets whistlen at his eare,
> And his dim eyes see nought but death and drere:
> Oh happy Plough-man were thy weale well known;
> Oh happy all estates except his owne!
>
> (IV, vi, 44–49; Davenport, 1949, 70)

The conclusion echoes a famous passage in Virgil (*Georgics*, II, 458–459):

O fortunatos nimium, sua si bona norint
agricolas [...]

[Oh how very happy farmers would be, if only they knew their own good fortune.]

The "angry bullets", however, are very much of Hall's own time. So, too, are the concerns about social mobility, which suggest that Hall saw satire as a socially conservative force. If he seeks to "Check the misordred world", this supposes a pre-existing order which should be restored. Nevertheless, it is not just the lower orders who are to blame. Hall's attacks on grasping landlords, enclosures, the decay of hospitality and the sort of *nouveaux riches* who want a domestic chaplain as a status symbol but have no intention of offering him a decent stipend show an equal concern with what he sees as the obligations of the rich towards the poor. His ideal society is an ordered, hierarchical one, in which the different ranks know their respective places and fulfil their duties towards each other.

Hall's references to identifiable persons are relatively few, and his criticisms are directed more at types than individuals. He recognised, however, that he might still give offence, and in a prose postscript to *Virgidemiae* defended himself with a version of the "If the cap fits" argument: "Art thou guiltie? complaine not, thou art not wronged: art thou guiltless? complaine not, thou art not touched" (Davenport, 1949, 98). In spite of this, Hall's satires attracted official disapproval. In 1599, the Archbishop of Canterbury and the Bishop of London listed them with other books of a satirical or erotic character by various authors which were to be burnt and forbidden to be reprinted. Although *Virgidemiae* was reprieved at the last minute, most of the other books on the list were in fact burnt by officials of the Stationers' Company. This official response to what was viewed as "disturbing comment on topical social problems" did not suppress satire in English entirely, and the first part of *Virgidemiae* was reprinted in 1602, but it may have been enough to limit the development of verse satire in the first half of the seventeenth century. Hall also produced a prose satire in Latin, *Mundus Alter et Idem*, which was published c. 1605, but it appeared against his wishes and with a probably fictitious continental imprint. For the rest of his long life, Hall was known almost exclusively as a clergyman, and it was not until the following century that we find *Virgidemiae* being praised by Alexander Pope and reprinted once more (Davenport, 1949, xvii, xxvii–xviii).

The great revival of interest in classical authors that heralded the Renaissance led to developments in education which were to prove favourable to a flowering of satire. From the sixteenth century onwards, British schools, like those elsewhere in Europe, placed an enormous emphasis on the study of Latin, and, to a lesser extent, Greek authors. While Latin prose writers were not neglected, much attention was given to poets. As Sullivan and Boyle note, Martial was especially prominent. Because of their concision, epigrams offered convenient short texts for school use, and since the collection known as the *Greek Anthology* was not fully published until the early nineteenth century, Martial long remained the best-known ancient epigrammatist. He was an important model for schoolboys' efforts in Latin verse, and was also, from the sixteenth century onwards, widely translated into English. An indication of its possible usefulness can be seen in the story of how, as an Oxford undergraduate, the prolific miscellaneous writer Thomas Brown (c. 1663–1704) was offered a reprieve from expulsion for some offence by the Dean of Christ Church, Dr John Fell, if he could produce an extempore translation of an epigram by Martial. The epigram, apparently chosen by Fell, was as follows:

> Non amo te, Sabidi, nec possum dicere quare:
>   hoc tantum possum dicere, non amo te.
>
> (Martial, *Epigrams*, I, xxxii)

Brown is said to have "immediately render'd [it] into English thus":

> I do not love you Dr. Fell, But why I cannot tell;
> But this I know full well, I do not love you Dr. Fell.
>
> (Brown, 1713, 166–167)

This is not entirely literal, as the fact that "hoc tantum possum dicere" means "I can say this much" rather than "But this I know full well" indicates. Nevertheless, it is a close paraphrase, with only the substitution of Fell's name for that of Martial's Sabidius. Fell apparently forgave the audacity of the translation, Brown went on to graduate (Jones, 2004), and his version was long repeated with minor variations, though Sullivan and Boyle were probably overstating the case when they claimed it was still "known to every schoolboy" in the late twentieth century (1996, 135). Even when allowance is made for the possibility of some embroidery in the telling, it demonstrates the cultural capital attached to the translation of classical poetry, and the period's delight in the idea of imitation, that ancient literature could readily be adapted to modern circumstances, no matter what historical differences prevailed. As William Hay (1695–1755), a later translator of Martial, put it:

> What was practised at Rome, near seventeen hundred years since, is now going on at London. Shift but the scene, and you would think Martial was lashing our times. The cap fits exactly.
> (Hay, 1755, ii)

The parallel between Rome in the first century and Britain in the eighteenth was not necessarily a favourable one. When eighteenth-century poets referred to London as "Augusta", they were suggesting that London, like ancient Rome, had become the capital of a great empire, the centre of a flourishing civilisation. If ancient poets like Horace and Virgil praised the Emperor Augustus (reigned 27 BCE–14 CE) for restoring peace and prosperity to the Roman world after many years of civil war, in 1759 the Irish writer Oliver Goldsmith (1728–1774) suggested that "The Augustan Age of England" was "the reign of Queen Anne [1702–1714], or some years before that period", which he saw as a "period of British glory" when "taste was united to genius; and as before our writers charmed with their strength of thinking, so then they pleased with strength and grace united" (Prior, 1854, I, 149–150). Nevertheless, there were those who saw Augustus as a tyrant and Horace as a base flatterer, and used perceived parallels between ancient Rome and modern Britain in the eighteenth century as a means of criticising the latter (Weinbrot, 1988, 21–33). In his *The First Epistle of the Second Book of Horace, Imitated* (1737), Alexander Pope (1688–1744) suggested parallels between Augustus and King George II (reigned 1727–1760), whose Christian names were George Augustus. While some contemporaries naively viewed the poem as a panegyric, the parallels were ironic. Unlike Augustus, George was no patron of the arts. Pope also suggested, somewhat unfairly, that George (again, unlike Augustus) was lacking in military distinction, and that, by allowing the government to be controlled by Sir Robert Walpole as an all-powerful prime minister, he reigned over a country stricken by moral decay (Butt, 1969, 189–231). While the parallel could be used both positively and negatively, the idea that such a parallel existed contributed to the popularity of imitation as a genre, and to the way in which it was often used for satirical purposes.

Translations from the classics played a major part in the development of English poetry from the sixteenth century onwards. Efforts by translators of Martial's Latin elegiac couplets "to reproduce in English a similar sharp precision and verbal economy" played a major part in the development of the English heroic couplet, that is, lines of iambic pentameter rhyming in pairs (Sullivan and Boyle, 1996, xxiv). While Pope was dismissive of "The Mob of Gentlemen who wrote with Ease" in the seventeenth century (Butt, 1969, 203), their interest in poetry as a prestige activity provided a climate in which professional writers like John Dryden (1631–1700) could flourish. A significant part of Dryden's output consisted of translation, and while his translations of Virgil (1697) were the best known, he was also responsible for translations of Juvenal and Persius published in 1692 (the introductory "Discourse concerning the original and progress of satire", all the Persius translations and five of Juvenal's sixteen satires were by Dryden himself). It was Dryden's practice in his translations, as much as in his other works, which established the heroic couplet as one of the most popular forms of poetry in English. As Pope put it:

> [...] Dryden taught to join
> The varying verse, the full resounding line,
> The long majestic march, and energy divine.

> (Butt, 1969, 217)

The enormous and long enduring popularity of Pope and his use of the heroic couplet for many of his original works as well as for his translations of Homer simply confirmed the situation. Throughout the eighteenth century, innumerable poets, good, bad and indifferent, whether professional writers of varying degrees of success or amateur versifiers who wrote only occasionally and for their own amusement, turned to the heroic couplet as a basic form of expression. It was widely used for composition in many different genres, including both the translation of Roman satire and the production of original satire in English.

Another important influence was the work of the French writer Nicolas Boileau Despréaux (1636–1711). Boileau's twelve satires, published at intervals between 1660 and 1705, were written in French alexandrines (twelve-syllable lines rhyming in couplets). Loosely based on the satires of Horace and Juvenal, they combined wittily expressed criticisms of aspects of contemporary French society with praise of King Louis XIV, and long ensured Boileau's place as one of the most important writers in the French literary canon. His *L'Art poétique* (1669–1674), while drawing on the *Ars poetica* of Horace, was more elaborate and systematic; Boileau was regarded as a major literary critic on the strength of this work, which Voltaire suggested was an improvement on its classical model. Finally, in *Le Lutrin* (1672–1683; "The Reading-Desk"), Boileau gave a satirical account of a squabble about precedence among the clergy of the Sainte-Chapelle in Paris, which proved to be extremely popular (Daunou, 1825–1826). Boileau's prestige soon extended across the channel, and there were several British editions of his works in French, as well as translations into English.

While there were classical precedents, such as the *Batrachomyomachia* ("The Battle of the Frogs and the Mice"), allegedly by Homer, which was translated into English by George Chapman (c. 1559–1634) and Thomas Parnell (1679–1718), it was *Le Lutrin* more than anything else which made the mock heroic a standard genre in the eighteenth century. Its use of a self-consciously lofty form of expression in order to describe low or trivial subjects could be an end in itself. An example is the *Muscipula* (1709) of Edward Holdsworth (1684–1746), which uses Latin hexameters modelled on Virgil to describe how the original Taffy became the hero of the Welsh nation because he invented the mousetrap to secure the safety of their supply of toasted cheese. One of the funniest things written in the eighteenth century, with numerous editions in Latin as well as

English translations, it depends on a national stereotype but is not really satirical (Money, 2004). On the other hand, *The Dispensary* (1699), by Sir Samuel Garth (c. 1660–1719), used *Le Lutrin* as a model for a mock-heroic poem which satirised a conflict between the Royal College of Physicians and the Society of Apothecaries about the provision of medicines for the poor in London, while also mocking the bad poetry of Sir Richard Blackmore, one of the physicians involved in the dispute. The high point of the poem is the battle between the physicians and the apothecaries, initially described in language suited to epic:

> The adverse Host for Action straight prepare;
> All eager to unveil the Face of War.

But it is soon revealed that the model is not Homer's *Iliad* but the *Batrachomyomachia*:

> To paint each Knight, their Ardour and Alarms,
> Wou'd ask the Muse that sung the Frogs in Arms.

The "stagg'ring *Braves*" attack each other, not with spear and shield, but with the tools of their healing trades, and they end up streaming not with blood, but urine:

> Each Combatant his Adversary Mauls,
> With batter'd *Bed-Pans*, and stav'd *Urinals*.
> On *Stentor's* Crest the useful Chrystal breaks,
> And Tears of *Amber* gutter'd down his Cheeks ...
> (Garth, 1741, 63–66)

After this, the conclusion of the poem is a little flat: in a parody of one of the best known passages in Virgil's *Aeneid*, one of the physicians descends into the underworld, where he meets the ghost of William Harvey (1578–1657), the discoverer of the circulation of the blood, who suggests that the contestants invite the Lord Chancellor to settle their differences by arbitration. Nevertheless, *The Dispensary* proved to be popular, and its influence can be seen in Pope's *The Rape of the Lock* (Tillotson, 1962, 112–115).

The heroic couplet was not without rivals. An alternative tradition looked to *Hudibras*, a poem by Samuel Butler (c. 1613–1680) first published in parts between 1663 and 1678. Butler satirised seventeenth-century Puritanism, partly by parodying classical literature and by drawing on the picaresque novel *Don Quixote* (1605–1615) by the Spanish writer Miguel de Cervantes (1547–1616), but mainly by consistent use of his chosen verse form. This was what came to be known as the Hudibrastic couplet in iambic tetrameter, that is, eight-syllabled lines rhyming in pairs. The shorter lines and the quick return of what were often deliberately incongruous rhymes produced ludicrous effects, in some ways reminiscent of Skelton. Modern readers are likely to find *Hudibras* heavy going, as it assumes a knowledge of seventeenth-century religious divisions and disputes which is no longer common. It was long popular however, and the Hudibrastic couplet was used by other satirists, including Ebenezer Cook, author of *The Sot-Weed Factor: Or, A Voyage to Maryland* (1708), which is often regarded as the earliest American satire. Superficially an attack on the degraded and uncivilised manners of the American colonists, it has also been viewed by modern critics as a satire on the bumbling incompetence of the English narrator who is unable to adapt to colonial conditions, and, in its use of such a dual satire, a significant predecessor of later American humorists like Mark Twain (Ford, 2003). The Hudibrastic couplet was also sometimes employed for the sake of variation, as for example in the work of Philip Francis (1708–1773), who produced what became a popular translation of the complete poems of Horace (1742–1746) in which he employed a range of metrical forms which to some extent responded to the variety to be found in Horace's own writing. Francis turned most of Horace's satires into heroic couplets, but for the one about Priapus and the witches (see Chapter 3), his use of the Hudibrastic form in his translation helps to emphasise the ludicrousness of the situation:

> In Days of Yore our Godship stood
> A very worthless Log of Wood.
> The Joiner doubting, or to shape Us
> Into a Stool, or a Priapus,
> At length resolv'd for Reasons wise,
> Into a God to bid me rise;

> And now to Birds and Thieves I stand
> A Terror great. With ponderous Hand,
> And something else as red as Scarlet,
> I fright away each filching Varlet.
> (Francis, 1756, III, 103).

Metrical variation could be used to excellent effect in other ways. *The New Bath Guide* by Christopher Anstey (1724–1805), first published in 1766, offered a satirical portrait of an English spa town. In some ways, this was an easy target, since the medicinal reputation of the thermal springs drew together in the shared pursuit of health and amusement a wide range of different sorts of people who would not otherwise have associated with each other in the very class-conscious society of the time. There was also an enormous disparity between the claims of eighteenth-century medicine, that the spa waters were beneficial whether taken internally or externally, and the actual results. This, and the fact that, whether drunk or bathed in, the waters came from the same source, were easy to mock. As Anstey pointed out, the most fashionable visitors were in effect drinking the same water that anybody and everybody, including maids like Tabby, were bathing in:

> So while little Tabby was washing her Rump,
> The Ladies kept drinking it out of a Pump.

However, what made *The New Bath Guide* a popular success for the best part of a century was Anstey's use of different narrative voices for his descriptions of the town, often expressed in different metrical forms. His frequent use of anapaests (feet consisting of two unstressed syllables followed by a stressed one) and ingenious, if sometimes imperfect, rhymes kept the entire work going at a brisk pace over some 1,600 lines:

> So when we had wasted more Bread at a Breakfast
> Than the poor of our Parish have ate for this Week past [...]

At the same time, Anstey's parodies of literary styles, from Dryden's ode on *Alexander's Feast* (1697) to contemporary Methodist hymns, provided additional variety and amusement for the well-read who made up his target audience (Anstey, 1994).

Nevertheless, in satire, as in many other genres, the heroic couplet remained the dominant form in English poetry from the later seventeenth century through to the early nineteenth. The range of material covered is enormous, from Pope's attacks in his *Imitations of Horace* on what he saw as the political corruption of Sir Robert Walpole's government, to *The Lousiad*, in which Peter Pindar (pseudonym of John Wolcot, 1738–1819), poking fun at the alleged appearance of a louse on King George III's plate during a dinner at Buckingham Palace, managed to stretch out his material over five cantos that he published between 1785 and 1795:

> The Louse I sing, who, from some Head unknown,
> Yet born and educated near a Throne,
> Dropp'd down – (so will'd the dread decree of Fate,)
> With legs wide sprawling on the Monarch's plate [...]

With so many satires, and so many satirists, the modern critic needs to be cautious of generalisations. It can perhaps be suggested, however, that the satirists of this period, whether more or less ferocious in their attacks, are united by the idea that their society as a whole, if not the individual targets of some satire, could, in fact, be improved, and that their own work might contribute to this. When Dryden damned bad writers in *MacFlecknoe* (1676) and Pope did the same in *The Dunciad* (developed over the period 1728–1743), each presumably expected to win readers over to their own views of what constituted good literature. In his long poem *Absalom and Achitophel* (1681), Dryden adapted the biblical story of King David and his rebellious son Absalom to comment on the politics of the Exclusion Crisis, when some politicians wished to exclude James, Duke of York and brother of Charles II, from succession to the throne, in favour of James, Duke of Monmouth, who, though he was Charles's son, was illegitimate. Dryden did not simply denounce the politicians who tried to persuade Monmouth to put forward his claims, but also urged Monmouth to resist their blandishments. Pope criticised some living individuals by name, or used pseudonyms which were readily identified by contemporaries. He claimed that

> [...] general satire in times of general vice has no force and no
> punishment: people have ceased to be ashamed of it when so
> many are joined with them; and it is only by hunting one or
> two from the herd that any examples can be made [...] if some
> are hung up, or pilloried, it may prevent others. And in my low
> station, with no other power than this, I hope to deter, if not
> to reform.
>
> (Butt, 1969, 313)

Pope claimed that he was an independent critic, beholden to no
one, a claim that had considerable substance in view of the commercial success of his writings and the fact that, as a Catholic,
he was ineligible for any government office. This was forcefully
stated in his *Epilogue to the Satires* (1738), where, in response to
the suggestion that he was "strangely proud", Pope replied in his
own persona:

> So proud, I am no Slave:
> So impudent, I own myself no Knave:
> So odd, my Country's Ruin makes me grave.
> Yes, I am proud; I must be proud to see
> Men not afraid of God, afraid of me:
> Safe from the Bar, the Pulpit, and the Throne,
> Yet touch'd and sham'd by *Ridicule* alone.
>
> (Butt, 1969, 324–325)

Satirists did not only issue denunciations, however. In *The Rape of the
Lock* (1712, enlarged 1714), Pope used an actual incident involving
two Catholic families with whom he had some acquaintance. Drawing
on Garth and Boileau, as well as on his own extensive acquaintance
with classical and modern writers, he developed this into a mock-
heroic poem which satirised the frivolity and superficiality of early
eighteenth-century high society:

> What tender Maid but must a Victim fall
> To one Man's Treat, but for another's Ball?
> When Florio speaks, what Virgin could withstand,
> If gentle Damon did not squeeze her Hand?

> With varying Vanities, from eve'ry Part,
> They shift the moving Toyshop of their Heart [...]
>   (1714, Canto I, 94–100; Tillotson, 1962, 152–153)

The satire is sometimes mild, even affectionate, and, as has been suggested (Weinbrot, 1988, 100–119), one effect of Pope's use of the mock-heroic is the implication that the society of his own time, for all its faults, is a considerable improvement on that which gave rise to the original heroic style that the mock-heroic rejects, the society which gave birth to the Homeric epics from whose translation Pope was to make a fortune. Conveniently ignoring the long wars between Britain and France, which were still continuing when he began the *Rape*, Pope suggests that, in sharp contrast to the often detailed and gruesome descriptions of death in close, hand-to-hand combat in Homer, warfare in English society has become a matter of card games, dying no more than lovers swooning at the sight of their beloveds, or, perhaps, more intimate contact: for many of Pope's contemporaries, the couplet "Nor fear'd the Chief th'unequal Fight to try,/Who sought no more than on his Foe to die" (1714, V, 77–78; Tillotson, 1962, 206) was unduly suggestive, since "dying" was often used as a synonym for "orgasm".

The process is taken a stage further by Samuel Johnson (1709–1784). In 1738, he published *London*, a poem in which Juvenal's third satire was adapted to Johnson's own time. He returned again to Juvenal with the publication in 1749 of *The Vanity of Human Wishes*, an imitation, as the eighteenth century understood the term, of Juvenal's tenth satire. It was longer and more elaborate than *London*, and has a clearer purpose. Some sections paraphrase Juvenal fairly closely, while many substitute later examples for the historical figures referred to by Juvenal. Where Juvenal uses the rise and fall of Sejanus to illustrate the absurdity of political ambition (Chapter 3), Johnson substitutes Cardinal Wolsey, and his tone is melancholy rather than jeering. Juvenal dismisses Hannibal's crossing of the Alps as the action of a madman, which ultimately achieves no more than the entertainment of schoolboys. Johnson is more sombre on the fate of Charles XII (King of Sweden 1697–1718):

> His fall was destin'd to a barren strand,
> A petty fortress, and a dubious hand;

> He left the name, at which the world grew pale,
> To point a moral, or adorn a tale.

Like Juvenal, Johnson points out the dangers inherent in the pursuit of learning, or the desire for longevity and beauty. Whereas Juvenal allows that "mens sana in corpore sana" ("a healthy mind in a healthy body") is something desirable, he concludes by suggesting that all prayer is in fact useless. Johnson, on the other hand, ends by advocating a specifically Christian resignation to the will of heaven (Rudd, 1981). Once again, as with *The Rape of the Lock*, the contrast between the modern poem and its classical antecedents suggests that, while modern society certainly has its faults, it remains preferable to what went before. The popularity of the poems suggested that this was a concept to which readers were attracted. As James Boswell (1740–1795), Johnson's companion and biographer, put it, "the *Vanity of Human Wishes* is, in the opinion of the best judges, as high an effort of ethic poetry as any language can show" (quoted Rudd, 1981, xiii). Since satire was far from entirely synonymous with invective or negative criticism, it could shade into more general morally and ethically informed discussions of society and human nature, such as Pope's *Essay on Man* (1734) or *The Traveller* (1764) by the Irish writer Oliver Goldsmith (1728–1774). While modern critics might not see these as satirical in nature, the distinction between satirical and philosophical poetry was not so clear-cut at the time, and works like these can be seen as following in the tradition of classical works such as Horace, *Satires* II, vi, advocating contentment with one's lot, or the Restoration poet Rochester's more acerbic *Satyr against Mankind*.

Formal verse satire was a complex and sophisticated literary medium, and the factors which ensured its popularity during the long eighteenth century may well be those which have led to its subsequent eclipse amongst the reading public. The use of rhyme and strict metrical forms allowed for striking sound effects, which gave added emphasis to the points being made. Johnson's *London* (ll. 176–177) offers a good example of regular form:

> This mournful truth is ev'ry where confess'd,
> SLOW RISES WORTH, BY POVERTY DEPRESSED [.]

But the expectation of regularity could also be manipulated to advantage, as is seen in another of Johnson's couplets:

> There mark what ills the scholar's life assail,
> Toil, envy, want, the patron, and the jail.
>
> (*Vanity of Human Wishes*, II, 159–160)

While the first line is a perfectly regular iambic pentameter, the second still has five stresses, but not where they might be expected, so that they fall like hammer blows:

> Tóil, énvy, wánt, the pátron, and the jáil.

Rhyme can draw attention to incongruous associations, as in Pope's reference to the royal palace at Hampton Court, where matters of state are juxtaposed against trivia:

> Here Thou, Great *Anna*! whom three Realms obey,
> Dost sometimes Counsel take – and sometimes Tea.
>
> (*Rape of the Lock*, 1714, III, 7–8)

"Obey/Tea" was an exact rhyme in the period, and the couplet makes a nice contrast between Queen Anne, reigning at the time Pope wrote, as a sovereign exalted by her office and as an individual human being sometimes engaged in mundane activities. A well-chosen rhyme can provide a devastating conclusion to an argument, as when Charles Churchill (1732–1764), at the beginning of his *Gotham* (1764), questions "The claim of EUROPE to the *Western World*":

> Never shall One, One truly honest man,
> Who, blest with LIBERTY, reveres her plan,
> Allow one moment, that a Savage Sire
> Could from his wretched race, for childish hire,
> By a wild grant, their All, their Freedom pass,
> And sell his Country for a bit of glass.
>
> (Churchill, 1774, III, 2–3)

While some sections or individual couplets had the directness and concision of epigrams, it was the case that much formal verse satire depended for its impact on cumulative effects which built up over long passages or in the work as a whole. The 1712 version of *The Rape of the Lock* in two cantos (334 lines) is an amusing trifle, while the longer version in five cantos (794 lines) is much more elaborate and impressive. Such works make demands on their readers' attention and prior knowledge. Effects which depended on parody and allusion assumed that readers would be able to recognise the earlier texts to which reference was being made.

The publication of *Lyrical Ballads* (1798) by William Wordsworth (1770–1850) and Samuel Taylor Coleridge (1772–1834) is conventionally regarded as the starting point of Romanticism, and this movement brought about a major change in taste. While Romanticism meant different things to different people, broadly speaking it can be said to have led to a greater emphasis on the importance of emotion and personal expression in poetry. Literary artifice as a worthwhile end in itself was rejected in favour of poetry which was closer to ordinary, everyday speech. The "poetic diction" of the eighteenth century, which took it for granted that, with a few exceptions, such as the avowedly burlesque, everyday speech was precisely what was not wanted in poetry, rapidly came to be seen as old fashioned. This was the death knell of verse satire as it had been practised for so long. Perhaps the last major example of the traditional approach was *English Bards and Scotch Reviewers* (1809) by George Gordon Byron, sixth Baron Byron (1788–1824), which mocked early Romantics such as Wordsworth:

> Who, both by precept and example, shows
> That prose is verse, and verse is merely prose,
> Convincing all by demonstration plain,
> Poetic souls delight in prose insane;
> And Christmas stories tortured into rhyme,
> Contain the essence of the true sublime [...]
>   (McGann, 2008, 7)

In spite of Byron's protests, the reading public wanted something different from that to which it had previously been accustomed, and it already appeared that "[...] MILTON, DRYDEN, POPE, alike forgot,/ Resign their hallow'd Bays to WALTER SCOTT" (McGann, 2008, 5).

English Bards and Scotch Reviewers was an early work, and Byron's extensive and varied literary productions came to include love lyrics such as "Maid of Athens, ere we part" (1810) and long dramatic poems such as *The Corsair* (1814), which evoked what came to be thought of as the "Byronic hero", splendidly at odds with the entire universe. These were immensely popular, and have ensured that he is often classed among the Romantics he had criticised. While he continued to be an admirer of the Augustans, and continued to write satire, Byron changed his methods. He composed *English Bards and Scotch Reviewers* in heroic couplets, but his *The Vision of Judgment* (1822) took a different approach (McGann 2008, 939–968). On one level, this was a response to *A Vision of Judgement* (1821) by Robert Southey (1774–1843), whom Byron had previously mocked in *English Bards*. Using the pseudonym "Quevedo Redivivus" in allusion to the Spanish satirist and miscellaneous writer Francisco de Quevedo (1580–1645), Byron began with a prose introduction which attacked Southey for moving away from the radicalism of his youth to a political and social conservatism which revealed itself in literary terms in his *Vision*, a poem which described its author imagining the reception into heaven of the recently deceased King George III. Southey's poem gave a blandly favourable summary of the late king's reign, and was dedicated with obsequious flattery to the new monarch, George IV (Southey, 1821). Aspects of Byron's *Vision* parodied Southey's poem, such as the Archangel Michael calling Satan and the spirits of some of the king's dead opponents to give evidence as to whether George should or should not be admitted into Heaven. In some ways, the debate is similar to earlier satires which imagine celestial arguments over the future state of prominent historical figures, such as the ancient Roman satire, the *Apocolocyntosis* of Seneca, and the sixteenth-century dialogue known as *Julius Exclusus*, which is attributed to Erasmus (see Chapter 5). Byron did not imitate Southey's experiment in writing English hexameters modelled on classical Latin poetry, however, or use the heroic couplets which had so long been the standard form for verse satire in English, and which he had himself used effectively in *English Bards and Scotch Reviewers*. Instead, he employed the ottava rima stanza which he had perfected on the basis of Italian models in his *Beppo* (1818) and the earlier cantos of

his mock epic, *Don Juan* (1819–1824). This allowed for more colloquial language, though sometimes varied with deliberately comi-
cal double and even triple rhymes, but the stanza built up to a final
couplet which worked like a punchline. Byron argued that, while
George III was possessed of domestic virtues, this did not excuse the
fact that he presided over a system which was politically and socially
oppressive, and that the monarch gave a veneer of respectability to
the actions of his ministers. The king, "although no tyrant", was "one
/ Who shielded tyrants", and the indictment can be summed up in
part of the speech which Byron gives to Satan, and which demonstrates the workings of his chosen form:

> 'Tis true, he was a tool from first to last
> 　　(I have the workmen safe); but as a tool
> So let him be consumed! From out the past
> 　　Of ages, since mankind have known the rule
> Of monarchs – from the bloody rolls amass'd
> 　　Of sin and slaughter – from the Caesar's school,
> Take the worst pupil; and produce a reign
> More drench'd with gore, more cumber'd with the slain!
> 　　　　　　　　　　　　(McGann, 2008, 944, 953)

George III had presided over Britain's part in the American War of
Independence and the long wars with revolutionary and Napoleonic
France, and thus, Byron argued, bore ultimate responsibility for the
bloodshed these produced. Some allowance is made, nevertheless,
for the king's having been largely a figurehead, and Byron is at least
as interested in abusing Southey, who is brought onto the scene by
the devil Asmodeus, who had caught him in the act of writing the
very poem Byron is attacking, "a libel – / No less on History than
the Holy Bible". When Southey attempts to read some of his poetry
to the angels and devils assembled before the celestial gate to decide
on whether the king should be admitted, they all scatter, the devils
fleeing back to Hell rather than listen. Byron concludes his *Vision*
by saying

> All that I saw farther in the last confusion
> 　　Was, that King George slipp'd into heaven for one;

And when the tumult dwindled to a calm,
I left him practising the hundredth psalm.
(McGann, 2008, 963, 968)

Don Juan, by contrast, is not so much a verse satire as a long poem which includes satirical passages. These often demonstrate Byron's technical virtuosity, such as the following passage from the description of the hero's education, which points out the contradictions and occasional absurdities involved in straight-laced parents, like Juan's mother Donna Inez, wanting a classical education for their children because that was what was expected by upper-class conventions:

His classic studies made a little puzzle,
    Because of filthy loves of gods and goddesses,
Who in the earlier ages made a bustle,
    But never put on pantaloons or bodices;
His reverend tutors had at times a tussle,
    And for their Aeneids, Iliads and Odysseys,
Were forced to make an odd sort of apology,
For Donna Inez dreaded the mythology.

As Byron went on to add in a famous couplet, "[…] what proper person can be partial / To all those nauseous epigrams of Martial?" (McGann, 2008, 388). The literature of ancient Greece and Rome continued to enjoy great prestige, and a knowledge of it functioned as cultural capital, but its texts were unfortunately all too full of what the early nineteenth century regarded as obscenities. The satirical elements in *Don Juan* are, nevertheless, only one aspect of the very lengthy poem as a whole, which is a mock epic, a sort of picaresque novel in verse, and it is the hero's amorous and other adventures which take him all over Europe that serve as the main attraction for the reader.

Verse continued to be used for satire, sometimes very effectively, as with the criticism of religious hypocrisy in *The Latest Decalogue* by Arthur Hugh Clough (1819–1861):

Thou shalt have but one God only; who
Would be at the expense of two?
[…]

> At church on Sunday to attend
> Will serve to keep the world thy friend [...]
> (Clough, 1871, 142)

Clough's poem is only twenty lines long, but there have been occasional attempts at longer verse satires, such as R. F. Patterson's *Mein Rant* (1940), a parody of Hitler's *Mein Kampf* in a semi-Hudibrastic style which stretched the joke out to some seventy pages. Popular song and performance still sometimes use traditional tools for satirical purposes. In 1963, Michael Flanders and Donald Swann, whose recorded performances continue to be popular on CD, used the style of the Victorian comic song, combining a lively piano tune with the format of a rhyming ballad, in their *The Gasman Cometh: A Ballad of Unending Domestic Upheaval*. This lamented the middle-class householder's helplessness when confronted with tradesmen who fix one problem only to create another: "It all makes work for the working man to do" (Flanders and Swann, 1991). A rather different approach to a much grimmer issue appears in the Black British poet Linton Kwesi Johnson's *Liesense fi Kill*, released as a vinyl single in 1998. This tackled the issue of the unexplained deaths of black people in police custody, but several aspects suggest it can be interpreted as a satire rather than as a straightforward protest poem. Johnson the poet adopts the persona of a narrator reporting what he has heard from his co-worker Christine at a party, and the opening line, "Sometime me tink me co-worker crazy", and the later reference to "di way she love fi talk bout conspiracy" distance the poet from the inflammatory nature of the content and the possibly libellous nature of what is being suggested. At the same time, this scenario invites readers or listeners to consider whether it is really so crazy after all. The "licence fi kill" of the title is a phrase repeated several times in the poem which alludes to the James Bond character who had a "licence to kill" in Ian Fleming's series of espionage novels, and both James Bond and the British government's security agency MI5 are explicitly referred to in the poem before Christine makes her claim that "some police inna England got licence fi kill". The spelling "Liesense" in Johnson's original version of the title hints at the difficulties relatives of those who had died in custody and their supporters had at getting at the truth of what had really happened. As Christine points out, the dead cannot be asked exactly what happened to them:

Yuh can't ask Clinton McCurbin
Bout him haxfixiation
An yuh can't ask Joy Gardner
Bout her suffocation
Yuh can't ask Colin Roach
If him really shoot himself
An yuh can't ask Vincent Graham
Iffa him stab himself [...]
                                    (Johnson, 2012)

The names, and those of others mentioned later in the poem, are all real: Clinton McCurbin died in police custody in 1987, with a subsequent inquest verdict of "death by misadventure"; Joy Gardner died in a hospital in 1993 after suffering respiratory failure when she was restrained by officers from the Metropolitan Police Services's Aliens Deportation Group and had 13 feet of adhesive tape wrapped round her head and face; Colin Roach died of a gunshot wound while in a police station in 1983, an inquest later ruling that this was suicide; and Vincent Graham died in police custody in 1989 (Athwal, 2002). But, Christine suggests, one can and should ask those in authority and the politicians with ultimate responsibility:

[...]
But you can ask de PCA
Bout de licence fi kill
Ask de ACPO
Bout de licence fi kill
[...]
Yuh may ask Michael Howard
Bout de licence fi kill
An yuh can ask Jack Straw
Bout de rule of law
Yuh fi ask Tony Blair
If him is aware or care
Bout de licence fi kill
Dat plenty police feel dem got.
                                    (Johnson, 2012)

The PCA was Britain's Police Complaints Authority (replaced in 2004 by the Independent Police Complaints Commission), while the ACPO was the Association of Chief Police Officers. Michael Howard and Jack Straw were, respectively, Conservative and Labour politicians who occupied the position of Home Secretary from 1993 to 1997 and from 1997 to 2001, and, as such, had responsibility at a national level for policing, security and prisons. The Labour politician Tony Blair was prime minister from 1997 to 2007, and his Conservative predecessors Margaret Thatcher and John Major are also mentioned in the poem. Johnson's use of rhyme, repetition and rhythm, the last emphasised by his usually performing his work against a background of dub music, creates a sophisticated poem which may not convince the listener to believe in conspiracy theories or in the existence of an actual "licence to kill", but which compels them towards an acknowledgement that something is seriously wrong and demands investigation. The techniques used in the construction of *Liesense fi Kill* as a poem increase its impact beyond what might be expected from a purely factual prose protest against injustice, and make it something we can recognise as satire.

While Johnson's techniques have a long literary history, they are being used here in ways which pre-twentieth-century writers would scarcely have recognised, and the older style of formal verse satire seems to be completely dead. It cannot have the immediate impact of an epigram, a political cartoon or a YouTube clip, and many of those who do read poetry expect it to be something quite different. The knowledge of the Bible and of classical authors which satirists, like other eighteenth-century writers, could assume their readers possessed is now generally regarded as esoteric. Pope may survive in university departments of English, but when a columnist in a conservative British newspaper which prides itself on its coverage of the arts can dismiss him as "an 18th-century man of letters nobody reads anymore" (Dorment, 2014), it is clear that there has been an enormous change since the days when he was read by everybody who cared about literature in English and widely regarded as perhaps second only to Shakespeare. While changes in taste are inevitable, to abandon Pope and the other satirists of his era entirely is to ignore a major part of English literary history.

5

THE HEIRS OF LUCIAN

The second decade of the sixteenth century saw the publication of three satirical texts in Latin which rapidly came to enjoy a very wide circulation, and which were all sooner or later translated into vernacular languages. The first of these was the *Moriae Encomium*, known in English as *The Praise of Folly*, which was written by the Dutch humanist scholar Desiderius Erasmus (?1466 or 1469 – 1536) in 1509, and first printed in 1511, with expansions and revisions in later editions until 1532 (Erasmus, 1993). The original title involves a pun in Greek, suggesting that the work is not only the "praise of folly", but also the "praise of More", the More in question being Erasmus's friend Sir Thomas More (1478–1535), a scholar, lawyer and politician later beheaded for his refusal to accept King Henry VIII's divorce and assumption of the rôle of Supreme Head of the Church of England. In 1515, More began writing something which he completed the following year and which was first published in Louvain at the end of 1516 as *Libellus vere aureus nec minus salutaris quam festiuus de optimo reip[ublicae] statu, deq[ue] noua insula Vtopia*. The long-windedness of the title was kept in the English translation by Ralph Robinson which was first published in 1551 (revised edition published 1556) as *A fruteful and pleasaunt worke of the beste state of a publyque weale, and of the newe yle called Utopia*, though this omitted the original description of the text as "a truly golden little book". Robinson's translation has retained something of a canonical status for Anglophone readers, in spite of the existence of several later English versions, but while the original title is useful as indicating one possible reading of the text (not necessarily the author's), the book itself has come to be universally known simply as *Utopia* (Bruce, 1999). The third work, for which the most likely date of its first appearance in print was early in 1517, was published anonymously under many variant titles, but is usually known as *Julius Exclusus* ("Julius shut out [of Heaven]") and was a satire on the recently deceased Pope Julius II (reigned 1503–1513). While other authors have been suggested, modern scholarly opinion accepts it as a work of Erasmus (Sowards and Pascal, 1968). It was soon reprinted in several different places and read all over Europe, but its topicality meant that its influence was nothing like as long lasting as that of *The Praise of Folly* and *Utopia*. It was occasionally revived, in Latin or in translation: the Latin text was reprinted with a French translation in 1875 by Isidore Liseux, a Parisian publisher who specialised in texts which were erotic or "curieux", and who may have been motivated by the accusation of sodomy levelled at Julius II. The translator, Edmond Thion, included a dedication to the current pope, in which he contrasted the warlike and worldly spirit of Julius II with the humility of Pius IX, the "prisoner of the Vatican". In view of the latter's intransigent, if ultimately unsuccessful, efforts to retain his temporal power in the Papal States in opposition to the movement for the unification of Italy, and his support for the doctrine of papal infallibility, proclaimed as a dogma of the Catholic Church by the first Vatican Council in 1870, the comparison appears to be somewhat tongue in cheek, and suggests that this republication of *Julius Exclusus* was a manifestation of the anticlericalism often found in French public life, in spite of the formally respectful language of the dedication (Thion, 1875).

What the three works had in common was that they made use of approaches which went back to a particular strand in satirical writing in classical antiquity, and which in turn foreshadowed much later satire. This was what has come to be known as Menippean satire, after a writer in Greek known as Menippus of Gadara (third century BCE). Menippus came to be credited with the invention of the form, even though none of his own works survive, mainly because of his being frequently mentioned in the writings of the much later satirical author known as Lucian of Samosata (second century CE). Menippean satire is a term almost as imprecise as satire itself. As far as the surviving classical examples are concerned, its main characteristic is a much looser approach to form than the traditions of verse satire used by Horace and Juvenal, for example, which required adherence to a particular kind of metre. As a result, Menippean satire might refer to texts written in a mixture of verse and prose, or in prose alone, and from the later twentieth century onwards the term has come to be applied to a very wide range of works in different media, including Shakespearean plays, novels as different as Cervantes's *Don Quixote* and Lewis Carroll's *Alice in Wonderland*, and films, so that "Like a will-o'-the-wisp, the definition of Menippean satire seems always just beyond grasp" (Milowicki and Wilson, 2002).

Like Menippus, Lucian wrote in Greek, and both writers belonged to the Greek-speaking culture which was widespread in the ancient eastern Mediterranean, but Greek was perhaps the first language of neither: Menippus was referred to as a "Phoenician", while Lucian called himself a "Syrian", and although the site of his home town of Samosata is in what is now Turkey, it was part of the Roman province of Syria. The mother tongue of both writers may have been a language of the Semitic family such as Phoenician or Aramaic; if so, this would have meant that Lucian learned Greek as a second language and may explain the importance he attached to writing the carefully cultivated and archaising form of Attic Greek which was the mark of high literary culture in his time (as opposed to the *koine* or "common" Greek which was the popular speech and lingua franca of much of the eastern Mediterranean). An important consequence of this for the history of satire was that at a much later date Lucian became a prominent feature of the Western European educational curriculum. Indeed, when interest in Greek language and literature in the West revived in the Renaissance, both the content and the form of his works made them seem ideal as texts for students. Many of Lucian's works are relatively short, their entertainment value was high, and they were written in a pure style which provided what teachers regarded as a suitable model for imitation. Manuscripts of Lucian in Greek were brought to Italy in the fifteenth century; the first Latin translation of one of his works dates from the beginning of the century and was soon followed by others. By the early sixteenth century, a wide range of Lucian's works was available in printed editions, in both the original Greek and in different Latin translations, and translations in Italian and other vernacular languages were beginning to appear. According to one estimate, there were more than 270 printed editions of works by, or attributed to, Lucian before 1550. The best-known versions were a series of Latin translations by Erasmus and More, which appear to have been the result of active collaboration between them, and which were often printed together. More's translations of Lucian were printed at least thirteen times in his lifetime (more than twice the number of editions of *Utopia* which appeared before his death), and those of Erasmus were printed more than forty times between 1506 and 1550 (Thompson, 1939–1940). By the middle of the sixteenth century, Lucian had become a canonical part of the classical curriculum which long dominated Western education, and he retained this position until the early twentieth century (Marsh, 1998; Ligota and Panizza, 2007). Recent publications suggest Lucian is enjoying a revival as a pedagogic tool for the learning of Greek (e.g., Hayes and Nimis, 2015).

The Menippean tradition was also passed through classical Latin writers. The prolific Roman author Marcus Terentius Varro (116 BCE–27 BCE) reportedly composed 150 books of what were described as Menippean satires, and while these have survived only in fragments, they influenced later works, such as *Divi Claudii Apocolocyntosis* (often translated as "The Pumpkinification of the Divine Claudius"), attributed to Lucius Annaeus Seneca the Younger (c. 4 BCE–65 CE), and the *Satyricon*, attributed to Gaius Petronius Arbiter (c. 27–66 CE). The *Apocolocyntosis* appears to be more or less complete, while we have only parts of the *Satyricon*, though one of these, the *Cena Trimalchionis* ("Trimalchio's Dinner", or "Trimalchio's Feast") is of significant length, and is sometimes treated as a work in its own right. The *Apocolocyntosis* and the *Satyricon* are the only substantial survivors of ancient Menippean satire in Latin. Both experienced periods of obscurity as well as popularity in the Middle Ages, but the *Apocolocyntosis* was first printed in 1513, while incomplete editions of the *Satyricon* which started c. 1482 were eventually followed, after the discovery of a previously unknown manuscript, by the publication of the text as we now have it in 1669. Like the works of Lucian, they were to inspire many later writers (Eden 1984; Walsh 1997b).

Both the *Apocolocyntosis* and the *Satyricon* are in a mixture of prose and verse. One of the highlights of the surviving portions of the *Satyricon* is the character of Eumolpus, who is, at least in his own opinion, a poet and insufficiently appreciated genius. The reader is treated to two long poetic effusions by Eumolpus, one on the Trojan War and one on the Roman civil wars of the first century BCE. While there have been critics prepared to take both these and Eumolpus's pronouncements on art and literature seriously, it seems much more likely that the poems are parodies of contemporary writers such as the younger Seneca and his nephew Lucan (Marcus Annaeus Lucanus, 39–65 CE, author of an epic on the war between Caesar and Pompey in the previous century) (Walsh, 1997b, xxxii–xxxiv). On the other hand, the episode of the *nouveau riche* dinner party is almost entirely in prose, its vivid details creating a portrait of the vulgar upstart Trimalchio, who is perhaps Petronius's most enduring creation. At one point, a huge pig is brought in to the dining room, supposedly one of several which had earlier been displayed while still alive to the guests:

> We began to express surprise at the speed of the cooking, swearing that not even a farmyard cock could have been thoroughly roasted so quickly. Our surprise was all the greater because the pig seemed to be far bigger than the boar had been a little earlier. Then Trimalchio looked closer and closer at it, and said: "What's this? Has this pig not been gutted? By heaven, it hasn't. Get the cook, call the cook unto us."

The cook admits that he had forgotten to gut the pig, and for a moment it appears that he will be flogged as a punishment, and the guests beg for him to be let off. Trimalchio's mood appears to change:

> His face softened to a smile, and he said: "Well, then, since you are so forgetful you must gut it while we watch." The cook [...] seized a knife. Then with shaking hand he slit the pig's belly on each side. At once the slits widened with the pressure

of the weight inside, and sausages and black puddings came tumbling out.

(Walsh, 1997b, 39–40)

It becomes clear that this is not the original pig, but one that had been prepared earlier, and that the whole episode is an elaborate charade, designed to show off Trimalchio's wealth. It also suggests that Trimalchio enjoys the power which he possesses as master over his enslaved servants, even though he brags that he had been a slave himself and had become wealthy through his own efforts. This self-belief is not affected by his shameless admission that catering to the sexual desires of his former master and his wife was what had brought him freedom and the substantial legacy which provided the capital which enabled him to go on to become a multi-millionaire through trading and money-lending.

Petronius's Trimalchio became an enduring example of tasteless extravagance and ostentation. Scott Fitzgerald's earlier title for *The Great Gatsby* (1925) was "Trimalchio at West Egg" (Walsh, 1997b, xli). The film adaptation *Fellini Satyricon* (dir. Federico Fellini, 1969) was seen by a reviewer for *The New York Times* as "a surreal epic" (Canby, 1970), but the *New York Post* saw it as offering a "powerful contemporary parallel" (Archer Winsten, quoted Fava and Vigan, 1985, 138). In 1989, the well-known American cartoonist Robert Crumb compared the businessman and property developer Donald Trump to Trimalchio (Sorene, 2016), and an online search will show how the comparison has been taken up by others since Trump entered politics and became president of the United States of America, including an article with the title "Trimalchio in the White House" (Gander, 2017).

Whether the original Trimalchio was based on a particular individual is not something we will ever know; it seems more likely that he is a composite figure incorporating traits of several actual contemporaries (Walsh, 1997b, xxvii–xxxi). Menippean satire could, however, include attacks on particular persons: the *Apocolocyntosis*, written shortly after the recently deceased Roman emperor Claudius had been officially declared a god by the senate (54 CE), mocked Claudius as a bumbling fool but also portrayed him as a bloodthirsty tyrant who is, on that account, refused admission among the Olympian gods and sent by them to the underworld. In a mocking reference to Claudius's alleged fondness for dice games, which were, strictly speaking, illegal under Roman law, he is first punished by Aeacus, one of the judges of the underworld, by being made to play dice using a dice-box with a hole in the bottom of it. Whenever Claudius shakes the box in order to throw the dice, they fall out of the bottom instead. The text switches from prose to verse here, heightening the ludicrousness of the situation with a parody of the form and style of traditional epic, as eight lines of hexameters lead up to Claudius's frustration being compared to that of the mythological figure of Sisyphus, forever forced to roll a stone uphill only to have it roll back down as soon as he had reached the top. This is not punishment enough, however, and the text switches to prose once more as it ends with Claudius condemned to be forever the slave of Caligula, his predecessor as emperor. The return to prose perhaps serves to suggest that the claim made here in the *Apocolocyntosis* that Caligula had physically abused Claudius when they were both alive, in the manner of a master mistreating a slave, was no more than a matter of fact (Eden, 1984, 60–61).

In a similar fashion, the *Julius Exclusus*, composed soon after the *Apocolocyntosis* had first been printed, imagines Pope Julius II turned away from the gates of Heaven by St. Peter, who was commonly regarded as the first pope but who declares himself to be appalled by his successor's obsession with money, power and worldly pomp, all things which Julius was willing to obtain by corruption and force, but which St. Peter declares to be utterly opposed to the Christian Gospel:

Ita quo quisque in mundo est afflictior, hoc uberius delitiatur in Christo. Quo in mundo pauperior, hoc in Christo locupletior. Quo in mundo dejectior, hoc in illo sublimior et honoratior. Quo minus vivit in mundo, hoc magis vivit in Christo.
(Thion, 1875, 158–160)

[Thus in as much as anyone is more afflicted in the world, by so much more does he rejoice in Christ. In as much as anyone is poorer in the world, so much richer is he in Christ. The more he is cast down in the world, the greater and more honoured is he in Him. The less he lives in the world, the more he lives in Christ.]

Julius prided himself on the pope's customary title of "Vicar of Christ" and claimed that this gave him power over all earthly rulers, but he is shown to lack all understanding of Christ's true message of love and humility, never more so than at the end of the satire, when he threatens to return with an army to fight his way into Heaven:

> [...] auctis copiis meis, vi deturbabo vos istinc, nisi in meam deditionem veniatis. Neque enim dubito quin brevi sint ad me e bellorum stragibus sexaginta hominum millia huc perventura.
> (Thion, 1875, 168)

> [Having increased my forces, I will drive you out of there unless you surrender to me. For I doubt not that there are soon to come to me sixty thousand men from the carnage of the wars.]

Lucian was quite capable of personal invective, as is shown by his account of Alexander of Abonoteichus (c. 105–c. 170 CE), a self-proclaimed prophet who persuaded his followers to believe in the oracles of a man-headed serpent-god of his own invention called Glycon, who was, according to Lucian, a kind of puppet manipulated by Alexander himself. Another target was the Cynic philosopher Peregrinus who, having announced his intention to burn himself alive in a very public manner at the Olympic Games of 165 CE to give an example of how "to scorn death and be strong in the face of adversity", was allegedly taken aback by the failure of his devoted followers to beg him to remain alive, and who, when they enthusiastically urged him on, was obliged to go through with his promised self-immolation (Casson, 1968, 267–300; 364–382). As with much other Menippean satire, some of Lucian's effects are achieved by exaggeration and personal abuse, as in his portrait of the prophet Alexander:

> O Heracles the Protector, O Zeus the Guardian, O Castor and Pollux the Saviors! Throw a man in with his worst enemies, and keep him away from someone like Alexander! [...] you must conjure up in your mind, a soul composed of the most varied ingredients, one that blended deceit, trickery, lying, sharp practices, carelessness, nerve, recklessness, and tireless-ness in carrying out plans with trust, reliability, and the knack

of acting a better role, of looking white when the end in view
was black.

(Casson 1968, 270)

We should not necessarily take at face value, for example, Lucian's
claims that Alexander was a sexual predator on a grand scale as well
as a fraud, or that Peregrinus had murdered his own father. Lucian's
main concern, however, is not so much with Alexander or Peregrinus
as individuals, as with popular credulity and superstition more generally. If the work known as *On the Syrian Goddess* is indeed by Lucian,
something disputed by modern scholars, it is true that this is apparently devoid of satirical intent and gives a respectful account of the
cult of Atargatis at Hierapolis, the modern Manbij in Syria (Swain,
2007, 32–34). On the other hand, his tales of the Olympian deities, in
works such as the *Dialogues of the Gods* (e.g., Casson, 1968, 97–120),
are uniformly irreverent. Something of the sort can be found in earlier
Greek literature, such as the passage in Homer's *Iliad* (Book XIV)
where Hera "with false lying purpose" seduces Zeus in order to take
his attention away from the battle between the Greeks and the Trojans
so that he will not be able to intervene on behalf of the Trojans and
the Greeks will regain the upper hand (Lattimore, 1951, 1961, 302).
Lucian takes things a lot further, and in his writings Zeus and his fellow gods and goddesses are invariably squabbling narcissists who are
given to all too human failings. This was not necessarily a problem
for Renaissance readers, though combined with Lucian's derogatory
remarks about Christianity in his account of Peregrinus, who had been
a Christian for a while in his earlier career, it was enough to give him
a reputation as an atheist. This sometimes led to heated debate about
whether Lucian was in fact suitable for school use, as in nineteenth-
century Germany (Baumbach, 2007).

Most of Lucian's work is distinguished by a degree of frivolity. If
he mocks individuals or types, he does not take himself seriously. This
appears particularly in his *True Story*, a tall tale to end all tall tales
which parodies previous accounts of travellers' adventures, including
a number now lost to us as well as surviving authors such as Homer,
Herodotus and Thucydides. Unlike his predecessors, however, Lucian
claims for himself the virtue of truth, since he is ready to assure his
readers that he is indeed a liar: "The one and only truth you'll hear

from me is that I *am* lying" (Casson, 1968, 15). Even when allow-ance is made for other influences, such as the descriptions of Atlantis in Plato's dialogues *Timaeus* and *Critias* (fourth century BCE), it is Lucian's *True Story*, with episodes such as a trip to the Moon and of being swallowed, ship and all, by a whale, which is the ancestor of all imaginary voyages, alternative universes and far-off lands which function as a means of criticising the writer's own society. Lucian's *The Fly* (Harmon, 1913, 82–95) was essentially a short playful text, but it was later to popularise the genre of the mock encomium, much used by Renaissance and later satirists. One example is the praise of debt which François Rabelais (c. 1483–1552) puts into the mouth of Panurge in the Third Book of *Gargantua and Pantagruel*:

> Can you imagine how good I feel each morning when I see all those lenders around me, so humble, obsequious and prodi-gal with their bowings, or when I note that, should I bestow a more open countenance or a more cheerful welcome on one rather than the others, the scoundrel believes he will be paid off first and be first in the queue, taking my smile for ready cash.
>
> (Screech, 2006, 422–430, at 424)

Erasmus's *Praise of Folly* is a variation on the genre, because the text is presented as if spoken by the figure of Folly. Making use of the grammatical gender of the equivalents in both Greek and Latin, Erasmus makes Folly female, and the implications are spelt out by Holbein's drawings in the margin of one copy, where Folly is shown as a woman wearing the cap and bells of the traditional costume of the professional (usually male) Fool, and addressing her audience from a pulpit, a self-evident absurdity to most potential readers, who would remember St. Paul's advice that women should remain silent in church (I Corinthians, xiv, 34–35; I Timothy, ii, 11–12). After suggesting that fools have a more agreeable life of it than those who endeavour to be wise, and that life itself would not continue without the foolish behav-iour inseparable from sexual activity, Folly moves on to a wide range of topics, connected by the idea that they are all manifestations of herself. These include popular superstition, the satirist's common tar-gets of doctors and lawyers, the follies of philosophers and scholastic theologians, the vanity of authors, the absurdities of life at royal courts and the obsessive pursuit of money and prestige by higher ecclesiastical officials, up to and including the popes themselves. Although no particular persons are named, Folly insists that she is present everywhere, even if people refuse to recognise the fact:

> I doubt if a single individual could be found from the whole of mankind who is wise every hour of his life and doesn't suffer from some form of insanity. The only difference is one of degree. A man who sees a gourd and takes it for a woman is called insane because this happens to very few people. But when a husband swears that the wife he shares with her many lovers outdoes faithful Penelope, and congratulates himself on what is a happy delusion, no one calls him insane, because this is seen happening in marriages everywhere.
>
> (Erasmus, 1993, 60)

While Erasmus uses the character of Folly to satirise the failings of the Church as an institution, and the behaviour of many of those who claimed to serve it, he never mocks Christianity itself. On the contrary, there is a change of tone towards the end of the *Praise of Folly*, where Folly proceeds to show that the simple Christian piety of the unlearned might be regarded as foolish by many, but was in fact infinitely preferable to what passed for worldly wisdom. Particularly in the later versions of the text, this is supported by a wide range of biblical references which would be impressive and surprising in the assumed character of Folly as the ridiculous woman preacher, but which reminds us that Erasmus knew his Bible thoroughly and was responsible for an important critical edition of the Greek New Testament (first published 1516). As a modern editor of the *Praise of Folly* comments, the text "ends with a remarkable feat of double irony as it transforms itself from a mock encomium into a real one" (Levi in Erasmus, 1993, 115, n. 131).

Like other forms of satire, Menippean examples play with readers' expectations in different ways. More's *Utopia* includes some explicit criticisms of contemporary English society, including a famous denunciation of the practice of agricultural enclosures, by which landowners placed increasing emphasis on sheep breeding and the profits to be gained from the wool trade at the expense of other forms of agriculture, thus causing sheep to become "devourers of men", and a passage arguing against the use of capital punishment for crimes against property, even petty thefts (Bruce, 1999, 21–23; 25–26). The imaginary commonwealth of the Utopians, with its community of goods and its relegation of gold to base uses such as chamber-pots and fetters for criminals, offers a number of provocative comparisons with sixteenth-century England and other European societies. Whether Utopia is in fact to be regarded as an ideal, as "the beste state of a pub-lyque weale" in Robinson's translation of the title, is another matter. It is not just that the equality of Utopian citizens depends to a signifi-cant extent on the labour of those whom More's text explicitly calls *servi* ("slaves"; "bondmen" in Robinson's translation), rather like the way in which the democracy of ancient Athens and the equality of its citizens depended on the wealth of the state which was produced by slaves working in appalling conditions in the silver mines of Laurium. When we read that the Utopians rejected the use of professional law-yers, "For they think it most meet that every man should plead his own matter" (Bruce, 1999, 94), we may smile because we remember that More was himself a lawyer. The contrast between the description of the Utopians' general tolerance in matters of religion (even if this does not extend to atheists) and what we know of More's personal involvement in the burning of heretics is more disturbing (Bruce, 1999, xxv, 106–110). The text itself offers a number of indications that, like Lucian's *True Story*, we should be cautious about taking it at face value. Even Raphael Hythloday, the imaginary traveller who provides the account of Utopia, says

> [...] whether they believe well or no, neither the time doth suffer us to discuss, neither is it now necessary. For we have taken upon us to show and declare their laws and ordinances, and not to defend them.
>
> (Bruce, 1999, 85)

Hythloday's name is constructed from Greek words which suggest that he is a peddler of nonsensical fables, and the Greek etymology of "Utopia" might suggest not only a "good place" but, alternatively, "no place". More's play on Greek roots shows that the Utopian capital

Amaurote is the "shadowy city", and it stands on the river Anyder, whose name means "without water". In a letter to a friend of Erasmus which appeared in the second edition of the book, More assured him, with somewhat heavy-handed irony, that it was all true, and that

> [...] even if I had wished to abuse the ignorance of the unlearned, I should certainly not have omitted to insert indications by which scholars would easily have been able to see through my design. If I had done nothing else I should at least have given such names to the prince, the river, the city, the island, as would have warned the skilful reader that the island exists nowhere, that the city is of shadows, the river without water, and the prince without people.
>
> (Bruce, 1999, 137–138)

This passage indicates one of the main problems of Menippean satire. Even if, as with Erasmus's defence of unlettered piety, it expresses sympathy with those who are not highly educated, it is very much a genre composed by intellectuals and dependent on verbal ingenuity and wordplay, literary allusions and the writers' assumption that their readers will appreciate in-jokes.

An outstanding example of this is Rabelais, a writer known by reputation to many more than have actually read him. The term "Rabelaisian" suggests bawdy or vulgar humour, especially of a sexual or scatological nature. This is certainly to be found in the works with which he is chiefly associated, and which are usually referred to as *Gargantua and Pantagruel*: *Pantagruel* (first published 1531 or 1532), *Gargantua* (1535), *The Third Book of Pantagruel* (1546), *The Fourth Book of Pantagruel* (1546) and *The Fifth Book of Pantagruel*, which was not published until 1564, more than 10 years after the death of Rabelais, and which may or may not be based on materials left by him. One example would be the episode in which the child-giant Gargantua, after experimenting with many and varied alternatives, comes to the conclusion "that there is no bottom-wiper like a downy young goose, provided that you hold its head between your legs" (Screech, 2006, 249). In his famous study of *Rabelais and his World*, first published in Russian in 1965, the Russian critic and theorist Mikhail Bakhtin argued that Rabelais drew his inspiration from "the medieval culture of folk humour", which Bakhtin saw as liberating:

> [...] the medieval culture of laughter was the drama of bodily life (copulation, birth, growth, eating, drinking, defecation). But of course it was not the drama of an individual body or of a private material way of life; it was the drama of the great generic body of the people, and for this generic body birth and death are not an absolute beginning and end but merely elements of continuous growth and renewal.
>
> [...]
>
> The serious aspects of class culture are official and authoritarian; they are combined with violence, prohibitions, limitations and always contain an element of fear and of intimidation [...] Laughter, on the contrary, overcomes fear, for it knows no inhibitions, no limitations. Its idiom is never used by violence and authority.
>
> (Bakhtin, 1984, 71, 88, 90)

There is plenty of eating and drinking in Rabelais, nearly always associated with good fellowship, even if there is not actually that much of "Rabelaisian" humour in the sense of references to copulation and defecation. It is easy to see why many readers have come to see his work as a joyous celebration of life, feeling that, in the words of a modern translator, in Rabelais "the mechanics of sex, crapulence and gluttony are amusing as part of a wider vision of what men and women are, or may become" (Screech, 2006, xix). Modern readers are less likely to be troubled by the parodic references to the Bible which sixteenth-century ones found dangerously close to blasphemy and which Rabelais himself sometimes censored in later printings of his work during his lifetime. Some of his targets, such as the pedantry of scholastic theologians, may now seem like fair game. We may indeed be inclined to think that, in reading Rabelais, we are entering "a wise world of kaleidoscopic laughter" (Screech, 2006, xl), that his work functions as a satire on the human condition, something which makes us reconsider our very natures in an ultimately liberating fashion.

For some readers, this effect is produced by the ending of the *Fifth Book*, when the mystic word of the long-sought Divine Bottle turns out to be "Drink!", and this is then read backwards into all that has come before to produce a reading that Rabelais is arguing for an existentialist acceptance of our place in the universe. We may compare the ending of another Menippean satire, Voltaire's *Candide* (first published 1759), where, after many misadventures which are as diverting for the readers as they are painful for the characters involved, Candide finally rejects the philosophical speculations of his companion and sometime mentor Pangloss, with "Cela est bien dit ... mais il faut cultiver notre jardin" ("That is well said, but we need to till our garden".)

That the *Fifth Book* may not actually be by Rabelais is one problem, but there are others. Bakhtin's references to "the medieval culture of folk humour" may seem over-generalising, and there is no getting around the fact that a great deal of Rabelais, far from being "folk humour", is extremely learned, to the extent that most modern readers will require extensive annotation to make any sense of it. Rabelais had translated parts of Lucian (Screech, 2006, xxv), and Lucian's influence can be seen in, for example, the imaginary voyage in search of the Divine Bottle (which begins in the *Fourth Book*) and the strange sights they encounter during the course of it. Rabelais has read More's *Utopia*, and there are frequent references to Erasmus, especially his *Adagia*, an annotated collection of Greek and Latin proverbs first published in 1500 and greatly expanded in later editions (Screech, 2006, xli). We may also wonder if it is really true, as Bakhtin suggests, that the folk laughter he sees at the heart of Rabelais "knows no inhibitions, no limitations". Rabelais mocks scholastic theologians and their pretensions to be "magistri nostri" ("our masters"), and he ridicules some aspects of the Church as an institution, with which he had had a somewhat difficult relationship: he had been a Franciscan friar, and later became a Benedictine monk before giving that up to become a physician. He had broken his religious vows to father several children. He does not, however, question Christianity itself, and although he was associated with several individuals who became prominent Protestants, he himself remained a Catholic priest until his death. Bakhtin's claim that the idiom of laughter "is never used by violence and authority" is also at odds with several passages in Rabelais. While lawyers are a traditional target for the satirist, one passage in the *Fourth Book* where they are attacked, literally as well as metaphorically (Screech, 2006, 697–714), depends on the idea that there is something inherently funny in an aristocrat having his social inferiors beaten up as an alternative to paying his debts. The nobleman organises a fake wedding to coincide with the arrival of a Chicanous, or bailiff, who wants to serve him a writ. Mock fights were customarily organised at weddings because the blows were supposed to remind those who received them of the happy occasion, but here the Chicanous is invited in order to give him a real beating up:

> Towards the end, buffets from fists began to fly about; but when it came to the turn of Chicanous they regaled him so thoroughly with great biffs from their gauntlets that he stood there all battered and bruised, with one eye poached in black butter, eight fractured ribs, his breast-plate stoven in, his shoulder-blades in four quarters and his lower jaw in three pieces.
> And all done with a laugh.
>
> (Screech, 2006, 701)

A long-running theme, which begins in the *Third Book*, is Panurge's struggle to decide whether he should get married because he desires a wife, or avoid marriage because he is afraid of becoming a cuckold. In Rabelais, as in many other authors, cuckoldry is only amusing because it is a subversion of what is perceived as the natural order of things, in which a woman ought to be subjected to the control of her husband.

One is left wondering about the function of Menippean satire. Is it essentially a matter of preaching to the converted? What is the purpose, for example, of the mockery of popular superstition which we can find in Lucian, in Erasmus, and More, in Rabelais, if it does not appear to offer any questioning of the social conditions which lead people to feel that they have to have something supernatural in which to believe? It can seem uncomfortably like a manifestation of intellectuals' disdain for those who do not share what they consider to be their superior education, a disdain which inevitably becomes a form of class bias in times and places where education is treated as a commodity to be bought and sold. If we think of the satirist as a sort of resistance fighter in a cultural guerrilla war against forces of conservatism and oppression, it is a little disconcerting to discover that the final piece of biographical information which we have about Lucian is that in his old age he became a well-paid official in the service of the Roman imperial government in Egypt (Swain, 2007, 36–41). If the purpose of satire is to change the world, or at least change the ways in which we think about it, do writers like Lucian, or More, or Rabelais, do more than elicit complacent smiles from those who already share their points of view?

Nevertheless, Menippean satire proved not to be a rigid and unchanging genre. With hindsight, something which might appear to be pointing a way forward is *The Isle of Pines* (1668), by Henry Nevile or Neville (1620–1694). Like More's *Utopia*, this is a text which turns out to be more conservative than might at first appear to be the case. There is an imaginary voyage, whose narrator, George Pine, records how he was the only male survivor of a shipwreck which leaves him and four women on an otherwise uninhabited island somewhere near Madagascar. He proceeds to have children by all of them, so that by the time he is eighty, many years later, he is the patriarchal ruler of a society consisting of some 1,789 of his own descendants. Some have seen this as "a fantasy of absolute sexual liberty, a wish-fulfilment of individual phallic and paternal transcendence" (Bruce, 1999, xxxviii). Traditional boundaries are happily transgressed: after first sleeping with the two maidservants, Pine also sleeps with the daughter of his former master, and then with the enslaved black woman. But as a modern editor notes, the text was published in two parts, one of which provides a framing narrative which tells us what happened on the island many years later. In the framing narrative, which is ignored by some critics who have only read the other part, a visiting Dutch ship puts in at the island and finds the current patriarch to be William Pine, the grandson of George Pine. This not only allows for a plausible reason for how George Pine's narrative gets back to England, but also tells how the Dutch provided William Pine with the force needed to crush a rebellion against his authority. Taking the two parts together, *The Isle of Pines* could be seen as making a case for the importance of firm government in a colonial context, and as advocating a more Dutch approach to colonisation, that is, one which placed a greater emphasis on economic development (Bruce, 1999, xxxvi–xlii). William Pine attributed the growth of quarrelling and dissension among the inhabitants, and of crimes and "mischiefs" of all sorts (including "whoredoms, incests, and adultery"), to "the neglect of hearing the Bible read", while the Dutch captain commented that "where the hedge of government is once broken down, the most vile bear the greatest rule" (Bruce, 1999, 201, 207–208). The text also manages to suggest that interracial sex is subversive of good order in society. George Pine notes that he was "willing to try the difference" but that he only had sex with the black woman "in the night and not else; my stomach would not serve me, although she was one of the handsomest blacks I had seen, and her children as comely as the rest". After George Pine's death, the two major troublemakers are children of this relationship (Bruce, 1999, 198, 202, 207).

In some ways, Nevile's short text looks ahead to William Golding's novel *Lord of the Flies* (1954), in which a group of British schoolboys, marooned on an island by a plane crash and thus freed from the restraints of civilisation, rapidly descend into savagery. A different sort of parallel, more revealing in terms of literary history, is with *Robinson Crusoe* (1719). Daniel Defoe's hero, unlike George Pine, is alone on his island for many years. Even after the arrival of Friday, there is no suggestion of sexuality in the text. By prayer and hard work, Crusoe develops his relationship with God, and accumulates material goods, which he lists with a meticulous attention to detail which would have been a credit to a professional accountant. In spite of the various encounters with cannibals, after the initial shipwreck not very much actually happens, and modern readers may well find Crusoe a rather bloodless and unappealing figure. Nevertheless, Crusoe's combination of spiritual introspection and capitalist accumulation appealed to the burgeoning middle class among Defoe's contemporaries, and the text enjoyed enormous popularity, both in its original version and in numerous adaptations and translations in other languages. Many have hailed *Robinson Crusoe* as the first modern novel, and in his *Anatomy of Criticism* (first published 1957), the influential Canadian critic Northrop Frye (1912–1991) treated Menippean satire as something which shaded into other forms of fiction (Frye, 1971, 303–314). Frye's comment that "The Menippean satire deals less with people as such than with mental attitudes" can certainly be applied to *Robinson Crusoe*. What mattered to Defoe's readers was not the precise details of how Crusoe built up herds of goats or stores of grain to provide for his future, but rather how these demonstrated an attitude of self-reliance, of trusting in the idea that God helps those who help themselves.

In a period when trade at home and abroad, the development of overseas colonies and the activities which supported this, such as the slave trade in which Crusoe took an active part, were providing increasing alternatives to traditional forms of wealth and influence, this offered great attractions.

Two other eighteenth-century examples deserve mention. The first is *Gulliver's Travels* (1726), in which Jonathan Swift (1667–1745) created an imaginary voyage in the Lucianic tradition. Some of the details, such as the coloured threads which reward obsequious courtiers in Lilliput and which allude to the ribands of British orders of knighthood at the court of George I, or the Academy of Lagado, where the professors engage in pointless activities such as endeavouring to extract sunbeams from cucumbers or developing a breed of sheep without wool, which satirises the scientists of the Royal Society, refer specifically to Swift's own time. The same is true of Gulliver's explanation of the British constitution, which leads the King of Brobdingnag to "conclude the Bulk of your Natives, to be the most pernicious Race of little odious Vermin that Nature ever suffered to crawl upon the Surface of the Earth". But other aspects, especially the description of the ideal state of the rational, horse-like Houyhnhnms and their subject race of brutish Yahoos, who bear a frightening resemblance to humans, have always been seen as having a much wider application. It seems that for Swift, as for Gulliver himself, we are all Yahoos, and the reader is inexorably drawn to the same conclusion. The pretensions of birth, wealth and education are all ruthlessly exposed as folly, and we are left, perhaps, with the possibility that once we recognise this, we can then begin to make something worthwhile of ourselves, even if Gulliver's final word on the subject is a rejection of "so absurd a project as that of reforming the Yahoo Race in this Kingdom [...] I have now done with all such visionary Schemes for ever" (Swift, 2005, 10).

If Gulliver comes to regard the usual social distinctions as utterly pointless, they are at the heart of *The Expedition of Humphry Clinker* (1771). Written by Tobias Smollett (1721–1771), a Scot who had made a successful literary career in London, this was, among other things, an attempt to educate readers about the variety of the British Isles, since, as one of the characters puts it, "What, between want of curiosity, and traditional sarcasms, the effect of ancient animosity, the people at the other end of the island know as little of Scotland as of Japan" (Smollett, 1998, 214). The book takes the form of an epistolary novel, allowing for multiple points of view as the family of a Welsh country squire travel the length and breadth of Britain. The letters are written by the conservative squire, his husband-hunting sister, his young niece and her brother, who is an Oxford student. We are treated as a result to opposing opinions: the squire is horrified by the bustling modernity of London, for example, while his niece finds it exciting. A few of the letters are written by a Welsh lady's maid, and while some humour is extracted from the way in which she is portrayed as no more than semi-literate, her acute observations of human nature ensure that she is much more than a figure of fun. Other voices, including Scottish and Irish ones, are heard through the accounts of the letter writers. The result is a broad panorama of society combined with vividly realised characterisation and a number of satirical passages, such as the description of the levee held by the Duke of Newcastle, a former prime minister who was much less important than he had once been, but who clung to whatever marks of flattering respect he could get:

> [...] he wheeled about; and, going round the levee, spoke to every individual, with the most courteous familiarity; but he scarce ever opened his mouth without making some blunder, in relation to the person or business of the party with whom he conversed; so that he really looked like a comedian, hired to burlesque the character of a minister [...]
>
> (Smollett, 1998, 113)

One of the most significant passages is the account of a ball and dinner to which the cawdies or errand boys (in fact, grown men) of Edinburgh invite the nobleman and gentlemen attending the Leith races. The cawdies sit down with their guests at table as equals, and after dinner one of their number gives a series of witty and satirical toasts directed against many of the upper-class guests. Afterwards, the cawdies leave their seats and stand each behind a guest's chair, like footmen, saying "Noo we're your honours' cawdies again". The message is clear: class distinctions are part of society and are not going to go away, but their arbitrary and ultimately pointless nature is recognised by all people of sense. And, at the end, one of the noblemen has to pay the bill for the lavish entertainment (Smollett, 1998, 226–228). Nevertheless, while the suspension of the usual conventions of social behaviour in eighteenth-century Britain is striking, it is also clear that it is purely temporary. The cawdies are at liberty to mock their "betters" to their faces only within the particular circumstances of this one occasion. Like the mediaeval carnival festivities at the heart of Bakhtin's interpretation of Rabelais, the cawdies' dinner allows them to let off steam before returning to what both they and their upper-class guests would have considered to be their rightful places in the social order. Satirical mockery is succeeded all too quickly by the renewal of deference.

With Smollett's text, we seem to be moving away from the Lucianic tradition towards something more like the modern novel. If, as Frye argues, "no sharp boundary lines can or should be drawn", and that in a text like Henry Fielding's *Tom Jones* (1749) "Squire Western belongs to the novel, but Thwackum and Square have Menippean blood in them" (Frye, 1971, 309), we are close to suggesting that any novel with satirical elements in it can be claimed as an example of Menippean satire, and indeed a very wide range of novels have been classed as such by modern critics, and the term has also been applied to films. The field which bears the strongest resemblance to ancient predecessors, and which can trace its ancestry back to Lucian's *True Story*, is that of alternative universes and imaginary worlds. While much science fiction functions purely on the level of entertainment, texts such as Aldous Huxley's *Brave New World* (1932), with its castes based on genetic engineering and preserved by government-sponsored drug use; George Orwell's *Nineteen Eighty-Four* (1949), in which the supremacy of the Inner Party is secured by the ubiquity of propaganda, surveillance and terror; or Ursula Le Guin's *Left Hand of Darkness* (1969), which invites us to imagine a world whose inhabitants have no fixed gender identity, all work, in Frye's formulation of the defining characteristic of Menippean satire, by dealing "less with people as such than with mental attitudes". It is not so much, however, the attitudes of traditional targets, "pedants, bigots, cranks, parvenus, virtuosi, enthusiasts, rapacious and incompetent professional men of all kinds", and "their occupational approach to life as distinct from their social behaviour" (Frye, ibid.), which we are invited to consider, but our own.

6

THE "CHARACTER" AS SATIRE

In 1592, the French scholar Isaac Casaubon (1559–1614) published an edition of a hitherto little-known ancient text and, in so doing, seems to have stimulated the development of a new satirical form which was to become popular across Europe for some two centuries, and whose effects continue to the present day.

Casaubon's book was called *Theophrasti Characteres Ethici, sive Descriptiones morum Graecè* ("The Moral Characters of Theophrastus, or Descriptions of manners in Greek"; Casaubon, 1592). Theophrastus was an ancient Greek philosopher (c. 371–c. 287 BCE) who is mentioned by Chaucer's Wife of Bath in her Prologue, and by the Merchant in the Tale of January and May, because he was referred to by St. Jerome as the author of a work attacking marriage (now lost). He was a significant pioneer of scientific botany, and his *History of Plants*, rediscovered in the fifteenth century, was influential in the Renaissance. The *Characters*, or what we have of them, are a collection of thirty short pieces which exist in a number of mediaeval manuscripts. Their first appearance in print was an edition of the first fifteen by the German humanist Willibald Pirckheimer (1470–1530), who added a Latin translation (Pirckheimer, 1527). Later sixteenth-century editions published the first twenty-three, as at first did

Casaubon, though his second and third editions (1599, 1612) took the total to twenty-eight by drawing on a previously unused manuscript. The final two were not printed until the eighteenth century (Diggle, 2004, 37–57). The distinction between the *Characters* as known to modern classical scholars and how they were interpreted by Casaubon and others is important to the history of the development of the character as a satirical genre.

What Theophrastus originally wrote would appear to have been a series of short prose sketches of different types of human behaviour, such as the Chatterbox, the Country Bumpkin, the Penny-pincher, the Tactless Man and so forth. At its best, the style is succinct, saying much in a short compass and making good use of telling detail. In places, however, it is obscure, though it can be argued that this is not necessarily how it was actually composed by Theophrastus, whose very name, suggesting divine eloquence, was conferred on him by Aristotle (he is said to have been originally called Tyrtamus). The *Characters*, as we now have them, "are nothing more than the very best that editors have been able to make of what is probably the corruptest manuscript tradition in all of Greek literature" (Diggle, 2004, 20). At an early date, a preface was added, suggesting that the *Characters* should be read as moral examples so that readers could be made aware of the sort of behaviour they should avoid. All of the sketches were supplied with introductory definitions of the personality traits being illustrated, and several were given moralising epilogues. While this additional material is now rejected as spurious, all of it was accepted by most older editors, including Casaubon, as being by Theophrastus himself. There is the further problem that some material has been lost: while we have no way of telling whether there were originally more than the thirty characters we now have, the text as it stands has gaps and there are places where it does not make sense, and conjectural emendation will take us only so far. This makes it difficult to see any purpose in the work, since, once the spurious additions are rejected, "the work lacks all ethical dimension. Nothing is analysed, no moral is drawn, no motive is sought" (Diggle, 2004, 12). The suggestion of the Italian classical scholar Giorgio Pasquali (1885–1952) that the sketches "were conceived as illustrative show-pieces for a course of lectures on ethics, a few moments' light entertainment amid more serious matter" can be no more than a plausible conjecture (Diggle, 2004, 15).

As interpreted by Casaubon, however, the *Characters* became something rather different. The Greek text took up only forty-two pages of a small volume, and though Casaubon added more than five times as much in the way of detailed annotation, what really mattered was his Latin translation, which made the work available to a much wider range of readers across Europe, and the preface in which he claimed a moral purpose for it:

> Argumentum autem et subjectum scripti istius philosophicum plane est: de moribus enim hominum hic agitur, et ad bene honesteque vitam degendam nobis hoc scripto praeire Theophrastus voluit ...
>
> (Casaubon, 1592, Prolegomena 7)

> [Moreover, it is clear that the topic and theme of this work is a philosophical one: it treats of the behaviour and morals of human beings, and Theophrastus wished by this work to persuade us to pass our lives in an upright and virtuous manner ...]

Casaubon's translation was "regularly reprinted with the Greek text until the nineteenth century" (Botley, 2014, 483). By accepting the added material as genuine, and by his insistence on the moral character of the work, he was influential in giving it a much wider appeal and helping to suggest that it was of universal applicability.

Something of the effect of this can be seen in the English translation of Theophrastus which was published in 1616 and attributed to John Healey. This "relies heavily" on Casaubon's Latin version (Considine, 2004a), and the translator's introductory note refers explicitly to Casaubon as "that great Magazine or Storehouse of all learning". It goes on to claim that Theophrastus "hath deserued well of virtue and good manners; having very liuely and sharpely described those deformed vices which flourished in his time, but raigne in ours". As we have seen with examples like William Hay's imitations of Martial (Chapter 4), the belief that human nature was essentially unchanging allowed ancient texts to be adapted as criticisms of contemporary society. The didactic nature of Healey's version can be seen from these extracts, which are all passages considered spurious by modern classicists but which were included in Casaubon's text of Theophrastus and his Latin version:

> I therefore, O *Policles*, hauing a long time obserued the diuers dispositions of men [...] hauing conuersed with all sorts of natures bad and good, and comparing them together: I took it my part to set down in this discourse their seuerall fashions and manners of life. For I am of opinion, my *Policles*, that our children will proue the honester and better conditioned, if we leaue them good precedents of imitation: that of good children they may proue better men [...]
>
> Garrulity is a slippery loosenesse, or a babbling of a long inconsiderate speech [...] These kind of men are to be shunned, with great warines [sic] and speed, as a man would preuent or out-run an Ague. For 'tis a miserable condition, to continue long with those which cannot distinguish the seasons of businesse and leisure.
>
> (Healey, 1616, "Theophrastus Characters" 2, 12, 15)

Even before Healey's translation appeared, the *Characters* were known in Britain, and the earliest references to them by a writer in English appear to be the paraphrases of two passages which appear in Ben Jonson's *Volpone* (Act III, Scene ii; Act IV, Scene i), which was probably first performed in early 1606 and printed the following year (Parker, 1999, 171, 220). Jonson was also

> among the first playwrights to apply the art of "character-writing" to the portrayal of dramatic figures [...] In the first act of *The Magnetic Lady* (acted 1632; published 1640), several figures in the play are described according to their social status, their habits, their manners, and their morals, and the word "character" is used twice in the play in reference to these passages.
>
> (Blank, 2000, 272)

This marked an important shift in the meaning of the term, since the word "character" in English had long been used with almost exclusive reference to written or printed letters or symbols, and by the sixteenth century, to personal styles, so that when Shakespeare's Claudius refers to "Hamlet's character" (*Hamlet*, IV, vii, 51), he is not talking about his personality, but his handwriting (Blank, 2000, 268). In the opening of *Twelfth Night*, Viola's reference to the Captain's "fair and outward character" (I, ii, 51) suggests the idea that someone's likely conduct can be determined from their appearance: she trusts him because she thinks he looks trustworthy, and "character" here primarily means external features. In spite of King Duncan's "There's no art/To find the mind's construction in the face" (*Macbeth*, I, iv, 11–12), this was, and perhaps remains, a widespread belief. By the time an audience saw Jonson's *Magnetic Lady*, however, a further meaning had been given to "character" by three popular publications which all drew to some extent on Theophrastus.

The first of these, published in 1608, was *Characters of Vertues and Vices* (Hall, 1608), by Joseph Hall, whom we have previously met as the author of verse satires (Chapter 4). Hall's *Characters* were reprinted with his *Meditations and Vowes, Diuine and Morall* (1621) and as part of his collected works (1625 and 1628). They were versified in English by Nahum Tate (1691), while a French translation by Jean Loiseau de Tourval appeared in 1610 and was republished in 1619 and 1634, and another translation, by Urbain Chevreau, appeared in 1659. There was also a German translation by Georg Philipp Harsdörffer (1696).

In 1614, the London bookseller Lawrence Lisle published a poem with the title *A Wife, now a Widowe*. No author's name was given, but the poem was by Sir Thomas Overbury (bap. 1581, d. 1613), and in it the never-married Overbury described his ideal wife, emphasising the importance of her usefulness and obedience. The poem sold well, and was soon reissued with Overbury's name on the title page and the addition of, it was stated, "many witty Characters, and conceited Newes, written by himselfe and other learned Gentlemen his friends" (Overbury, 1614). The prose "Characters", modelled on Hall, were, as described at the head of the collection, "Witty descriptions of the properties of sundry Persons" – a summary which, like the Characters themselves, left a degree of ambiguity as to whether they dealt with "Persons" in the sense of human individuals or roles which those individuals adopted, perhaps only temporarily, as Shakespeare's Peter Quince said that "one must come in ... and say he comes to disfigure, or to present, the person of Moonshine" (*Midsummer Night's Dream*, III, i, 59–61). "The collection was a great success, and Lisle issued a series of progressively augmented editions [...] By 1622 an eleventh edition had appeared, with eighty-two characters ..." Nevertheless, in spite of the claim on the original title page, none of the characters were actually by Overbury, though some were by the dramatist John Webster and others have been attributed to different authors of the period, including John Donne, though without much certainty. It is clear that some of the collection's popularity was the result of clever, if unscrupulous, marketing on the part of Lisle, who was exploiting the fact that Overbury was a well-known courtier who had fallen from royal favour and had died in the Tower of London in mysterious circumstances: he was alleged to have been poisoned, and sensational murder trials followed in 1615 (Considine, 2004b). The lingering air of scandal ensured that the collection was still being reprinted in the following century (Overbury, 1756) and has kept Overbury's name in academic use as useful shorthand for a group of miscellaneous pieces of largely uncertain origin.

The third work was by John Earle (b. between 1598 and 1601; d. 1665), who was, like Joseph Hall, an Anglican clergyman who eventually became a bishop. *Micro-cosmographie, or, A Peece of the World Discovered; in Essayes and Characters* was published anonymously in 1628 by Edward Blount (who had earlier been responsible for the publication of Healey's translation of Theophrastus), but "was soon known to be Earle's work". It proved to be "immensely popular and went through many editions in the seventeenth, eighteenth, and nineteenth centuries, in the course of which the original fifty-four characters were augmented to seventy-eight" (Spurr, 2004).

Something of Earle's methods, and how the "character" could be turned to satirical purposes, can be seen in his treatment of a popular target for satirists of many different periods, the "meer dull physician":

> [...] he is distinguished from an empiric, by a round velvet cap and doctor's gown, yet no man takes degrees more superfluously, for he is doctor howsoever. He is sworn to Galen and Hippocrates, as university men to their statutes, though they never saw them; and his discourse is all aphorisms, though his reading be only Alexis of Piedmont, or the *Regiment of Health*.

> The best cure he has done, is upon his own purse, which from a lean sickliness he hath made lusty, and in flesh [...] He tells you your malady in Greek, though it be but a cold, or head-ach; which by good endeavour and diligence he may bring to some moment indeed. His most unfaithful act is, that he leaves a man gasping, and his pretence is, death and he have a quarrel and must not meet; but his fear is, lest the carcass should bleed.
>
> (Earle, 1934, 10–11)

The physician wears academic dress in order to appear different from an "empiric", that is, someone who professed to treat sickness but who had no formal academic training. Earle undercuts the distinction by pointing out that "he is doctor howsoever", since in the seventeenth century, as in more recent times, the title of "Doctor" was commonly accorded to medical practitioners whether or not they actually possessed the degree of Doctor of Medicine, as opposed to a Bachelor of Medicine degree, a lower qualification that would still have conferred the right to practise. Earle continues by noting that the physician was "sworn to Galen and Hippocrates", that is, he affected reverence for two ancient Greek authors who were still regarded as important sources of medical knowledge in the seventeenth century. The fact that these texts were in Greek gave physicians a reputation for learning, but Earle suggests that, in some cases, the physician paid as little attention to them as academics generally did to the university statutes they swore to obey, and that the physician's reading actually consisted only of popular health manuals available in English. Insofar as the physician does understand Greek, the only use he makes of it is to baffle his patients into accepting expensive treatment which may make a minor ailment into a matter of moment, something genuinely serious which might even lead to the death of a patient. Earle uses the popular belief that the wounds of a corpse would flow with fresh blood in the presence of its murderer to suggest that the physician avoids the actual deathbed because he is afraid of others recognising his responsibility for the fatal consequences of the treatment he has prescribed. In accordance with a long-lasting theme in the treatment of the medical profession in literature, Earle also suggests that the physician's greatest success, and, by implication, his main concern, is in improving the condition of his purse. For a much later example, we may compare the "Physicians of the Utmost Fame" in the poem *The Chief Defect of Henry King* by Hilaire Belloc (1870–1953), which appeared in his *Cautionary Tales* (1907): "They answered, as they took their Fees, / 'There is no Cure for this Disease'". In view of what we know of the inadequacies of seventeenth-century medicine, Earle may not be that far from the unvarnished truth, but we should note that the title of his "character" indicates that his target is the "meer dull physician". He leaves open the possibility that other physicians may be genuinely knowledgeable and enjoy better success. Earle's target is not medicine or medical practitioners as such, but the pretensions of the "meer dull physician" who affects an unjustified superiority over the "empiric", even though there is in fact little difference between the two of them. While it is probable that not even the "meer dull physician" used Greek all the time in the manner suggested, Earle's emphasis on selected detail, and a degree of exaggeration, show how the "character" shares some similarities with caricature in the visual arts (Chapter 8). Just as the caricature concentrates on aspects of external appearance, often exaggerated for effect, so the "character", as the seventeenth century understood the term, dealt with observable behaviour and often achieved its effects by selection and exaggeration or distortion. Both can achieve a boldness and immediacy of effect, but such a result is very different from the gradual revelation of interior life in what we think of as character in a novel of the nineteenth century or later, especially when we see that character developing over time in the text. The seventeenth-century "character", by contrast, is a representation of a human type which is assumed to be fixed and unchanging.

Hall, "Overbury" and Earle remained the best-known examples, but they stimulated a fashion which saw the publication of numerous individual characters or collections of them, with one estimate claiming that "Over two hundred 'characters' or books of characters, are said to have been published between the years 1605 and 1700" (M'Cormick, 1894, 107). Hall's vocabulary shows the development of changes in terminology. His Superstitious Man "weares Paracelsian characters for the tooth-ache", that is, he seeks a cure in the use of magical symbols (1608, 90). Where the Hypocrite is concerned, however, "In whose silent face are written the characters of Religion, which his tongue & gestures pronounce, but his hands recant" (1608, 71–72), the term means he affects the appearance of a pious man, even if his conduct shows that he is nothing of the sort. More generally, Hall uses both "Character" and "Characterisme" to mean what we would now refer to as a character sketch. In a preface, Hall explicitly stated that his purpose was like that of the ancient moral philosophers, who offered examples to their readers, "whereby the ruder multitude might even by their sense learne to know vertue, and discerne what to detest" (1608, A5 v–r). In other words, "Charactery", or the writing of character sketches, might lead readers to better behaviour "by their sense", their natural reason, even without an appeal to revealed religion. Hall may refer to "the best of vertues, religion" (1608, 45), but explicitly religious exhortation plays little part in this text. He praises Theophrastus as "that ancient Master of Moralitie" (1608, 2), and there are some places where there is a degree of overlap. Hall's "Male-content", for example, who "is a slaue to enuie, and loseth flesh with fretting, not so much at his owne infelicitie, as at others good", bears a resemblance to Theophrastus's Ungrateful Grumbler (Hall, 1608, 99–105; Diggle, 2004, 115). Both give the character of the Superstitious Man, and while the details may be different – the one in Theophrastus takes fright if a weasel crosses his path, while in Hall it is a hare – both writers give the same general impression of someone obsessed by omens or ritualistic behaviours which appear meaningless or stupid to others (Hall, 1608, 87–91; Diggle, 2004, 110–113). Some details look like direct borrowings: Hall says of the Covetous Man that "If his seruant breake but an earthen dish for want of light, hee abates it out of his quarters wages", where in the case of Theophrastus's Penny-Pincher, "When a slave breaks a pot or a dish he deducts the cost from his rations" (Hall, 1608, 127; Diggle, 2004, 97). Other classical writers may have provided some inspiration. When they read of Hall's Busie-Bodie, "What euerie man ventures in Guiana voyage, & what they gained he knows to a haire", some contemporaries might have been reminded of a similar individual in an epigram by Martial (Hall, 1608, 79; Martial, IX, xxxv).

While he has a few references to contemporary events, such as the Gunpowder Plot (1605) or the Great Frost of 1608, when the Thames froze over (Hall, 1608, 151, 81), Hall talks in generalities. His work is divided into two parts: the first consisting of nine virtuous characters worthy of imitation, such as the Honest Man, the Humble Man and the True Friend, while the second part describes fifteen types whose behaviour is to be avoided, such as the Flatterer, the Covetous Man and the Distrustful Man. There are suggestions that Hall is thinking primarily of people with a certain level of wealth and position in society. The Vainglorious Man, for example, "neither vouchsafes to name any not honorable, nor those without some terme of familiaritie; and likes well to see the hearer looke vpon him amazedly, as if he said, How happy is this man that is so great with great ones!" (Hall, 1608, 135). Nevertheless, except for the Good Magistrate, none of the types of behaviour described is specifically associated with any particular class or occupation. Hall does tend to talk in platitudes, which are only occasionally redeemed by touches of figurative language, such as the conclusion to his character of the Humble Man:

> He is a lowly valley sweetly planted, and well watered; the proud mans earth, whereon he trampleth; but secretly full of wealthie mines, more worth than he that walks over them; a rich stone set in lead; and, lastly, a true Temple of God built with a low roofe.
>
> (Hall, 1608, 31)

These descriptions, such as the comparison of the Humble Man with "a rich stone", that is, a precious jewel, set in lead rather than gold, emphasise that external appearances can be deceptive. They appear to suggest that the social hierarchy is a fact of life, in the same way that the proud man tramples the earth, but the presence of the "wealthie mines" below and the reference to "a true Temple of God built with a low roofe" rather than being a grandiose building, which would immediately command attention, indicate that real merit is not necessarily either obvious or generally appreciated. Hall as satirist hints at how the values of early seventeenth-century society may not be those of a higher, eternal truth, something which his readers need to appreciate in order to "learne to know vertue, and discerne what to detest".

Like Hall's, the Overbury characters, and those in Earle, have some direct echoes of Theophrastus. For example, Earle's "sordid rich man ... loves to pay short a shilling or two in a great sum, and is glad to gain that when he can no more" in a manner reminiscent of Theophrastus's Repulsive Man, who in Casaubon's edition is given a passage misplaced from another character which says, in

Healey's translation, "If he be to pay 30. pound hee will be sure it shal want 3. groats" (Earle, 1934, 104; Casaubon, 1592, 66; Healey, 1616, "Theophrastus", 48; Diggle, 2004, 157). Overbury and Earle also introduce a number of new features, however. The much larger number of characters in these two collections allows for the inclusion of a greater range of types than we find in Hall: a significant proportion of the new characters are devoted not to types of behaviour as such, but to particular occupations, to which, indeed, stereotyped patterns of behaviour are attributed. We even get characters of places, such as a prison (Overbury) or a tavern, and Paul's Walk, in the old St Paul's Cathedral in London (Earle). While Hall might say "It is no shame for vs to learne wit of Heathens" (1608, A5v), referring to wit in the sense of wisdom, both the writers of the Overbury characters and Earle were much more concerned with "wit" as it was often understood in the seventeenth century, as a capacity for saying things in an amusing manner which drew attention to the writer's own verbal ingenuity. This often involved plays on words which are likely to seem overdone and contrived to modern readers, but it was a style greatly admired at the time, even if Earle gave a hostile sketch of the "meer empty wit" without any learning to sustain his facetiousness, and whose "bubbles and flashes, darted out on a sudden [...] if you take them while they are warm, may be laughed at; if they are cool, are nothing" (1934, 78–80). To give two of the shorter examples: "A very whore" is described in Overbury as "the cook and the meat, dressing herself all day, to be tasted with the better appetite at night" (1756, 223), while Earle notes how the cook of an ostentatious banquet sets out his dishes in the order they are meant to be eaten, while suggesting that there will be more food than can actually be consumed:

> ... he seems to have great skill in the tactics, ranging his dishes in order military, and placing in the forefront meats more strong and hardy, and the more cold and cowardly in the rear; as quaking tarts and quivering custards, and such milksop dishes, which scape many times the fury of the encounter.
>
> (1934, 62–63)

The comparison of the cook with a general in command of an army is a striking one, while the "quaking tarts and quivering custards" at the back of the arrangement of prepared dishes are for show rather than consumption: they are like "cowardly" soldiers who will escape danger when braver ones fall in combat, since the guests will have filled themselves on the "more strong and hardy" main courses.

While there are some positive sketches, such as the "Noble Spirit" (Overbury, 1756, 94–95) or the "grave divine" (Earle, 1934, 8–9), the negative, obviously satirical ones are more common and more striking. In the manner of the satirist, Earle may mock the "mere great man" whose "virtue is, that he was his father's son, and all the expectation of him to beget another" (1934, 104), but it is apparent that the authors of the "Overbury" characters and Earle all write from the perspective of educated, upper-class male adherents of the Church of England, who are familiar with court life and who are confident of their superiority to those outside their own circle. It is this sense of moral superiority, and the writers' expectation that it will be shared by their readers, that gives a satirical bite to their descriptions. The country gentleman who has little knowledge of the fashionable world, the town merchant, servants and tradesmen are all treated with some degree of disdain. Both collections mocked the alleged Welsh obsession with pedigrees (Overbury, 1756, 104; Earle, 1934, 67), and Overbury's sketch of "A drunken Dutchman resident in England" included what has become one of the enduring staples of anti-immigrant propaganda: "They swarm in great tenements like flies; six households will live in a garret" (Overbury, 1756, 175). Religious differences produce the strongest expressions of contempt. In Overbury, the "precisian" (i.e., Puritan) is assumed to be "varnished rottenness", a hypocrite:

> He can better afford you ten lies, than one oath, and dare commit any sin gilded with a pretence of sanctity; he will not stick to commit fornication or adultery, so it be done in the fear of GOD, and for the propagation of the godly, and can find it in his heart to lye with any whore, save the whore of BABYLON.
>
> (1756, 147)

With Earle's "she precise hypocrite", the target is not alleged sexual misconduct, but a complacent self-satisfaction in religion: "She doubts of the virgin Mary's salvation, and dares not saint her, but knows her own place in heaven as perfectly as the pew she has a key to" (1934, 50).

A somewhat different, and extremely influential, approach to the writing of characters was adopted in the work of the French writer Jean de la Bruyère (1645–1696), whose *Les Caractères, ou Les Mœurs de ce Siècle* ("The Characters, or The Manners of this Century") was first published in 1688. The book went through three further editions during the same year, and four more editions in the author's lifetime considerably expanded the text. A ninth edition which appeared a few weeks after his death added nothing further, but included some textual changes which are accepted by some, though not all, modern editors as the work of La Bruyère himself (Bury, 1995, 10–21).

The final text includes 1,120 of what La Bruyère called "remarks". Some of these are brief observations, some as short as a single sentence, about aspects of human nature. These are not unlike the *Maxims* of his contemporary François, Duc de La Rochefoucauld (1613–1680), which were first published in 1664. La Rochefoucauld's apothegmatic comments can themselves be seen as a type of satire of manners:

> Nous avons tous assez de force pour supporter les maux d'autrui.
> [...]
> Si nous n'avions point de défauts, nous ne prendrions pas tant de plaisir à en remarquer dans les autres.
>
> (Lafont, 1976, 46, 48)

> [We are all strong enough to endure other people's misfortunes.
> [...]
> If we had no failings at all ourselves, we would not take so much pleasure in noticing those of other people.]

We may compare these examples from La Bruyère:

> Qui est plus esclave qu'un courtisan assidu, si ce n'est un courtisan plus assidu.
> L'esclave n'a qu'un maître: l'ambitieux en a autant qu'il y a de gens utiles à sa fortune.
>
> (Bury, 1995, 334)

[Who is more of a slave than an assiduous courtier, except for
a more assiduous courtier?

The slave has only one master; the ambitious man has
as many of them as there are people useful to his way in
the world.]

However, La Bruyère explicitly rejected the term "maxims" for what
he himself was writing, and his shorter "remarks" are mingled with
longer comments and character sketches which sometimes extend
over several pages. The variation in length is an important feature of
the collection as a whole, and helps to prevent the feeling of eating too
many sweets at once, which is liable to affect the reader of a collection
of epigrams.

La Bruyère's observations focus on the urban life of Paris and that
of the royal court at Versailles, but nevertheless his work is much
more varied and wide-ranging than that of Earle or the Overbury writers and offers a vivid panorama of French society in the later part of
the reign of Louis XIV. Combined with the fact that La Bruyère is
generally regarded as a superb exponent of French prose style, this
has ensured that he has remained a much more significant figure in the
French literary canon than Hall or Earle have usually been considered
in the English one.

La Bruyère emphasised his own indebtedness to tradition. While he
seems to have been influenced by both Casaubon and the English writers of characters (Bury, 1995, 15–17), he introduced his *Characters*
with his own translation of Theophrastus into French. He emphasised
that much could still be learnt from Theophrastus, since he took the
view that human nature was essentially unchanging:

> Or ceux dont Théophraste nous peint les mœurs dans ses
> Caractères étaient Athéniens, et nous sommes Français [...]
> et si [...] nous considérions [...] qu'ainsi il y a deux mille ans
> accomplis que vivait ce peuple d'Athènes dont il fait la pei-
> nture, nous admirerons de nous y reconnaître nous-mêmes,
> nos amis, nos ennemis, ceux avec qui nous vivons, et que cette
> ressemblance avec des hommes séparés par tant de siècles soit
> si entière.
>
> (Bury, 1995, 69)

[Indeed those whose manners and customs Theophrastus describes for us in his Characters were Athenians, and we are French, and if we take into account that therefore it was a full two thousand years ago that those Athenians were living, we will be astonished to recognise in that description ourselves, our friends, our enemies, those with whom we live, and to see how the resemblance to men separated from us by so many centuries can be so complete.]

He accepted the idea that the work of Theophrastus had a moral purpose, and laid claim to this himself. His own Characters were introduced with a Latin quotation from Erasmus:

Admonere voluimus, non mordere; prodesse, non laedere; consulere moribus hominum, non officere.

(Bury, 1995, 115)

[We wish to warn, not to bite; to be helpful, not to harm; to promote morality, not to hurt it.]

Nevertheless, taken as a whole, La Bruyère's work seems to suggest that these two elements are mutually contradictory. The satirist claims that his purpose is to bring about the improvement of society by making people aware of their failings, but if it is claimed at the same time that human nature is unchanging, this could be read as suggesting that all such efforts will be in vain. One of La Bruyère's modern editors describes him as "profoundly pessimistic" (Bury, 1995, 32), and we may note how his description of Theophrastus previously quoted continues as follows:

En effet les hommes n'ont point changé selon le cœur et selon les passions, ils sont encore tels qu'ils étaient alors, et qu'ils sont marqués dans Théophraste, vains, dissimulés, flatteurs, intéressés, effrontés, importuns, défiants, médisants, querrelleux, superstitieux.

(Bury, 1995, 69)

[As a matter of fact, men have not changed in the slightest as far as their hearts and their passions are concerned, they are still such as they were then, and as they were recorded as being in Theophrastus, vain, dissimulating, sycophantic, self-seeking, shameless, tiresome, mistrustful, scandal-mongering, quarrelsome, superstitious.]

The ways in which these characteristics express themselves may change in different periods, however, and the attraction of La Bruyère, both for his contemporaries and for modern readers, is the way in which his sketches bring to life "les mœurs de ce siècle", the manners and customs of his own century.

An important part of this is the variety of his material. Some of his characters are simply representatives of social types, such as the ecclesiastical pluralist (quoted here in full):

> Ce garçon si frais, si fleuri, et d'une si belle santé est seigneur d'une abbaye et de dix autres bénéfices; tous ensemble lui rapportent six vingt mille livres de revenu, dont il n'est payé qu'en médailles d'or. Il y a ailleurs six vingt familles indigentes qui ne se chauffent point pendant l'hiver, qui n'ont point d'habits pour se couvrir, et qui souvent manquent de pain; leur pauvreté est extrême et honteuse: quel partage! Et cela ne prouve-t-il pas clairement un avenir?
>
> (Bury, 1995, 269–270)

> [This lad, so fresh, so ruddy-complexioned, and with such good health, is the lord of an abbey and ten other benefices, which altogether bring him an income of a hundred and twenty thousand livres, which he gets paid in nothing but gold coin. Elsewhere there are a hundred and twenty pauper families who have no heating at all in winter, who have nothing to wear, and who often lack bread. Their poverty is extreme and shameful – what a distribution of wealth! And does not this plainly prove that there is a life to come?]

La Bruyère's indignation is clear: the suggestion that there will be some justice in an afterlife is not an excuse for accepting the lack of it in this one. Not all pluralists were young, of course, but by making his representative of the type a "garçon", a mere lad, La Bruyère emphasises the capricious injustice of a system which exploited church revenues as a means of providing for the younger sons of noble families: the lad has done nothing to deserve this, but on the other hand he has not done anything actively to secure it, for example, by being an accomplished politician and networker. It is simply something which has happened to him as a result of being born into the right sort of family. At the same time, he is an abstraction – there were many such individuals in the France of the Ancien Régime, and there is no reason to think that La Bruyère had any particular one in mind.

On the other hand, some of his sketches were what were thought of, not as "characters", but as "portraits". The subjects might be referred to by pseudonyms, usually of a classicising nature, but the portraits were so sharply drawn that many contemporaries had no difficulty in identifying them as real individuals, and keys circulated to help readers who were unsure. One example is "Théodas", who is introduced after brief sketches of two figures who are unnamed but clearly meant for the writer of fables, Jean de la Fontaine (1621–1695), and the dramatist, Pierre Corneille (1606–1684), both described as distinguished writers who were indifferent conversationalists and awkward in company (Bury, 1995, 473–474). Théodas was Santolius Victorinus (Jean-Baptiste Santeul, 1630–1697), who was perhaps the last person to become a celebrity purely on the strength of his ability to write Latin verses. No aristocratic family occasion was complete without a Latin poem by Santolius to celebrate it, something which brought him both cash rewards and dinner invitations, but his colossal vanity and equally colossal social ineptitude were notorious. La Bruyère called him "un enfant en cheveux gris" ("a child with grey hair") and suggested that his literary talents were almost like those of another personality within him:

> [...] mais permettez-lui de se recueillir, ou plutôt de se livrer à un génie, qui agit en lui, j'ose dire, sans qui'l y prenne part, et comme à son insu; quelle verve! quelle élévation! quelle images! quelle latinité! Parlez-vous d'une même personne? me direz-vous; oui, du même, de Théodas, et de lui seul.
>
> [... but let him gather himself together, or, rather, give himself over to a genius which works within him, without him having any part in it, and as if he were unaware of it: what

animation! what grandeur! what images! what Latinity! Are
you talking of the same person? you will ask me; yes, the same,
Théodas, and him alone.]

La Bruyère goes on to describe how a combination of wisdom and
folly exhibited itself along with physical tics:

> [...] disons-le sans figure, il parle comme un fou, et pense
> comme un homme sage; il dit ridiculement des choses vraies,
> et follement des choses sensées et raisonnables; on est surpris
> de voir naître et éclore le bon sens du sein de la bouffonnerie,
> parmi les grimaces et les contorsions [...]
>
> [... let us say it plainly, he talks like an idiot and thinks like
> a wise man, he says true things in a ridiculous manner, and
> rational and judicious things as if he were a madman; one is
> surprised to see good sense come into being and blossom in
> the bosom of buffoonery, in the midst of grimaces and contor-
> tions ...]

This is clearly not a type, but "Théodas, et ... lui seul" ("Théodas
himself"), something perhaps given additional emphasis by the way in
which La Bruyère, possibly thinking he has been unduly harsh, concludes the portrait:

> Je commence à me persuader moi-même que j'ai fait le portrait
> de deux personnages tout différents: il ne serait pas même
> impossible d'en trouver un troisième dans Théodas; car il est
> bon homme, il est plaisant homme, et il est excellent homme.
>
> [I begin to think that I have given the portrait of two quite
> different characters: yet it would not be impossible to find a
> third in Théodas, for he is a virtuous man, he is an agreeable
> man, and he is a very kind man.]

Here La Bruyère keeps up the first-person address to the reader which
is a feature of some of his remarks but absent from earlier character writers.

The portrait of Théodas is in some ways reminiscent of the highly
finished watercolours of nineteenth-century public figures by Carlo

Pellegrini (1839–1889) which were reproduced as a regular feature of the English magazine *Vanity Fair* for 20 years. Although Pellegrini used the pseudonym "Ape" (from the Italian for "bee", rather than anything to do with primates), his sketches have little sting in them, though they can seem, as with perhaps his best-known work, the sketch of Oscar Wilde published in 1884, to evoke the subject's personality to a greater extent than we might expect from a photograph. By contrast, some of La Bruyère's other sketches are more like some of Hogarth's more savage caricatures, such as the portrait of a group of quack doctors, titled "The Company of Undertakers" (1736). The most extreme example is probably "Ménalque", the longest of the characters (Bury, 1995, 394–401). Ménalque is the absent-minded man, taken to implausibly ludicrous extremes:

> Lui-même se marie le matin, l'oublie le soir, et découche la nuit de ses noces: et quelques années après il perd sa femme, elle meurt entre ses bras, il assiste à ses obsèques, et le lendemain quand on vient dire qu'on est servi, il demande si sa femme est prête, et si elle est avertie.
>
> [He gets married in the morning, forgets about it in the evening, and sleeps away from home on his wedding night; a few years later he loses his wife, she dies in his arms, he attends her funeral, and the next day when he is told that dinner is served, he asks if his wife is ready and if she has been told.]

When Ménalque makes himself ridiculous in church by pulling a slipper out of his pocket instead of his prayer book, this may be included purely to amuse the reader, but some of the character's other absurdities may have more point to them. When, for example, Ménalque mixes up two letters and sends them to the wrong recipients, La Bruyère highlights both the extremes of social divisions in late seventeenth-century France and how the grotesque artificiality of the conventional language of correspondence emphasised this:

> [...] il se trompe à l'adresse; un duc et pair reçoit l'une de ces deux lettres, et en ouvrant y lit ces mots, *Maître Olivier, ne manquez, sitôt la présente recue, de m'envoyer ma provision de foin* ... Son fermier reçoit l'autre, il l'ouvre, et se la fait

lire, on y trouve, *Monseigneur, j'ai reçu avec une soumission aveugle les ordres qu'il a plu à Votre Grandeur* ...

[... he makes a mistake when it comes to writing the address; a *duc et pair* (a member of the highest rank of the nobility below the royal family) receives one of these two letters, and on opening it reads these words, *Master Oliver, do not fail, as soon as you have received this letter, to send me my supply of hay* ... His tenant-farmer receives the other, he opens it, and gets it read to him, and there one finds, *Your Grace, I have received with a blind obedience the orders which it has pleased Your Highness* ...]

In the middle of this almost slapstick account, La Bruyère carefully includes the naturalistic detail about the tenant-farmer being illiterate and needing to have the letter read to him: the person reading, and perhaps others, will witness the farmer's puzzlement. Similarly, when Ménalque suffers a mishap at a royal reception, we may wonder whether he is the sole target of the joke, or if the incident is not contrived to suggest the vacuity of the courtiers' existence more generally:

Il entre à l'appartement, et passe sous un lustre où sa perruque s'accroche et demeure suspendue, tous les courtisans regardent et rient; Ménalque regarde aussi, et rit plus haut que les autres, il cherche des yeux dans toute l'assemblée où est celui qui montre ses oreilles, et à qui il manque une perruque.

[He enters the (royal) apartment, and passes under a chandelier where his wig catches and remains hanging. All the courtiers look at it and laugh. Ménalque looks at it too, and laughs louder than the others – he looks around the whole gathering to find who it is who is displaying his ears and who is missing a wig.]

Some of La Bruyère's range appears to be the result of his personal circumstances. He came from a Parisian legal family, and an inheritance allowed him to buy a government office (a common practice at the time) and this gave him both an income and a title of nobility, though he had been a commoner by birth. He spent the later part of his life in the household of the Duc de Bourbon, a member of the royal family. While he was involved in the literary controversies of the day, and made enemies as a result, his *Characters* brought him widespread recognition and the prestige of being elected to the Académie Française in 1693. Though he was very aware of social injustices, the general outlook of his work appears conservative. If he attacks hypocrites who make a parade of an insincere religious devotion, he also opposes those who turn worship into a public spectacle like an opera, and both because they encourage the equally undesirable free thinker. His views on women, especially learned women, are not unlike those of generations of misogynist writers before him. If he suggests that it is the duty of the rich to relieve the distresses of the poor, he is no revolutionary. He offers conventional praise to the king, and, if he highlights the more futile aspects of court life, he is scathing about non-nobles who develop ideas above their station, and praises those citizens of Paris who have learnt to live within their incomes and the importance of the idea that "ce qui est dans les Grands splendeur, somptuosité, magnificence, est dissipation, folie, ineptie dans le particulier" (Bury, 1995, 307; "that which among the great is splendour, sumptuousness, magnificence, is dissipation, folly and stupidity in the private individual").

A translation of La Bruyère was published in English in 1699, and other editions followed. He was a significant influence on the development of *The Spectator*, an enormously influential periodical edited by Joseph Addison (1672–1719) and Richard Steele (1672–1729) and originally published in the period 1711–1714 (Turner 1953). The *Spectator* consisted of prose essays, which, as Addison put it in the first number, hoped to contribute to the "Diversion or Improvement" of readers. While the essays covered a range of topics, including, for example, literary criticism, a significant number commented on contemporary society through the medium of character sketches. Many times reprinted in volume form, the *Spectator* remained popular until the early twentieth century. It inspired many imitations, and not only in English: it was soon translated into French, as *Le spectateur, ou Le Socrate moderne* (1714), which was published in several different editions in the Netherlands, France and Germany in the course of the eighteenth century, and the influence of the *Spectator* also led to what one critic has described as an "epidemic" of *moralische*

Wochenschriften ("moral weeklies") in German-speaking countries during the same period (Smeed, 1985, 87).

While the essays in the *Spectator* are relatively short, they are longer and more detailed than the characters in "Overbury" and Earle. The *Spectator* also revisits the same characters in different essays, with the result that, if we take together the essays featuring the supposedly typical country squire, Sir Roger de Coverley (as does Hampden, 1967), we may well feel that we are reading a continuous piece of prose fiction. Smeed indeed argues that the prominence of the character in periodical essays is an important influence on the development of the novel in both English and German. A significant difference, as Smeed points out, is that by the nineteenth century, writers and readers came to expect that characters in a novel might show some degree of change and development in the course of the text. This is not something which happens in the *Spectator*: Sir Roger is introduced as old and set in his ways, and while readers may feel that they get to know him in greater detail as they learn, for example, more details about his unsuccessful courtship of the Widow, he himself does not change. The question of the relationship between the character and the novel raises the wider issue of whether the character, in the Theophrastan sense, really counts as a distinct genre.

While the rediscovery of Theophrastus's *Characters* in the sixteenth century, and Casaubon's edition in particular, undoubtedly had some impact, it is also clear that other factors were at work. As more than one critic has pointed out, long before this, the description of character types was a significant part of ancient and mediaeval rhetorical training (Clausen, 1946; Smeed, 1985, 5–9). The stock character who is less of an individual than the representative of a type was an important feature of the Hellenistic New Comedy, and was employed by Roman and later playwrights. Shakespeare's Falstaff, for example, has many individualising traits, but is still recognisably a descendant of Theophrastus's Coward and Plautus's *Miles Gloriosus* ("The Swaggering Soldier") (Diggle, 2004, 137; Watling, 1965, 147–212). The Italian tradition of *commedia dell'arte* which developed in the sixteenth century is based on improvisation around stock characters, and the influence of this can be seen in works like Jonson's *Volpone*, where the names of many of the characters indicate their roles. The title character himself is "Volpone, or The Fox", indicating his craftiness and deceit; his chief servant, who eventually betrays him, is called Mosca, after the Italian for "fly", suggesting both his parasitic nature and the fly's tendency to feed on filth, while the lawyer is called Voltore, or "vulture", and other characters are given programmatic bird names. In more recent times, situation comedies for television have depended heavily on stock characters and audience expectations of them, such as the snobbish Hyacinth Bucket in *Keeping up Appearances*, which went through five series between 1990 and 1995 and became the BBC's most exported programme, or the geeks in *The Big Bang Theory* (premiered on the American CBS network in 2007 and ongoing).

It is also difficult to claim any sort of priority for Theophrastus. The Ancient Egyptian text sometimes referred to by modern scholars as "The Satire of the Trades" dates to the second millennium BCE. In it a scribe exhorts his son to study hard so that he, too, may become a scribe, as it is a much better rewarded and more enjoyable station in life than that of the manual labourers whose different types of occupation are described in off-putting detail: the fisherman "stinks more than fish roe", the potter "grubs in the mud more than a pig", the farmer's "fingers are swollen/And stink to excess" (Lichtheim, 1975, 184–192). The different sorts of women described by Semonides (Chapter 7) would seem very like Theophrastan characters if they were in prose, but predate him by some three centuries. If we accept that characters do not have to be in prose, there are many examples of character-like sketches in verse in later classical literature as well as more recent writing. The bore who accosts Horace as he walks through Rome is similar to Theophrastus's Chatterbox or Talker (Horace, *Satires*, I, ix; Diggle, 2004, 73, 87). If we look at Tennyson's poem *Northern Farmer, New Style* (first published 1869; Ricks, 1987, II, 688–690), the use of Lincolnshire dialect makes his subject seem highly individualised:

> Doan't thou 'ear my 'erse's legs, as they canters away?
> Propputty, propputty, propputty – that's what I 'ears 'em say [...]

Nevertheless, he is also a type: the man whose sole concern is money, and who cannot accept the idea of his son marrying for love.

Some apparent echoes of the Theophrastan tradition turn out to be not particularly close. The title of F. M. Cornford's *Microcosmographia*

Academica, being a Guide for the Young Academic Politician (originally published in 1908), might suggest a reference to Earle, but while Cornford does glance at the different sorts of people one might encounter on university committees, he is more concerned with the types of argument they might employ and satirising aspects of procedure. Much of the slim volume is rooted in the particular circumstances of early twentieth-century Cambridge, but some aspects have an enduring appeal, such as the summary of the classic obstructionist argument that "nothing should ever be done for the first time", or one suggestion for to how to stall things in a meeting: "Motions for adjournment, made less than fifteen minutes before teatime or at any subsequent moment, are always carried" (Cornford, 1973, 15, 19). However, the traditional character, as the short prose sketch of a social type, has shown a remarkable persistence: examples continued to appear throughout the nineteenth and twentieth centuries, and it can still be found in newspaper features such as the *Daily Telegraph*'s "Modern Stereotypes" (e.g., Mather, 2016).

7

SATIRE AND GENDER

A short poem by the Welsh writer of Latin epigrams, John Owen (1563/4–1622?), is, in a number of ways, typical of a theme which is all too prominent in the history of satire:

> Divitias Iobo, sobolemque, ipsamque salutem
>   Abstulit (hoc Domino non prohibente) Satan.
> Omnibus ablatis misero, tamen una superstes,
>   Quae magis afflictum redderet, uxor erat.
> [Owen, 1633, 69]

> [Since God forbade not, Satan Job bereav'd
> Of wealth, of health, of eke his children's life.
> With all else lost, the wretch still more was griev'd
> That one thing yet remain'd to him – his wife.]

Misogyny can, of course, be found in the earliest Western literature. In his *Theogony*, for example, the ancient Greek poet Hesiod (? eighth century BCE) describes the creation of the first woman, and how

> From her comes all the race of womankind,
> The deadly female race and tribe of wives

Who live with mortal men and bring them harm [...]
[Wender, 1973, 42]

The Greek word here translated as "race", γένος, almost suggests that Hesiod thought men and women were different species. He returns to the first woman in his other main work, the *Works and Days*, giving her the name Pandora and calling her "this ruin of mankind" (Wender, 1973, 61) in a manner which has led some commentators to see parallels with the biblical story of Eve in Genesis. Similarly, in both the *Iliad* and the *Odyssey*, the poet or poets we know as Homer (probably more or less contemporary with Hesiod) place the responsibility for the Trojan War on Helen herself, and not on patriarchal assumptions about honour and masculine control of women, and describe Helen as acknowledging and accepting this view.

Nevertheless, these expressions of misogyny do not in themselves constitute satire. Owen creates a poem which is satirical by techniques often found in satire on many different topics. In the first place, he takes an existing literary work as his starting point, in this case the biblical Book of Job (perhaps sixth century BCE). In the Bible, Job is a righteous and prosperous man whom God allows to be afflicted by Satan in order to demonstrate the steadfastness of his faith. He loses his property, his children and his health, and, at first, trusting in the fact that he has led an upright life, he despairs and questions God's treatment of him. Only when he finally acknowledges God's omnipotence and his own relative insignificance and inability to do anything which might allow him to have any sort of claim on God is he restored to health and prosperity. Secondly, Owen adapts his source to his purpose by selection and distortion. The Book of Job is over 13,000 words long in the Vulgate Latin translation (substantially more in the King James Version of the English Bible). Owen's epigram reduces it to 23 words, something which is only possible by leaving out several characters entirely – for example, Job's three "comforters", Eliphaz, Bildad and Zophar, together with another interlocutor, Elihu – and omitting any reference to the lengthy speeches which the biblical narrative attributes to them, as well as to those of Job himself, God and Satan. Job's wife receives only three brief mentions in the biblical text (Job ii, 9–10; xix, 17; xxxi, 10), of which only the first is of any real significance, where she suggests to Job that, after the disasters which have befallen him, his situation is so bad that he might as well curse God and die, after which Job rebukes her for speaking "as one of the foolish women speaketh". If this is enough to make her one of Job's afflictions, it is not much in comparison with the efforts of the "comforters" to persuade Job that he must have done something to deserve his fate. The biblical narrative is an extended attempt to answer the all-important philosophical and theological question of why bad things happen to good people. It says very little about gender relations, and does not appear to suggest that either Job's wife or "the foolish women" are intended to be representative of women as a whole. Owen, on the other hand, adapts it to reinforce a misogynistic stereotype about the wretchedness the married state inflicts upon the husband. Finally, he does so by careful use of literary form and technique. For an early seventeenth-century writer, the Latin epigram was an intrinsically gendered form, one which was learnt in all-male educational establishments and which few women, even among those literate in vernacular languages, could read. This gives Owen's poem the appeal of an in-joke. The Latin elegiac couplets are skilfully constructed in accordance with conventional norms, and we may note the use of parallels and antithesis. The third line is nicely balanced, for example, with what is lost mentioned in the first half of the line, and what remains in the second. The rôle of Satan and his importance is emphasised by his name being the final word of the first couplet. In a similar fashion, the epigram as a whole builds up to a climax by not revealing exactly what it was that remained until the conclusion, by putting the phrase "uxor erat" ("it was [his] wife") at the end of the second couplet. Such is the nature of the form, moreover, that many readers would feel invited to draw a parallel between the characters mentioned at the end of each couplet, that is, between Satan and Job's wife, and be led on to the reflection that not just Job's wife in particular, but wives more generally, could be viewed as having something Satanic about them, as being devilish afflictions sent to torment their husbands. In this, as in some other examples of satire, or of other types of composition intended to persuade, from advertisements to political speeches, the ingenuity of the manner in which something is expressed appears intended to encourage readers to overlook the inadequacies of the argument. While it could be argued that Owen's epigram is a self-conscious literary game whose very ingenuity signals that it should not be taken too seriously, the simple fact of its existence demonstrates the assumption of a fundamental misogyny shared by the writer and his intended readership.

A prominent theme in the history of satire has been its support of patriarchal norms. In this particular subgenre, women are presented as valued by male writers (and, by implication, male readers) predominantly or exclusively in terms of their sexuality. They are treated as sources of sexual pleasure for men, but women's own sexuality is seen as something to be feared and kept under control. This is sometimes explicitly linked to the idea that it is important for a man to know that the child who will inherit his property is truly his. Male dominance in any relationship is regarded as essential in order to secure this, and as a result, both the cuckold and the hen-pecked husband are treated as figures of ridicule. Women who venture to express themselves, the gossip, the scold, the bluestocking, all become targets for the satirist. Women are said to be interested in men only for material gain, but on the other hand, women who bring money into a marriage are criticised for exploiting this fact as a means of securing an unnatural domination over their husbands. The ideal is a heteronormative one, in that sexuality is assumed to be a matter of heterosexual relationships which will produce pleasure and/or children for the male partner, with the woman's feelings being regarded as being of secondary importance or even totally irrelevant.

These ideas are of course not the exclusive property of the satirist. Martial has a number of epigrams in which it appears that women are valued only for a sexually attractive appearance, while those who have lost their looks as a result of old age, or those who rely on make-up, are mocked. All these attitudes are brought together in the epigram (IX, xxxvii) in which Martial addresses a perhaps imaginary woman he calls Galla, whom he ridicules in obscene terms, saying that, in spite of her make-up, false teeth and false hair, and in spite of her offering a large sum of money, she cannot persuade the poet to have sex with her. Martial tells her

> et iaceas centum condita pyxidibus,
> nec tecum facies tua dormiat ...

> [and you lie down put away in a hundred boxes, nor may your face sleep with you]

This is a theme which can be found in many later writers, such as George Buchanan, whose works include a cycle of poems addressed to a prostitute he calls Leonora. Martial's satire is clearly a model here, though we may also see the influence of the earlier Roman poet Catullus (first century BCE), some of whose poems abuse his former lover, the woman he calls Lesbia (Ford, 1982, 87–91). Several of Buchanan's Leonora poems focus on her use of cosmetics, and one two-line epigram neatly equates this with her profession:

> Omnia quod, Leonora, putant te vendere, falsum est:
> Nam faciem, tibi quae caetera vendit, emis.
> (Buchanan, 1687, 351)

> [That, Leonora, thou sell'st all, 'tis falsely thought:
> The face which sells all other things for thee, 'tis bought.]

Parallels can be drawn with other works from different historical periods which overtly satirise women who set out to create a false impression through the use of make-up and other artificial aids to beauty, or who were simply thought of as paying undue attention to their appearance. The elaborate description of Belinda's toilette in Pope's *The Rape of the Lock* (1714) parodies epic scenes of heroes putting on their armour, and may have drawn some inspiration from another of Martial's epigrams (II, lxvi; Tillotson, 1962, 155–158; Sparrow, 1977). Perhaps the most extreme example in English is Jonathan Swift's ironically titled "A Beautiful Nymph Going to Bed" (1734), which describes a diseased prostitute removing her false hair, false eye, false eyebrows, false teeth and other contrivances. The effect is heightened by the relentless piling on of repulsive detail and the pace achieved by the use of lines which rhyme in pairs but are shorter than the heroic couplets commonly used in the period. The "nymph"

> Pulls out the Rags contriv'd to prop
> Her flabby Dugs and down they drop.
> Proceeding on, the lovely Goddess
> Unlaces next her Steel-Rib'd Bodice;
> Which by the Operator's Skill,
> Press down the Lumps, the Hollows fill,

Up goes her Hand, and off she slips
The Bolsters that supply her Hips [...]

(Fairer and Gerrard, 1999, 79)

These may seem to be obvious examples of works intended as satire. On the other hand, passages such as Hamlet's criticism of Ophelia's "paintings" in Shakespeare's play ("God has given you one face and you make yourselves another [...]", Act III, Scene I), or Bosola's comparison in John Webster's *The Duchess of Malfi* (1612–1613; Act II, Scene I) of the Old Lady's closet to "a shop of witchcraft" for the range of cosmetics with bizarre and disgusting ingredients which he presumes it must contain, express the same sort of attitude as parts of texts which also deal with other themes.

Something of how misogyny was shaped into satire can be seen in one of the most notorious examples of the genre, Juvenal's *Sixth Satire*. The poet begins by claiming that while chastity may have existed in the distant past, it has long vanished from the earth. He asserts that all women are unchaste and driven by lust, and that this is the source of all their other faults, which he proceeds to catalogue in exhaustive detail. Women will always put their lovers before their husbands, whom they will seek to dominate. They are always asking for expensive presents and getting into debt in order to show off. They are obsessed by jewellery and cosmetics. They will drive away their husbands' friends and mistreat the servants. Not only will they embarrass their husbands by keeping guests waiting, but they drink too much at dinner and throw up all over the floor. They demean themselves by consorting with actors and gladiators. Some even enter the arena themselves, sweating and grunting in what was seen as an unfeminine manner. Some women have sex with eunuchs in order to avoid conception, while others simply resort to abortion, but this is preferable to the habit which some women have of foisting supposititious children on their husbands. Women are utterly shameless, and will accuse their husbands of misconduct in order to divert attention from their own adulterous affairs, but even if they are caught in the act they will seek to brazen it out. They will pollute sacred rituals by using them as a cover for carrying on their liaisons. They pretend to have expertise in the law, or to know all about current affairs. Even worse are those who fancy themselves as literary critics. Women are superstitious and always ready to follow the latest fashion in imported religions. They rely on astrologers and fortune-tellers, some of whom double as herbalists and supply the spells and potions with which women seek to control their husbands, who are often driven out of their minds as a result. From there it is an easy step to the use of poisons – women are more than willing to kill their step-children in order to secure their inheritance. We should not wonder at the evil women in mythology, as real life examples are all around us, says Juvenal. Nowadays every street has its own Clytemnestra, the wife who in Greek mythology killed her husband Agamemnon on his return from the Trojan War. Clytemnestra used an axe, but poison is the more sophisticated modern approach. Nevertheless, if that doesn't work because her husband has been taking antidotes by way of precaution, the modern Roman woman is quite willing to finish him off with an edged weapon. While the poem is perhaps not quite as formless as some critics have suggested, Juvenal does seem to jump all over the place from one topic to the next, but the general thrust of his argument is clear enough: if women, and their sexuality in particular, are not tightly controlled, they will soon get away with anything and every-thing, up to and including murder.

Baldly summarised like this, the "extravagant Acrimony" of the Satire, as one eighteenth-century translator called it (Sheridan, 1739, xvi), seems so excessive that it may be hard to believe that it was ever taken seriously. Indeed, a number of modern critics have argued that the narrator's voice in the Satire is not the poet himself, but a distinct persona he has created, and that it is the misogynistic views of the persona which are the real target. Others claim that the Satire is a criticism of the way in which Roman *matronae*, that is, the wives of upper-class citizens, had abandoned the traditional modest and retir-ing ways which custom had prescribed for them in order to take a more active rôle in public life (Watson and Watson, 2014). Another of Juvenal's translators, John Dryden, identified the obvious problem, that Juvenal was constantly extrapolating from the particular to the general: "he is not to be excus'd for imputing to all, the Vices of some few amongst them". Dryden said that "The whole World must allow this to be the wittiest of his Satyrs; and truly he had need of all his parts, to maintain with so much violence, so unjust a Charge". In other words, Dryden claims, we can admire the ingenious manner in which Juvenal puts forward a flawed argument. Nevertheless, he noted, the

Satire had become "a Common-place from whence all the Moderns have notoriously stollen [sic] their sharpest Raileries [sic]" (Dryden, 1693, 86–87). Innumerable later writers found Juvenal a useful source for their attacks on women, and there were always those prepared to take him at face value, such as his translator Thomas Sheridan, who insisted that Juvenal's Satires

> express so just a Rage and Resentment against the unnatural and shocking Vices of the Age in which he lived, that he has scarce left any thing [sic] unsaid upon the Subjects he made choice of, and may serve as a Pattern to succeeding Times [...]
> (Sheridan, 1739, vi)

Juvenal's approach to his material can be seen in the passage he devotes to the alleged activities of Messalina (c. 17/20–48 CE), the wife of the Roman emperor Claudius, who reigned from 41 to 54 CE, a generation or so before Juvenal's own time.

> respice rivales divorum, Claudius audi
> quae tulerit. dormire virum cum senserat uxor,
> sumere nocturnos meretrix Augusta cucullos
> ausa Palatino et tegetem praeferre cubili
> linquebat comite ancilla non amplius una.
> sic nigrum flavo crinem abscondente galero
> intravit calidum veteri centone lupanar
> et cellam vacuam atque suam; tunc nuda papillis
> prostitit auratis titulum mentita Lyciscae
> ostenditque tuum, generose Britannice, ventrem.
> excepit blanda intrantes atque aera poposcit.
> [continueque iacens cunctorum absorbuit ictus.]
> mox lenone suas iam dimittente puellas
> tristis abit, et quod potuit tamen ultima cellam
> clausit, adhuc ardens rigidae tentigine volvae,
> et lassata viris necdum satiata recessit,
> obscurisque genis turpis fumoque lucernae
> foeda lupanaris tulit ad pulvinar odorem.
> (Juvenal, VI, 115–132; text adapted from
> Watson and Watson, 2014, 62)

[Look at the rivals of the gods. Hear what Claudius put up with. When the wife felt her husband to be sleeping, the imperial whore, daring to assume a night-time hooded cloak and prefer a mat to the Palatine bed, departed in the company of a single handmaid. And thus, concealing her black hair with a blonde wig, she entered the brothel, stuffy behind its old and patchwork curtain, and the empty cubicle which was her own. Then she stood forth naked, with gilded nipples, falsely assumed the identity of Lycisca, and displayed the belly which brought forth thee, o nobly born Britannicus. She received in an alluring manner those who came in and demanded their money. <Lying down she unceasingly takes in the thrusts of all.> All too soon the ponce was dismissing his girls and the best she could do was to be the last to shut up her cubicle, still burning with the swelling of her stiff parts, and depart, tired out by her men but not yet satisfied, and besmirched with darkened cheeks and foul with the smoke of the lamp she carried the smell of the brothel to the marriage bed.]

Messalina was executed in 48 CE, apparently as a result of her alleged involvement in a conspiracy to overthrow her husband and replace him as emperor with their son, Britannicus, who was still young. As a result, surviving sources are biased, and it is impossible to know how much truth there is in the hostile stories about her. Juvenal did not invent the idea that Messalina was exceptionally promiscuous – Pliny the Elder (died 79 CE) claimed that she had outdone a prostitute in a sexual endurance contest – but he shapes it in his own way. The passage concludes a series of vignettes about sexually immoral women whose social status increases in each case until it reaches the empress, who is presented as the supreme example of alleged female sexual insatiability. Other stereotypes are brought into play: the association of feminine concern for appearance with deceit and immorality is signalled by Messalina's disguising herself with a hooded cloak and a wig in order to sneak out to the brothel. The disguise may also be seen as a stage costume, fitting in with Juvenal's earlier passage (ll, 60–77) about the erotic obsession of *matronae* with stage performers of various kinds, all regarded as being of low social status. Pantomime in particular was seen as dangerously arousing and indecorous (Watson and Watson, 2014, 42–43, 96–100). The literal as well as moral filthiness of the brothel is emphasised. Some effects are achieved by juxtaposition and contrast. The passage begins with the imperial family being referred to as rivals of the gods, while it concludes with Messalina returning to the marital bed, here called a "pulvinar", a word often associated with the couch of a divinity, and suggesting something very different from the "teges", the mat on which she has been plying her trade as a prostitute. Messalina is first spoken of as "uxor", a wife, but in the next line she is a "meretrix", a whore, and not only that, but a "meretrix Augusta", an "imperial whore", an oxymoronic phrase which emphasises the enormous gap between her exalted status and the social degradation of the common prostitute to which, so the poet would have us believe, her excessive libidinous desires led her. While "Augusta" became a general term for an empress, it was in the earlier empire a specific title of honour which Claudius had actually refused to give to Messalina; Juvenal ahistorically uses it here for the sake of the verbal effect, and probably also in a deliberate echo of the way in which the earlier Roman poet Propertius (first century BCE) had called Cleopatra a "meretrix regina", a "whore queen" (Watson and Watson, 2014, 112–113). Cleopatra was regarded in Roman literature as someone who had ensnared first Julius Caesar and then Mark Antony with her sexual wiles, thus endangering the Roman state, and by associating Messalina with her in this way, Juvenal is able to suggest that uncontrolled female sexuality is a threat not just to social norms but to the empire itself. Other details are chosen with equal care. The gilded nipples may be implausible, but they do not merely add to the theme of cosmetic enhancement of any kind as something to be associated with promiscuity, but also serve to remind the alert reader of the heifer with gilded horns which Juvenal suggests earlier in the poem (l, 48) should be sacrificed as a thank-offering to Juno, goddess of matrimony, by any man fortunate enough to find a genuinely chaste woman as his bride. Standing in front of her cubicle, displaying herself for sale, Messalina enacts a parody of a religious rite, an image which further contributes to Juvenal's obsessive claims that the behaviour of Roman women subverts all established order and morality. She assumes the name of the prostitute Lycisca, which adds a further layer of deceit but which has other implications as well.

The name is Greek, and the use of Greek as an affectation by Romans, especially in erotic contexts, is one of Juvenal's bugbears. The fact that it means "little she-wolf" may suggest a parodic echo of the story of Romulus and Remus suckled by the she-wolf, one of the foundation myths of Rome. If this is so, it adds further emphasis to the idea that Messalina, and, it would seem as far as the poet is concerned, Roman women more generally, mock all that is sacred by their behaviour. The line in brackets is normally regarded by modern editors and commentators as a later interpolation, and Juvenal does not use the most blatant obscenities which can be found in other Roman poets such as Horace and Martial, but when Messalina leaves the brothel, his language is deliberately crude and leaves nothing to the imagination. In a final touch, he uses the words "tentigo" and "rigidus", which are normally employed in the context of male sexual arousal (Watson and Watson, 2014, 114), once more suggesting that female sexual desire is unnatural and to be condemned: Messalina's transgressive behaviour blurs the boundaries of gender as well as class. Juvenal's message – or that of the persona he creates – may not be very different from that which we find in Hesiod, but it is put forward with a great deal more in the way of literary artifice.

One of the major problems with satire is that it is often open to misinterpretation. The modern classicist Mary Beard believes that in Juvenal's Sixth Satire it is the misogynistic character of the speaker which is being ridiculed. She makes a comparison with Alf Garnett, the character played by Warren Mitchell in the British television sitcom *Till Death Us Do Part* (created by Johnny Speight, aired on BBC1, 1965–1975). Garnett expressed appallingly racist and sexist opinions which the show was intended to ridicule, but, to Speight's disappointment, there were viewers who sympathised with him. As Beard (2012, 76–77) says of Garnett:

> Was he pillorying racism, or making it easier to condone?
> The trouble with satire [...] is that the literal minded are always liable not to get it. And the satirist is inadvertently taken to support the very views s/he is attacking.

Modern readers are confronted with a similar problem when reading *The Wife of Bath's Prologue* and the *Tale* which follows it

(Cigman 1975), one of the best-known parts of *The Canterbury Tales* by the English poet Geoffrey Chaucer (c. 1343–1400). In her Prologue, the Wife is presented as giving her fellow pilgrims on the way to Canterbury an account of her own life in which she describes how she has been married five times and succeeded in bringing all of her husbands under her control. She follows this with the Tale of a knight at the court of King Arthur. The knight was facing the death penalty for a rape which he had committed, but the queen secured a reprieve for him on condition that he could discover within a year and a day the answer to the question "What thing is it that women moost desyren?" (l, 905). The knight receives so many different responses in his search for the answer that he begins to despair. Eventually, however, he encounters an old woman who is described as spectacularly ugly: "A fouler wight ther may no man devyse" (l, 999). She assures him that she can give him the correct answer, if only he will promise to fulfil whatever request she shall next make of him. He assents, and returns to the royal court, where the queen and all her ladies accept the answer he is now able to give:

> "My lige lady, generally," quod he,
> "Wommen desiren to have sovereyntee
> As well over hir housband as hir love,
> And for to been in maistrie him above!
> This is your mooste desyr, thogh ye me kille:
> Doth as yow list, I am at your wille."
> (ll, 1037–1042)

> ["My liege lady, in all cases," he said, "women desire to have sovereignty over their husbands and lovers, and to rule over them. This is your greatest desire, though you kill me for saying so – do as you please, I am at your disposal."]

At this point, the old woman appears, and demands that the knight fulfil his promise by agreeing to marry her. He is appalled at the suggestion, but can only comply. The marriage takes place, and the newly wedded pair are described as being in bed together, with the knight feeling very sorry for himself. The wife tells him off for despising her for being low-born and old. She tells him that true nobility is to be found in a person's conduct, rather than their ancestry, and makes a point shared with Juvenal's Eighth Satire:

> For, God it woot, men may wel often fynde
> A lords sone do shame and vileynye [...]
>   (II, 1150–1151)

> [For, God knows, it is often the case that men find a lord's son behaving in a shameful and reprehensible manner.]

She goes on to remind him that Christ chose the life of a poor and humble man during His earthly existence, and refers explicitly to Juvenal to suggest that poverty has something to be said for it, paraphrasing the same line (Juvenal, X, 22) referred to by Walter of Châtillon and William Langland (above, Chapter 4):

> Verray poverte it singeth properly;
> Juvenal seith of poverte mirily:
> "The povre man, when he goeth by the weye,
> Bifore the theves he may singe and pleye."
>   (II, 1191–1194)

> [True poverty, by its very nature, is able to sing. Juvenal wittily says of poverty: "The poor man, when he is travelling, can sing and be happy in front of thieves."]

She insists that the old are entitled to respect, suggests that having an ugly wife will protect him from becoming a cuckold, and then offers him a choice. She can remain old, ugly and faithful, or she can be young and beautiful, but then he must take his chances with the consequences. The knight agonises over this, cannot make up his mind, and finally asks her to decide. This appears to be the right answer:

> "Thanne have I gete of yow maistrie," quod she,
> "Sin I may chese and governe as me lest?"
> "Ye, certes, wyf," quod he, "I holde it best."
> "Kis me!" quod she, "We be no lenger wrothe;
> For by my trouthe, I wol be to you bothe!

This is to seyn, ye, both faire and good [...]"
(II, 1236–1241)

["Have I then secured control of you," she said, "since I may choose and decide things as I please?" "Yes, indeed, wife," said he, "I consider that to be best." "Kiss me!" she said, "we are no longer quarrelling with each other, for I swear to you that I will be both, that is to say, both beautiful and faithful ..."]

She invites him to take a good look at her and, indeed, the ugly old woman has been transformed into a beautiful young one, and we are told that they lived happily together for the rest of their lives. This may appear to be suggesting that the perfect marriage is one founded on mutual respect and forbearance. While this is a message which is likely to appeal to many modern readers, a consideration of the Tale in the context of the Wife of Bath's Prologue, and of the *Canterbury Tales* generally, indicates that other readings are possible.

The Wife of Bath is a vividly realised character, from her broad-brimmed hat and her scarlet stockings to the gap in her front teeth (General Prologue, 1, 603), which in Chaucer's England, as in some other cultures at the present day, is taken as a sign of sexual vigour and enthusiasm. Above all, she talks. Her Prologue is the longest of any of the individual Tales, and as long as Chaucer's General Prologue to the *Canterbury Tales* as a whole. She regales her fellow pilgrims with intimate details of her marriages, and sets out her views on marriage and gender relations at great length. She claims the right to control her own body, is unabashed in her fondness for sexual pleasure and asserts that her own "experience" is of equal value with "authority", that is, the Bible and the writings of the Church Fathers, when it comes to discussing such matters. In one passage, she alludes to Aesop's Fables (Malvern, 1983):

Who peynted the leoun, tel me who?
By God, if wommen hadde writen stories,
As clerkes han, withinne hire oratories,
They wolde han writen of men moore wikkednesse
Than all the mark of Adam may redresse.
(II, 692–696)

[Who painted the lion, tell me who? By God, if women had written stories, the way men of the Church have done within their oratories, they would have written about more sinfulness on the part of men than all men since the time of Adam would be able to put right.]

In Aesop's fable, a man is travelling with a lion, with whom he is having an argument about which of them is stronger. When they pass a sculpture of a man strangling a lion, the man says that this proves that men are stronger. The lion's response is that the images would be different if they were created by the lions (Temple and Temple, 1998, 47). In the same way, the Wife of Bath rejects the bias that she sees as inherent in ecclesiastical writings on sexuality and gender rôles.

All of this makes many modern readers respond to her with enthusiasm. The Wife has been interpreted as a satirist whose target is the prevailing misogyny of her time, "through the gift of satire granted her by Chaucer" (Malvern, 1983, 241). However, several aspects of her Prologue may lead us to question this interpretation. The views on sexuality which she puts forward are precisely those which popular preachers of Chaucer's time inveighed against (Green, 2008). Any of Chaucer's readers with a relatively thorough knowledge of the Bible would have questioned the Wife's treatment of it. Her quotations from the Bible are often distorted by being taken out of context, and she explicitly rejects passages which do not suit her purpose, an approach which believing Christians would have found unconvincing, if not positively abhorrent. She appears to be an unreliable narrator. For example, she claims to have paid her fourth husband back in kind for his affairs, but only by arousing his jealousy by being flirtatious with other men:

I made him of the same wode a croce;
Nat of my body, in no foul manere,
But certeynely, I made folk swich cheere
That in his owene grece I made him frye,
For anger, and for verray jalousie.

(ll, 484–488)

[I made him of the same wood a stick to beat him with, not of my body, in any shameful manner, but indeed I behaved to

other people in such a provocative fashion that I made him fry
in his own grease from anger and sheer jealousy.]

This seems to amount to a claim that she did not actually commit
adultery, but other passages, such as the General Prologue's mention
of "other companye in youthe" (l, 461) or her own reference to her
"walkinge out by nighte" (l, 397), or her statement that because of the
influence of her horoscope "I koude noght withdrawe / My chamber
of Venus from a good felawe" (ll, 617–618) suggest that her sexual
activity was not confined to the marital bed. The same goes for this
comment to one of her husbands:

> He is to greet a niggard that wolde werne
> A man to lighte his candle at his lantern;
> He shal have never the lasse light, pardee —
> (ll, 333–335)

> [He is excessively miserly who would prevent another man
> from lighting his candle at his lantern, as this will not make
> him have any less light for himself, by God.]

The fact that this is an echo of a classical text well known to mediaeval readers, Ovid's *Ars Amatoria* (III, 93), as is the Wife's admiring
glances at her future fifth husband, Jankyn, at her fourth husband's
funeral (ll, 595–599; cf. *Ars Amatoria* III, 431), suggests that her
libido is to be seen as both excessive and unchristian. It may also
suggest that the Wife is to be seen as learned, a quality which many
mediaeval readers would have viewed as undesirable in a woman.

We also need to view the Wife of Bath in the context of the Tale
of the Clerk of Oxenford, which comes a little later in the series and
appears to be a response to hers. The Clerk tells the story of "patient
Griselda", a reworking by Chaucer of a story found in several previous literary versions in mediaeval Europe. A young woman of humble
origin is married to a nobleman who decides to test her devotion to
him. He takes away her two children from her in turn, and allows her
to believe that they have been murdered. He sends her back to her
father, and then summons her to his palace once more, instructing her
to take charge of the preparations for his marriage to a new bride. Only

when she accepts all this uncomplainingly does he reveal that the new bride is in fact her own daughter, who, together with her brother, is safe and sound. He explains that he has only been testing her, and now restores her to her former position as his wife, proclaiming his love for her. If the Wife of Bath tells her third husband that the example of Job suggests that he should put up with whatever behaviour she chooses to inflict on him, since men are supposed to be more rational than women and therefore endowed with more patience (ll, 431–442), the Clerk refers to Job in order to claim that women can outdo men in patience and long-suffering (ll, 932–938).

The moral of the Clerk's Tale would appear to be that the perfect marriage is one in which the wife submits uncomplainingly to her husband's every whim. This certainly seems to be the view of the Host, who declares that it would have been worth more to him than a barrel of ale if his wife had heard this story. This sentiment is only partially qualified when the Clerk's Tale is immediately followed by the Merchant, who, after lamenting that his own wife is a "shrewe", tells his Tale of the old knight January and his young wife May, who deceives the knight and commits adultery with his servant Damyan. After the Merchant has finished his Tale, the Host comments that his own wife is a "labbyng shrewe" and "hath an heep of vices mo", but "Thereof no fors", apparently suggesting that he has decided it is worth putting up with her faults, since she is not actually an adulteress (Benson, 1988, 153–168). The *Canterbury Tales* treat the theme of marriage in different ways, and there is no point in speculating whether Chaucer intended any one of them to be definitive. It is clear, however, that we should be cautious in reading the Wife of Bath's Prologue and Tale in isolation, as is often done in teaching school and university students, and thinking of her as some sort of proto-feminist. Just as the modern reader's sympathy for Dido should not make us fail to see that for Virgil she is basically an obstacle which his hero Aeneas must overcome in order to proceed on his way and fulfil his divinely appointed mission to set in train the events which will lead to the founding of Rome, so we need to try to see the Wife of Bath as mediaeval readers might have done. While different interpretations are open to us, we should at least consider the possibility that she is an almost Juvenalian horror story, the perfect example of everything a wife should not be, as far as most of Chaucer's contemporaries were concerned: "Eventually, the humour of the Wife's

Prologue turns out to be largely at her own expense, although she never realises this", and even the "mastery" she claims to have achieved over her husbands may be overstated (Cigman, 1975, 7).

One aspect which may confirm this is the age disparity between the Wife and her fifth husband, Jankyn, who was twenty at the time of their marriage, while the Wife admits to being forty. The horror which the knight in her Tale evinces at the idea of being a young man married to an old woman is one which would have been shared by many mediaeval readers. Significant age differences in married couples were potentially open to ridicule whichever way they went: we may compare the January and May story in Chaucer's The Merchant's Tale. Nevertheless, in many cultures the marriage of an older man and younger woman has always been more socially acceptable than the other way around, and the suggestion made by the old woman in the Wife of Bath's Tale, that "filthe and elde ... Been grete wardeyns upon chastitee" (ll, 1215–1216), is a particularly long-lived and pervasive misogynistic trope. It reappears, for example, in the song *Ugly Woman* (1934) by the Trinidadian calypsonian Roaring Lion (stage name of Rafael de Leon, 1908–1999), in a manner which demonstrates clearly that it is not a rejection of conventional standards of beauty but a reassertion of the importance of masculine control of women:

> ... if you make an ugly woman your wife,
> You can be sure you'll be happy in all your life,
> For she would never do things in a funny way
> To allow the neighbours to have anything to say,
> And she wouldn't disregard her husband at all
> By exhibiting herself to Peter and Paul.
> So from a logical point of view
> Always love a woman uglier than you.
> An ugly woman gives you your meals on time
> And always try to make you happy in mind ...
>   (de Leon, 1934)

Roaring Lion's song was later adapted as *If You Wanna Be Happy*, which became a Number One hit on the Billboard Hot 100 in the United States of America for the singer Jimmy Soul (James Louis McCleese, 1942–1988) in 1963. Anyone who looks at the many versions of this which are readily available online, including covers in French (Claude François, 1963), Dutch (by the Surinamese singer Max Woiski, Jr., 1963) and Cantonese (George Lam, 1984), will have ample evidence of the apparently almost universal popularity of this kind of misogynistic satire.

In his Prologue, another of Chaucer's characters in the *Canterbury Tales*, the Reeve, uses "shrewe" to refer to a scoundrel without distinction of gender (Benson, 1988, 78). By the early seventeenth century this meaning, while still current, was becoming obsolete, and the predominant meaning was that of "a scolding or turbulent wife" (Oxford English Dictionary, "shrew", n. 2), the sense in which it is used by Chaucer's Merchant. The most famous shrew in English literature is of course Katherina in Shakespeare's *The Taming of the Shrew*, for which one or more versions of the "patient Griselda" story may have furnished material (Hodgdon, 2010, 62–63). Shakespeare's play has been deeply controversial almost from the start, and many critical accounts and stage productions have endeavoured to suggest that it should be viewed in an ironical manner and that we should feel that the playwright is sending up the misogynistic attitudes displayed by Petruccio and other characters (Hodgdon, 2010, 71–131). Nevertheless, there will probably always be readers for whom the play remains a dispiriting account of an arranged marriage in which the bride is literally starved into submission, and in which it is hard to find any evidence of satire at all.

A rather more complex view of gender relations can be seen in the comedies of Molière (pen-name of the French playwright Jean-Baptiste Poquelin, 1622–1673). In *Les Femmes Savantes* ("The Learned Ladies", 1672), for example, the character of Philaminte is treated as a figure of ridicule because of her intellectual pretensions, in a manner which goes back to Juvenal's mockery of the Roman woman who ventured to compare Virgil and Homer (VI, 434–437). Her husband Chrysale complains that

Il n'est pas bien honnête, et pour beaucoup de causes,
Qu'une femme étudie et sache tant de choses ...

(II, 7)

[It is not proper behaviour, for many reasons, that a woman should study and know so many things.]

He laments that in his parents' generation, women's books were "un dé, du fil, et des aiguilles,/Dont elles travaillaient au trousseau de leurs filles" ["a thimble, some thread and some needles, with which they worked at their daughters' marriage outfit"] (Ton-That, 2007, 62). Philaminte practically swoons with delight when Vadius is introduced as a man who knows Greek, but when her daughter Henriette is less impressed, Philaminte's response suggests that this is not because she actually understands Greek herself:

Philaminte

Quoi! Monsieur sait du grec! Ah! permettez, de grâce,
Que, pour l'amour du grec, Monsieur, on vous embrasse.

(Ils les baise toutes, jusqu'à Henriette qui le refuse.)

Henriette

Excusez-moi, Monsieur, je n'entends pas le grec.

Philaminte

J'ai pour les livres grecs un merveilleux respect.

(III, 3; Ton-That, 2007, 91)

[Philaminte: "What, Monsieur knows Greek! Ah! do allow us the favour, for the love of Greek, that we kiss you." Stage direction: He kisses all the women, except for Henriette, who rebuffs him. Henriette: "Excuse me, Monsieur, I don't understand Greek." Philaminte: "I have a marvellous respect for Greek books."]

Nevertheless, Molière's target here is linguistic and cultural pretension generally, and in the same scene his satire (with echoes of Horace and Juvenal) is directed at the two male pedants, Trissotin and Vadius. In an extremely funny exchange which mocks the preciosity fashionable in some literary quarters in Molière's time, they begin by flattering each other, but a clash of egos soon develops and ends in mutual accusations of bad writing and plagiarism (Ton-That, 2007, 91–97). The voice of reason in the play is represented by Henriette and by the kitchen-maid, Martine, who claims that

> Quand on se fait entendre, on parle toujours bien,
> Et tous vos biaux dictons ne servent de rien.
>
> (II, 6; Ton-That, 2007, 57)

> [When one makes oneself understood, one always speaks well, and all your loverly maxims are quite useless.]

Unsurprisingly, however, Molière is not that far removed from the conventions of his time. The plot of *Les Femmes Savantes* turns on Philaminte's desire to marry Henriette to Trissotin so that she can have an intellectual as a son-in-law, and she is willing to use her parental authority to overcome her daughter's objections. Chrysale is a stereotypical hen-pecked husband, and his brother Ariste has to point out to him not only the absurdity of Philaminte's high opinion of Trissotin as a wit and a philosopher, but also that "C'est une chose infâme /Que d'être si soumis au pouvoir d'une femme" ("It is a shameful thing to be so submissive to the power of a woman"; II, 9; Ton-That, 2007, 71). At the end of the play, Trissotin is exposed as a fortune-hunter, and Henriette is able to marry her preferred suitor, Clitandre, but only because Chrysale has finally reasserted his authority as head of the household and insisted that his support for Henriette's choice must prevail over his wife's wishes. Patriarchal norms have been restored.

The late seventeenth and early eighteenth centuries saw a proliferation of anti-feminist verse satires in Britain (Nussbaum, 1984) which drew on the Juvenalian tradition both directly and indirectly, through French adaptations such as Boileau's Tenth Satire, which was in turn adapted in English by Lady Mary Wortley Montagu (1689–1762) (Halsband and Grundy, 1993, 210–214). Anti-feminist elements appeared in satires on other topics, and the grotesque misogyny and personal abuse is sometimes such as can still startle modern readers. A notorious example is Pope's treatment of Eliza Haywood (?1693–1756). Haywood was in her time an extremely popular writer, some of whose works, such as the short novel *Fantomina: Or, Love in a Maze* (1725), have been rediscovered by modern critics and treated as serious explorations of women's position in eighteenth-century society. She had offended Pope, however, by some comments on his friend Martha Blount, and as a result, Pope mentions her in the parody of the descriptions of heroic games in Homer and other epics which he included in his attack in *The Dunciad* (1728) on those he considered to be bad writers. He suggests that she is immoral by conventional standards by attributing to her "Two babes of love", i.e., illegitimate children, though evidence for this having any connection with reality is lacking. He refers to a published portrait of her (1723), engraved by George Vertue after James Parmentier, and comments on the fact that it shows her in an informal and somewhat décolleté dress by referring to her breasts as "cow-like-udders", and, in some early versions of the text, talking about "her fore-buttocks to the navel bare". As if this were not enough, Pope made her the prize in a pissing contest between two booksellers (Sutherland, 1963, 119–124).

Pope had at one point been a friend of Lady Mary Wortley Montagu, but after they fell out, she was abused by him in an even worse manner than his treatment of Haywood. In his *First Satire of the Second Book of Horace* (1733), Pope wrote how one should dread "From furious Sappho scarce a milder Fate" than the slander, poison or hanging one might receive from those mentioned in the preceding lines, since one would be "P—x'd by her Love, or libell'd by her Hate". Contemporaries readily identified "Sappho" as Lady Mary, as she did herself. Pope's lines referred to the fact that Lady Mary had introduced inoculation for smallpox into England in 1721, but also clearly suggested that she herself had "the pox", i.e., syphilis, and that she was little better than a prostitute (Butt, 1969, xv–xvii, 13). A response called *Verses addressed to the Imitator of the First Satire of the Second Book of Horace* was probably written by Lady Mary and John, Lord Hervey (1696–1743), another ex-friend of Pope's. This accused Pope of failing to understand the difference between satire and invective:

> *Horace* can laugh, is delicate, is clear;
> You, only coarsely rail, or darkly sneer [...]
>   Satire shou'd, like a polish'd Razor keen,
> Wound with a Touch, that's scarcely felt or seen,
> Thine is an Oyster-Knife that hacks and hews;
> The Rage, but not the Talent to Abuse;
> And is in *Hate*, what *Love* is in the Stews.

Nevertheless, the *Verses* did not hesitate to attack Pope on the score of his personal appearance, calling him an "angry little Monster", referring to his "wretched little Carcase", and suggesting that his physical deformity was "the Emblem of thy crooked Mind,/Mark'd on thy Back, like Cain, by God's own Hand" (Halsband and Grundy, 1993, 265–270).

Pope got his revenge in his *Epistle to Dr Arbuthnot* (1734). In the same way as did texts like Juvenal's Ninth Satire or Chaucer's portrait of the Pardoner, Pope drew on the widespread acceptance of the idea that homosexual inclinations or behaviour were abnormal, morally reprehensible and, therefore, inherently ridiculous. He focused on Hervey's well-known bisexuality and referred to him as Sporus, a historical figure claimed by ancient writers such as Suetonius (probably best regarded as a scandalous gossip-monger rather than a historian) to have been a boy castrated on the orders of the Emperor Nero and then married to him. While Pope began by suggesting that Hervey was too feeble a creature for a satirist to be worth bothering about – "Who breaks a Butterfly upon a Wheel?" – he announced his intention to "flap this Bug with gilded wings,/This painted Child of Dirt that stinks and stings", and went on to associate Hervey's sexuality with satanic evil:

> Fop at the Toilet, Flatt'rer at the Board,
> Now trips a Lady, and now struts a Lord.
> *Eve*'s Tempter thus the Rabbins have exprest,
> A Cherub's face, a Reptile all the rest;
> Beauty that shocks you, Parts that none will trust,
> Wit that can creep, and Pride that licks the dust.
> (Butt, 1969, 117–120)

The viciousness of Pope's attack reduced Hervey to silence and put an end to his pretensions as a writer.

Juvenal was not the only literary predecessor on whom anti-feminist satirists could draw. Pope adapted both Chaucer's January and May story and the Wife of Bath's Prologue to eighteenth-century tastes in what were styled as translations (Tillotson, 1962, 3–78). Pope's final word on the subject was *Of the Characters of Women: An Epistle to a Lady*, first published in 1735 and revised and expanded in 1744 (Bateson, 1951, 38–71). This bears a strong resemblance to a poem by the ancient Greek writer Semonides of Amorgos (seventh century BCE) which has been claimed as "the earliest work of European literature to have women for its theme" (Lloyd-Jones, 1975). Drawing on Hesiod as well as on prevailing ideas about gender, Semonides described ten different types of women. Some resembled the sea, for their unpredictable changes of temper; some were inert, like the earth-woman, whose only interest was in eating. The rest were compared to animals, such as the slovenly pig-woman, the idle but lascivious ass-woman, or the woman who was like a proud mare, obsessed with her looks. All the types were treated negatively, except for the bee-woman, whose industry would cause her husband's property to increase, but even the bee-woman hardly compensated for the generalising (though possibly incomplete) conclusion which followed, claiming that women were "the greatest plague that Zeus has made". His modern editor has suggested that Semonides perhaps did not intend to be taken entirely seriously. Nevertheless, his work was given a wide circulation in later centuries by its inclusion in an anthology of Greek poetry published in 1560, where it was accompanied by a translation into Latin verse by George Buchanan (Lloyd-Jones, 1975, 102). This was later included in collected editions of Buchanan's poems (Buchanan, 1687, 348–351), and the translation itself, and the fact that it appeared in the context of other misogynistic poems by Buchanan himself, suggested that the views expressed by Semonides were to be taken at face value. The poem received a further boost to its circulation in 1711 when Joseph Addison (1672–1719) included a paraphrase of it in English prose in *The Spectator*, a series of periodical essays which were frequently reprinted and retained considerable influence well into the nineteenth century (Lloyd-Jones, 1975, 105–109). Addison commented, "That the following Satyr affects only some of the lower part of the sex, and not those who have been refined by a polite education, which was not so common in the age of this Poet". He commended Semonides's "great penetration in this diversity of female characters", and suggested

> What vice or frailty can a discourse correct, which censures the whole species alike, and endeavours to shew by some superficial strokes of wit, that brutes are the more excellent creatures of the two? A Satyr should expose nothing but what is corrigible, and make a due discrimination between those who are, and those who are not proper objects of it.

Whether or not as a result of direct influence, Pope's *Of the Characters of Women* took a similar approach. He did not treat "the whole species" of women in the same manner, but listed examples of different foibles under fictitious names, many of which contemporaries assumed to be identifiable with actual people. He ended the poem with a passage praising his unnamed "Friend" (Martha Blount) as superior to other women:

> The gen'rous God, who Wit and Gold refines,
> And ripens Spirits as he ripens Mines,
> Kept Dross for Duchesses, the world shall know it,
> To you gave Sense, Good-humour, and a Poet.

The concession seems rather like the exception Semonides made in favour of the bee-woman, in that it fails to overcome the negative impression the poem gives of women as a whole. The virtues of the female "Friend" need the male poet to render them complete, and if Pope suggests that woman is Heaven's "last best work", he does so in a manner which scarcely seems to question established notions of masculine superiority:

> And yet believe me, good as well as ill,
> Woman's at best a Contradiction still.
> Hev'n, when it strives to polish all it can
> Its last best work, but forms a softer Man [...]

Male satirists did not have it all their own way. Mary, Lady Chudleigh (1656–1710) was the author of a number of poems which offered a vigorous criticism of contemporary gender relations, such as *To the Ladies*, which began "Wife and Servant are the same,/But only differ in the Name" (Ezell, 1993, 83–84). Lady Mary Wortley Montagu's response to Swift's "The Lady's Dressing-Room" showed a talent for personal invective as well as sexual and scatological humour by suggesting that Swift had been moved to compose his misogynistic sketch as result of being embarrassed by impotence during a visit to a prostitute (Halsband and Grundy, 1993, 273–276). Nor was the authorship of such poems confined to aristocratic ladies: *The Woman's Labour* (1739) by Mary Collier (?1688–1762), a washerwoman and self-educated poet, responded in well-turned verse to *The Thresher's Labour* by Stephen Duck (1705–1756), which had disparaged the contributions of working-class women, whom Duck dismissed as "prattling Females" (Thompson and Sugden, 1989).

Nussbaum (1984, 158) notes how Swift and Pope combined their satirical attacks on some women with the idealisation of others – Swift's Stella, Pope's Martha Blount – and suggests that "When anti-feminist satire begins to blend with romance, however, it brings about its own demise for a time". By the end of the eighteenth century, this particular vein had exhausted itself, as part of the change in literary fashion which saw the decline of formal verse satire more generally. Male and female writers continued to debate aspects of gender relations, but explored these in other genres, such as fiction and essays (Nussbaum, 1984, 158). Some of the most interesting manifestations of feminist satire have taken the form of fictions exploring imaginary universes such as Ursula Le Guin's *Left Hand of Darkness* (Chapter 4) or utopias such as that in Charlotte Perkins Gilman's novella *Herland* (first published 1915), in which three stereotypically masculine explorers from the United States of America discover in the Amazon a large, happy and successful society consisting solely of women who reproduce by parthenogenesis. Occasional literary works have continued to treat gender issues in verse, such as *The Princess* (1847), by Alfred, Lord Tennyson (1809–1892), which discussed the question of higher education for women in serio-comic blank verse and which formed the basis of the comic opera, *Princess Ida* (1884) by W. S. Gilbert (1836–1911) and Arthur Sullivan (1842–1900). New forms have come into existence, such as televised situation comedy, but in some cases, themes appear to continue from much older predecessors. In the British sitcom *Keeping Up Appearances* (1990–1995), for example, the attempts at social climbing of the character Hyacinth Bucket, who insists that her name should be pronounced "Bouquet", include repeated expressions of pride in the alleged intellectual achievements of her son Sheridan, in a manner not very different from the desire of Philaminte in Molière's *Les Femmes Savantes* to be able to show off an intellectual as a son-in-law.

The importance of popular song in this context should not be underestimated, though this often connects gender with other issues. An outstanding example is the nineteenth-century British song of unknown authorship, *She was poor but she was honest*, which can be found in various versions in print (e.g., Auden, 1938, 476–477) as well as in audio recordings such as those by the music hall comedian Billy Bennett (William Robertson Russell Bennett, 1887–1942) (Bennett, 1997, track 7). The details may differ, but the plot is always the same: the poor girl is seduced by a rich man who then abandons her to a life of disgrace and increasing misery which culminates in suicide. The chorus is more or less invariable:

> It's the same the whole world over;
> It's the poor that gets the blame,
> It's the rich that gets the pleasure,
> Isn't it a blooming shame?

The message is clear enough: the poor are metaphorically, as well as literally, screwed by the rich. The same theme of the connections between sex, class and money can be found half a world away, in one of the sharpest and most bitter songs by the Grenadian/Trinidadian calypsonian The Mighty Sparrow (stage name of Slinger Francisco, b. 1935). In *No Money, No Love* (1969), Sparrow sings how

> Ivy pack up she clothes to leave
> Because John was down and out
> All alone he was left to grieve
> She had a next man in South [...]

Again, the chorus says it all:

> We can't love without money
> We can't make love on hungry belly
> Johnny you'll be the only one I'm dreaming of
> You're my turtle dove
> But no money no love [...]

Although Johnny "plead with she to get she to understand", Ivy refuses to change her mind. His response is to "nearly kill she wid blows" so that "the South man don't want she now". Sparrow's criticism of the oppressive nature of poverty does not, however, subvert the continuance of masculine dominance in such circumstances. In his earliest hit, *Jean and Dinah* (1956), which has remained popular throughout his career, Sparrow celebrated the departure of the American sailors from Trinidad following the closure of the naval bases conceded to the United States by the British colonial authorities during the Second World War. The song announces, "Yankees gone and Sparrow take over now", and lines like "we have things back in control" or "We are going to rule Port of Spain" are, in part, an expression of nascent national pride and anti-colonial sentiment. However, the "things" Sparrow and his male friends now "have ... back in control" are the prostitutes like Jean and Dinah, and the other "girls in town", who because "No more Yankees in Trinidad ... have to make out how they could". Here, as in so many other instances, the triumphalism and the satire are gendered.

8

SATIRE AND THE VISUAL ARTS

Evidence of the human urge to give an idea visual expression dates back to long before we have any record of what we might call literature, or even of language itself. Werner Herzog's documentary *Cave of Forgotten Dreams* takes us into the Chauvet Cave in southern France, where the extraordinary paintings, including vividly naturalistic horses, stags, bison, lions, bears and even rhinoceroses, date back as far as 32,000 years ago (Herzog, 2010). Since the Chauvet Cave was first discovered in 1994, the use of uranium series dating has suggested that a painting in El Castillo cave in northern Spain is at least 40,800 years old, raising the possibility that some cave art may have been created not by modern humans, but by Neanderthals (Jones, 2012). Cave paintings and related forms of rock art, such as petroglyphs, that is, images created by engraving a rock surface rather than by applying pigments, are found in many different parts of the world (Brodrick, 1948; Dubelaar, 1986). Even with recent advances in scientific techniques, however, such as the uranium series dating which has allowed paintings in Church Hole in Cresswell Crags in England to be dated to over 12,000 years ago (Bahn and Pettitt, 2009), establishing the chronology of a given site can be difficult, but trying to establish what such images might mean is even more difficult. Thurman (2008) notes the very diverse theories developed about the Chauvet paintings in less than 20 years since their first discovery, but herself indulges in speculation about one of the best known of the cave paintings from Lascaux, also in southern France, which were found in 1940. This shows the sketchy outline of a human figure, which is stretched out and perhaps lying down. Next to him is a more naturalistic bison, and the scene is usually understood as showing a hunter who has been gored by the bison, with a line near the human figure representing the spear which he has dropped. Some more or less circular lines coming from the bison's belly are assumed to be its intestines, and it has been suggested (Brodrick, 1948, 20) that the bison, having killed the hunter, has been gored in turn by the woolly rhinoceros pictured to the left, apparently moving away from the scene. Thurman observes that the bison's head is turned away from the hunter and comments, "but it might have an ironic smile. Could the subject be hubris?" If so, we might be looking at an example of visual satire from 16,000 to 18,000 years ago, but we would do well to note Bahn and Pettitt's warning against the all too common tendency to over-interpret prehistoric art.

Even in historic times, when we have written records to provide some sort of socio-cultural context for visual images, confidence in interpretation is often impossible. A case in point is a wall painting from an ancient Roman villa at Gragnano, near Pompeii, which is now in the National Archaeological Museum in Naples (Balch, 2008, 94–95). This shows three more or less human figures, the one in the centre carrying another on his shoulder and leading the third, shorter figure by the hand. The figure being carried appears to be holding a box. To anyone familiar with the *Aeneid*, the great epic poem by Virgil, the subject is instantly recognisable: it is Aeneas carrying his father Anchises and leading his son Ascanius, taking them away from the destruction of Troy and beginning the journey which will eventually lead to the foundation of Rome. The box Anchises is carrying contains their household gods, and the scene is one of the best known from the most familiar work of Roman literature, a poem which had become a school text within a few years of its author's death, and which was in effect the foundation myth of the Roman Empire. Yet the Gragnano painting is a grotesque caricature: the three figures have dog-like heads, and Aeneas and Ascanius have clearly represented long tails and exaggerated penises. There are other ancient representations of the same scene without the elements of caricature: a coin issued by Antoninus Pius (Roman emperor 138–161 CE) shows Aeneas, Anchises and Ascanius in exactly the same arrangement as the Gragnano painting, and may be connected with the celebrations of what was considered to be the ninth centenary of the founding of Rome which were held during the emperor's reign (British Museum collections, 1896,0608.26). The painting looks like a caricature of the image on the coin, though it is possible that both derive from a common earlier source. This gets us no nearer to an understanding of the painting, however. Is it simply an example of the impulse to mock the sacred which can be found in many different cultures at different times, or is there perhaps an element of political satire? The only possible answer is that we have no way of knowing.

Similar problems beset the interpretation of the so-called Alexamenos graffito. This is a crude image scratched on plaster, discovered on a wall in an ancient building on the Palatine Hill in Rome in the nineteenth century, and now in the Palatine Museum. The building in which it was found was completed towards the end of the first century, and estimates for when the graffito was made range from this point to the late third century. The image shows what appears to be a crucified human figure with the head of an ass. The head is turned towards another figure drawn next to it, that of a man standing with one hand raised towards the one who is crucified, so that the two seem to be looking at each other. There is an accompanying inscription in Greek, which has been interpreted by various scholars as meaning something like "Alexamenos worships a god", or "his god". There is nothing to indicate who was responsible for the image and the inscription, and we do not know who Alexamenos was, though, in view of the fact that the building in which the graffito was found was part of the imperial palace, it is possible that he was part of the household of the Roman emperor. The usual interpretation is that the graffito is mocking Alexamenos because he was a Christian; if so, it would be one of the earliest known representations of the crucified Jesus. Other readings are possible, however, such as that the donkey-headed god is an attack on Judaism rather than Christianity, and modern attempts at understanding are necessarily conjectural (Yarbrough, 2012; Smith, 2012).

Those who worked in the palace at the time, however, presumably knew who Alexamenos was, and enough about him to make sense of the graffito. In the same manner, a puzzling section of the Bayeux Tapestry may have been clear enough to contemporaries, though perhaps less so to us. One of the most famous mediaeval works of art, the Tapestry is a piece of embroidery some 70 metres in length showing the events leading up to the invasion of England by William, Duke of Normandy, in 1066, and ending, at least in its present condition, with the defeated English fleeing from the Battle of Hastings. It is generally accepted that the Tapestry was created within a generation of the events it depicts, and possibly only a few years after them. The Tapestry is not simply documentary: its earlier scenes, especially that showing Harold making a solemn oath to William, are intended to justify the invasion by claiming that William, and not Harold, had the better claim to the English throne after the death of the childless King Edward the Confessor (Thorpe, 1973). Nevertheless, one scene has baffled viewers for centuries and led commentators to seek some sort of meaning in it by suggesting that it might be political or social satire. In the middle of the images showing a visit to Normandy by Harold while King Edward was still alive, we see a woman standing in what looks like a doorway. Standing next to her is a man identifiable as a cleric by his tonsure, who is touching, or perhaps stroking, her face. In the border panel immediately below is a crouching man who is completely naked, his genitals carefully detailed. One hand is stretched out and seems to be gesturing at the woman. Just to the left in the border, and possibly connected with the same scene, is another naked or near-naked man who seems to be doing something to a piece of wood with an axe or adze. Above the two main figures are the words "ubi unus clericus et Aelfgyva" ("where a cleric and Aelfgyva"). Aelfgyva was an Anglo-Saxon woman's name, and presumably that of the woman shown here. There is no obvious connection with what comes before or after in the Tapestry. Comparison with other mediaeval works of art allows us to conclude that the face-touching gesture is in some way sexually suggestive. The naked man apparently gesturing at Aelfgyva may or may not be relevant. The top and bottom borders of the Tapestry are mostly filled with depictions of real or imaginary animals and appear to be purely decorative, except towards the end, where the battle scenes overflow into the bottom border.

Nevertheless, there are three other places in the border showing naked human figures; these are some distance from the Aelfgyva scene and there is no reason to assume that they have any relevance to it. It is presumed that the Aelfgyva scene was a satirical reference to some sort of sexual scandal, perhaps affecting the legitimacy of some other potential claimant to the English throne. The absence of other verbal or visual clues suggests the reference was obvious to at least the first generation of the Tapestry's viewers. Modern scholars are unable to settle even which of various historical figures called Aelfgyva might be meant, with three relatively recent articles carefully reviewing all the evidence and coming to different and incompatible conclusions (McNulty, 1980; Campbell, 1984; Freeman, 1991).

The Alexamenos graffito was essentially private, and in the immediate aftermath of its creation would have been seen by very few people, far fewer than the many who have looked at it, or at least at reproductions of it, in the century and a half since its rediscovery some 2,000 years afterwards. The Bayeux Tapestry, by contrast, was a much more public document, but this needs some qualification. While its early history is obscure, we know that at least by the late Middle Ages it was kept in Bayeux Cathedral and brought out to decorate the building on special occasions (Thorpe, 1973, 58). But an embroidered hanging, or a wall painting like that in the Gragnano villa, cannot be passed easily from one person to another like the words of a satirical song. To have any chance of getting their message it was necessary to be in a particular place, sometimes even to be in a particular place at a particular time. It was not until a number of related changes occurred in Western European culture in the fifteenth century that it became possible to have visual satire with something approaching mass appeal.

The first of these was the revival in Western Europe of interest in the literatures, arts and cultures of ancient Greece and Rome which we conventionally refer to as the Renaissance. One aspect of this was the stimulus it gave to the development of portraiture. While a portrait in oils or a marble sculpture might be seen by only a few, for the first time since the days of the early Roman empire, lifelike images of contemporary rulers began to appear on coins, including ones of relatively low value which circulated widely. Once standardised and realistic representations of the actual appearance of public figures became widely known, the art of the caricaturist and the visual satirist could begin to flourish. The second was the development of printing, which made possible the widespread dissemination of images as well as text. While printing, including the printing of texts using moveable type, had been known in China for centuries, it is not found in Europe until about the late fourteenth century, where it may have begun as a means of decorating textiles. The westward transmission of paper manufacturing, another Chinese invention, which reached Spain in the twelfth century, Italy by about 1275 and Germany a century or so later, provided a material which was not only ideal for printing on, but also much cheaper than the treated animal skins on which most European texts had been laboriously written out by hand for most of the Middle Ages. The earliest European printed images are believed to date from the late fourteenth century; the earliest which can be dated precisely is from 1418. In the early fifteenth century, printed images of a religious character, sometimes with a few lines of text forming part of the image, were being produced in enormous quantities. While many of these were woodcuts, the use of engraving on metal for printing purposes was also developed in the fifteenth century, something which grew out of the arts of coinage and decorative engraving on precious metals. Johannes Gutenberg (c. 1398–1468), the discoverer of the use of moveable type in the West, came from a family involved in the production of coinage, and both he and his sometime business partner, Johann Fust (c. 1400–1466), who later set up in printing for himself, had connections with goldsmithing (Mayor, 1971). After Gutenberg's pioneering work in the 1450s, printing spread rapidly, and by 1500 there were about a thousand printing presses across Europe. Germany and Italy were still the major centres, but printing could be found from Oxford to Constantinople, and from Sweden to Sicily, although in many places it long remained subject to varying levels of control by secular and religious authorities. By 1539, it had reached Mexico, and it continued to spread across the world in the seventeenth and eighteenth centuries. The development and spread of printing allowed both texts and images to reach much wider audiences than ever before, and this benefited verbal and visual satire as well as other genres.

In some ways, printing was simply a faster and cheaper way of disseminating existing materials: Bibles, saints' lives, secular texts which had become accepted as part of the canon of Western literature like the classics of ancient Greece and Rome. Some of this can be seen in one of the best-known examples of visual images in early printing, the series of woodcuts known as the Dance of Death by Hans Holbein the Younger (c. 1497–1543). Completed in 1526, although only published for the first time in 1538, these continue a theme found in many examples of mediaeval art. Death comes to all, rich and poor, high and low. The skull in the decorative border of a manuscript, or the elaborate tomb which shows the bishop in his ecclesiastical vestments on one level and a naked and decaying corpse below it, serve to convey the "Memento mori" message that, irrespective of social status, we all must die, and that we should repent and amend our lives while we can. The Dance of Death itself, a visual representation of a series of figures, in which living representatives of different ranks in society alternate with skeletons or corpse-like creatures who come to take them away from this world, was popular in the fifteenth century, with the oldest known example being a mural in the Cimetière des Innocents in Paris, dating from 1424–1425, which was destroyed in the seventeenth century. The Dance's reminder that we can take nothing out of this world can be seen as a criticism of the pretensions of the rich and powerful, and there is an anticlerical streak in the depictions of high-ranking ecclesiastics. Holbein's designs are very much in this tradition, but they also introduce new elements, some of them satirical, which depend on the new technologies of mass production. There is a mixture of those figures for whom Death is a peaceful end to a well-spent life, and, more critically, those whom it seizes in the midst of their misconduct or folly. Targets of anticlerical satire are balanced by images of the virtuous. The parish priest, for example, is shown calmly performing the duties of his office: he is taking communion to the sick. The terrified abbot, by contrast, is fat as a result of good living, and the skeletal figure of Death who drags him away in spite of his protests mocks his pretensions by assuming his mitre and crozier. The judge is taken in the act of receiving a bribe, the nun while entertaining her lover. The emperor is dispensing justice, apparently taking the side of a poor female suppliant and rebuking a nobleman. The king is at the table enjoying worldly pleasures, but it is Death who is pouring out the cup from which he must drink. These, and the dozens of other images in the series, only exist for us and could only be made popular in their own time as a result of the skill with which the accomplished craftsman Hans Lützelburger (d. 1526) cut Holbein's designs into wooden blocks which could be used for printing (Clark, 1947). The fact that the emperor has the features of Maximilian I (Holy Roman Emperor 1486–1519) and the king those of François I (king of France 1515–1547) implies that at least some of those who viewed the woodcuts could be expected to recognise them, as the result of the existence and circulation of realistic portraits on coins and medals.

Durable and easily portable, medals lent themselves both to propaganda and satire. One example from the Reformation is a medal attributed to Friedrich Hagenauer and produced at Cologne around 1544. One side shows the head of a pope which, when turned the other way up, becomes the head of a devil. The other side shows a cardinal's head coupled in a similar manner with the head of a fool or jester (Metropolitan Museum of Art, 60.55.58). The way images could be transferred from one medium to another can be seen in the fact that those from Hagenauer's medal reappeared as a print on paper in England around 1689, at a time when the "Glorious Revolution" had replaced the Catholic king James II with the Protestant William III (British Museum 1868,0808.3336). In spite of competition from other methods of circulating images, the satirical medal has survived into the twenty-first century, one example being a US official 10 cent piece mounted in a metal surround with brief texts accusing the administration of President Barack Obama of being socialist and intent on raising taxes, including "Comrade, can you spare a dime?", echoing the popular Depression-era song by E. Y. "Yip" Harburg and Jay Gorney, "Brother, can you spare a dime?" (Coin People, 2013).

Nevertheless, print and paper long remained the most important means of disseminating images. One of the first to realise their possibilities to the fullest was the English painter and engraver William Hogarth (1697–1764). While he could produce conventional portraits and grand paintings on historical or religious subjects in a traditional manner, Hogarth was best known in his own time and after for what he called his "modern moral subjects", which were satires of contemporary society. The first of these were the two series, *The Harlot's Progress* and *The Rake's Progress*. Although these began as oil paintings, it was always Hogarth's plan to reproduce them as engravings, as he realised that he could make a better income from selling many copies of engravings to a wider public than from selling individual paintings or even sets of paintings to wealthy patrons. While he enjoyed the benefits of some patronage, Hogarth was the son of a schoolmaster and unsuccessful publisher of textbooks who had got into debt as a result of an attempt to run a Latin-speaking coffee-house in London, and his success was mainly due to his own hard work and commercial acumen. Hogarth's prints showed a broad cross-section of British society, from extravagant aristocrats to the very poor, including marginalised figures such as black servants (Dabydeen, 1985). They were a great success, and helped to spread visual satire of high artistic quality among what was perhaps a far wider range of purchasers than ever before. This should not be over-stated, however. A Hogarth engraving was much cheaper than an oil painting, and could be bought by members of the middle classes as well as by the seriously wealthy, but they were beyond the reach of the labouring classes and the very poor whose patronage of the arts might occasionally extend to paying a couple of farthings for a printed ballad sheet illustrated by a crude woodcut. It was perhaps inevitable that a significant part of Hogarth's work reflected the ideals and aspirations of the expanding middle classes, and that his approach is often extremely conventional. The twentieth-century cartoonist David Low (1891–1963), a perceptive critic of his own art-form, summed up Hogarth's work by saying that "Virtue triumphs over Vice with sickening monotony" (Low, 1942, 8). This is best shown by his series of twelve engravings called *Industry and Idleness* (1747). Two poor boys from a similar background take different paths in life: the industrious apprentice prospers and eventually becomes Lord Mayor of London, while the idle apprentice falls into immorality and crime and is finally hanged. Hogarth intended that these images and those in other series such as *The Four Stages of Cruelty* (1751) should have an effect on the behaviour of people of the class he was depicting, and stated that because of this they were published as cheaply as possible. Nevertheless, each of the engravings in the *Four Stages* cost a shilling, or sixpence extra if on fine paper, which was more than a day's wages for many people. Hogarth was aware of the contradiction, and planned to produce woodcut versions which would be cheaper, but only two of these actually appeared (Bindman, 2004).

The works of later artists such as James Gillray (c. 1756–1815), Thomas Rowlandson (1756–1827) and Isaac Cruikshank (1764–1811), who made the late eighteenth and early nineteenth century into what is sometimes thought of as a great age of political caricature, were routinely displayed in the windows of the print-shops which published them for passers-by to see. As with Hogarth's prints, however, they remained relatively expensive and beyond the reach of the very poor and the majority of the working classes, who in any case could have had only a limited interest in satires of a political system from which they were largely excluded.

The extension of the right to vote, in Britain and elsewhere during the nineteenth century, accompanied technological developments such as steam-powered printing presses, paper made from wood pulp instead of the traditional rags, and new printing methods such as lithography. These meant that books and periodicals could be produced more cheaply and on a much larger scale than ever before. While the chief medium of visual satire in the eighteenth century was the separately published print, the nineteenth century saw the increasingly widespread use of illustrations in periodicals. By the end of the century, the development of photo-engraving meant that artists were no longer constrained by the limitations of particular reproductive techniques, such as wood engraving, but were able to draw in whatever style they liked and expect their work to be reproduced exactly. Illustrated satirical magazines began to appear, such as *Le Charivari* (1832–1937) in France, and *Punch* (1841–1992, 1996–2002; subtitled *The London Charivari*) in England. For much of his career, the French *Charivari* employed Honoré Daumier (1808–1879), a master of lithographic technique who was also a true radical. One of his best known illustrations is his caricature (1831) of the head of the "Citizen King", Louis Philippe (King of the French, 1830–1848), turning into a pear, which was based on a sketch by the future publisher of *Charivari*, Charles Philipon (1800–1861). Difficulties with censorship forced *Charivari* to concentrate on social rather than political satire, and while Daumier produced innumerable images mocking the follies and pretensions of middle-class professionals and petty functionaries for the magazine, some of his most striking and radical work was produced elsewhere. One example is a lithographic print of 1872 showing a group of emaciated corpses approaching a doorway. One is a woman leading a child, one is headless and another, draped in the remains of a military uniform, lifts a skeletal arm to point accusingly at the inscription over the doorway, which reads "Conseil de Guerre" ("Council of War"). In the aftermath of France's defeat in the Franco-Prussian War, this was banned by the censor (Mayor, 1971).

Censorship was less of an issue in Britain, but while there were accomplished political cartoonists such as John Tenniel (1820–1914), there was no British equivalent of Daumier. *Punch* specialised in the humour of snobbery, encouraging the upper and middle classes to mock the ignorance and social inadequacies of those they considered beneath them. Tenniel's best known work, apart from his illustrations for Lewis Carroll's *Alice in Wonderland* (1865), is perhaps "Dropping the Pilot", his 1890 cartoon in Punch showing the German chancellor, Otto von Bismarck, as a pilot leaving a ship while the young Kaiser Wilhelm II, who has just dismissed him, looks on. This shows both the good points and the limitations of Tenniel's work. As we can confirm by comparison with contemporary photographs, Tenniel's drawing offers good likenesses of the two men. On the other hand, there is a basic problem with the whole concept. As Low (1942, 20) noted, "The point of the situation which evoked this cartoon was that Bismarck's dismissal was an astonishing and unexpected event, but the leaving of a ship by the pilot is a perfectly normal and expected event – in no way a real parallel". Another side of Tenniel appears in a number of cartoons in *Punch* in which opposition to Irish nationalism took the form of grotesque, racist caricatures.

If Tenniel was only one of many artists who provided compelling evidence that visual satire could often be used in support of social and political conservatism, political upheavals also produced more radical versions, sometimes in surprising places. *Molla Nasreddin* (1906–1930) was an illustrated satirical magazine published successively in Tiflis (modern Tbilisi, Georgia), Tabriz (Iran) and Baku (Azerbaijan), in the Azeri and occasionally Russian languages. Published in predominantly Muslim areas, the magazine criticised the Muslim clergy, opposed European and American colonialism and called for modernisation, educational reform and equal rights for women. It succeeded in gaining readers across the Muslim world, from Morocco to India (Slavs and Tatars, 2012). In Germany between 1924 and 1933, the *Arbeiter-Illustrierte-Zeitung* ("Workers' Illustrated Paper") pursued a pro-Communist and anti-Fascist policy which led to its being driven out of Germany after the Nazi seizure of power, continuing in exile in Czechoslovakia and France before it finally ceased publication in 1938. One of the most prominent features of the paper was its use of illustrations by John Heartfield (1891–1968), who together with another superb visual satirist, George Grosz (1893–1959), developed the use of photomontage for satirical purposes in 1920. Some of Heartfield's photomontages are extremely detailed, but others have a stunning simplicity, such as his 1934 version of the Nazi swastika created from four axes dripping blood, with a caption associating Nazism with nineteenth-century German militarism by referring to a famous comment by Bismarck about "Blood and Iron". A long-lasting British publication has been *Private Eye* (1961 to date), which combines straightforward investigative journalism with satirical text and cartoons. The most famous recent illustrated satirical periodical is unquestionably the French *Charlie Hebdo* (founded 1970), whose constant pushing of the boundaries of what is or is not permissible to satirists will be discussed in our concluding chapter.

By the end of the nineteenth century, it had become possible to create pictures which moved. While a detailed discussion of film and television satire is beyond the limits of this book, some points can be made regarding what they suggest about the nature of visual satire and its relationship to texts. There is a very wide spectrum. At one end, we may place silent films like Fritz Lang's *Metropolis* (1927) or Charlie Chaplin's *Modern Times* (1936), in which the visual images of the dehumanising futuristic city or the production line are much more important than the words which appear on the inter-titles. When we finally hear Chaplin's voice towards the end of *Modern Times*, what he gives utterance to is a nonsense song. At the other end of the spectrum might be television programmes like *The Colbert Show* (2005–2014) in the United States of America or Britain's *Have I got News for You* (1990 to date) and *Mock the Week* (2005 to date), in which the satire of current events is predominantly verbal. The animated cartoon opens up alternative possibilities, and something like the film version of George Orwell's *Animal Farm* (1954; dir. John Halas and Joy Batchelor) could hardly have been made in any other way at the time, even though the development of computer-generated imagery made possible a later, and perhaps less successful, live-action adaptation (1999; dir. John Stephenson). On the other hand, the satire of American middle-class life in the cartoon series *Family Guy* (Seth MacFarlane, 1999 to date) is driven much more by what the characters say than by their appearance. The running joke that Brian the talking dog is by far the most intelligent member of the family could probably have been conveyed just as well by using CGI in a live-action format, although Stewie the psychotic baby with his fantasies of world domination might have been more difficult. *The Boondocks* (Aaron McGruder, 2005–2014) is much more acerbic than *Family Guy* in its approach to the continuing effects of racial issues on the lives of African-Americans who appear to have made it in material terms. The cartoon format allows for the inclusion of some fantasy elements, and characters like the rap star Thugnificent and the Uncle Tom figure, Uncle Ruckus, are to some extent visually exaggerated caricatures, but the satire is largely driven by the sharp comments of the young Freeman brothers, Huey and Riley, on the world around them, and not by the visual elements. *The Simpsons* (Matt Groening, 1989 to date) features numerous examples of both visual and verbal satire. The former include Blinky the three-eyed fish who is a result of radioactive pollution from Springfield's nuclear power plant, while a good example of the latter is the satire of conspicuous consumption in Mr. Burns's song "See my vest, made from real gorilla chest". This is given further layers of meaning by the fact that it is a parody of "Be our Guest" from the animated Disney version of *Beauty and the Beast* (1991), while the episode in which it appears is a parody of Disney's *One Hundred and One Dalmatians* (1961). A more direct connection to older traditions of visual satire can be seen in the British television show *Spitting Image* (created by Peter Fluck, Roger Law and Martin Lambie-Nairn, 1984–1996), in which politicians, members of the royal family and other well-known contemporaries appear as caricatured puppets of themselves. *Spitting Image* was adapted for the American market in 1986 with only moderate success, and has inspired similar programmes in many other countries, such as *Les Guignols de l'info* in France (Alain de Greef, 1988 to date), *The XYZ Show* in Kenya (Godfrey Mwampembwa, pen name Gado, 2008 to date) and *ZANEWS* in South Africa (Jonathan Shapiro and Thierry Cassuto, 2008 to date). The concept of the satirical puppet show was revived for British television with *Newzoids* (Citrus Television) in

2015. In the internet age, the true heirs of Hogarth are perhaps the creators of YouTube clips, in which anyone with editing skills can produce a combination of sounds and images which will create a satirical or simply mocking effect which viewers all over the world can absorb in under five minutes.

The question of immediacy of impact in visual satire is one which requires careful consideration. The history of the political cartoon is full of examples of visual shorthand which have their origin in the art of caricature. As Low (1942, 9–10) points out, the term caricature originally referred specifically to "trick likenesses" in which human subjects were drawn as something quite different, such as an old boot or a chair. While Hogarth did produce one caricature of a musician drawn as a musical note, he rightly insisted that this was not what his art as a whole was about. The term cartoon originally referred to rough sketches for designs to be worked up in another medium, such as tapestry or fresco, and only acquired its modern meaning when in 1843 John Leech (1817–1864) drew a series of satires which caricatured an exhibition of cartoons for frescoes in the new Houses of Parliament in London (Low, 1942, 18). While many nineteenth- and early twentieth-century cartoons used extremely naturalistic drawing, artists found the exaggerations essential to caricature a useful technique. The prominent nose and lanky frame of the British politician William Pitt the Younger (1759–1806, prime minister 1783–1801, 1804–1806) were exaggerated to serve as an easy means of identification, in the same way that cartoonists in the 1960s treated the noticeable height of French president Charles de Gaulle, and contemporary cartoonists often give Syria's president Bashar al-Assad a giraffe-like neck. However, when Gillray consistently portrayed Charles James Fox (1749–1806), the leading opposition politician in Pitt the Younger's time, with a heavy five o'clock shadow, it was more than a mark of identification, as it also helped to suggest that Fox was an untrustworthy villain as well as a dangerous radical. The five o'clock shadow was used to similar effect in the cartoons of US president Richard Nixon by Herblock (pen name of Herbert Lawrence Block, 1909–2001). In the later nineteenth century, Harry Furniss (1854–1925) exaggerated the fondness for high collars of the British prime minister William Gladstone (1809–1898, in office four times between 1868 and 1894), and more recent cartoonists have seized on the personal characteristics of politicians in the same way, such as the hairstyles of Ronald Reagan or Boris Johnson, or the grins of Jimmy Carter or Tony Blair. Cartoonists sometimes give their subjects props: Steve Bell's cartoons of John Major are by no means photo-realistic likenesses, but Major is instantly recognisable, not only by the heavy glasses which he did wear, but by the fact that Bell always drew him with his underpants outside his trousers. This portrayed Major as a somewhat shabbier version of Vicky's Supermac (see below); it was only in retrospect, several years after Major had ceased to be prime minister, that the image acquired an additional resonance when it was revealed that he had had an affair with a fellow Conservative politician, Edwina Currie (Bell, 2002). The showerhead in Zapiro's cartoons of South African president Jacob Zuma (Chapter 1) functions in a similar way.

Nevertheless, much of what we might class as visual satire is neither direct nor immediate in its effect, in the sense that the viewer can derive an immediate understanding from the visual elements alone. Many late eighteenth- or early nineteenth-century satirical prints included captions or speech bubbles consisting of sometimes lengthy quotations from literary texts such as Shakespeare or Milton. The viewer needed to be aware of the original context of the quotations, and to spend time considering how these were being applied to the contemporary figures illustrated in the prints (Taylor, 2012). A similar strategy can be seen in the cartoons which George Stronach (d. 1915) directed against Gladstone. A typical example shows Gladstone standing in an outdoor setting, with his hands crossed over his chest and his face turned slightly upwards with the eyes closed. If we have seen contemporary photographs of Gladstone, we can recognise the drawing as a reasonable likeness, but it is not at first obvious how to interpret it. Like many of Stronach's other cartoons, however, this is surrounded by a collection of quotations, from Shakespeare's *Winter's Tale* and *Coriolanus*, from Coleridge, from Samuel Butler's *Hudibras* and, in larger type than the rest, from Robert Burns's *Holy Willie's Prayer*. Only through reading these, and indeed only by being familiar with the whole of Burns's poem and not simply the few lines quoted, can we fully appreciate that, just as Burns portrayed Holy Willie as a hypocrite, the expression which Stronach has given William Gladstone is meant to be interpreted as one of sanctimonious humbug (Stronach, c. 1883).

Much nineteenth-century social satire, such as the *Punch* cartoons of George du Maurier (1834–1896), took the form of what Low described as the illustrated joke: the detailed and highly naturalistic drawing of a particular setting was in effect secondary to the text beneath, which often took the form of a brief exchange between two of the characters portrayed or a comment by only one of them. The most famous example is probably du Maurier's 1895 cartoon of a scene at an elaborately laden upper-class breakfast table, captioned "True Humility". Only when we read the dialogue underneath can we get the point:

Bishop: "I'm afraid you've got a bad egg, Mr. Jones."
Curate: "Oh, no, my Lord, I assure you that parts of it are excellent!"

Low saw a return in the twentieth century to what he called "the pure visual humour of character or situation which needs no words" (Low, 1942, 28, 48). Nevertheless, many modern political cartoons depend on the interplay between image and caption.

Indeed, it is questionable whether "pure visual humour … which needs no words" is actually possible. Some visual images need to be conceptualised as words, even words in a particular language, to make their point. When John Stuart, third Earl of Bute, was Britain's prime minister in 1762–1763, cartoonists often represented him by a drawing of a boot, a ploy which works only if the viewer is familiar with what the object is called in English. Just as literary satires can be interpreted in different ways, sometimes being read in a manner directly opposite to the intentions of their creators, so too can images. Holbein's Dance of Death engravings, for example, were recycled in different publications surrounded by different texts, so that different editions appealed to Protestant or Catholic purchasers even though there was no change in the pictures themselves (Davis, 1956). While John Major's image has perhaps never recovered from Bell's cartoons of him, these were based on the Supermac character created by the Berlin-born British cartoonist Vicky (pen name of Victor Weisz, 1913–1966). Supermac was intended to ridicule the prime minister of the day, Harold Macmillan (1894–1986, in office 1957–1963), and was based on the Superman of the comic books, though Vicky's character did not have his underpants on the outside, and was modestly attired in opaque tights. Nevertheless, in some quarters Supermac was seen in a positive light, and probably did Macmillan's reputation more good than harm (Benson, 2007, 142; Navasky, 2014, 120–122). An obvious recent case is that of the notorious cartoons first published in the Danish newspaper *Jyllands-Posten* in 2005 (Navasky, 2014, 180–185). Whether an image of a bearded man with a bomb in his turban is a satire on religious extremism or a blasphemous attack on the Prophet Muhammad is a question which is clearly never going to receive an answer universally agreed upon, although the link between radical Islam and terrorism is an essential element of the image's satirical intent.

Technical change continues to affect how we produce, exchange and consume images. Even in the early 1970s, Mayor claimed that "printed pictures, deaf to language, have gradually made Europe and then the Americas, Australia, and Japan into one condominium of the eye", suggesting that our experience of seeing was being globalised. More recently, the Chinese artist Xu Bing (b. 1955) has endeavoured to persuade us to reconsider how we think of language and its relationship to how it is expressed in visual terms. His *Book from the Sky* (1987–1991) consisted of several thousands of what appeared to be Chinese characters, but which were in fact meaningless inventions of his own. One aspect of this project was that it functions as a satire of the official attempts at the manipulation and control of language and expression in China, which included the introduction of a simplified form of the traditional Chinese script from the 1950s onwards. While this facilitated the spread of literacy, it also helped the communist government's control of how China's past was perceived by its citizens, as it was difficult for those educated using the new system to read texts printed before the establishment of the People's Republic in 1949. Xu Bing's *Book from the Ground*, on the other hand, used images based on emoticons and the kind of symbols we have become accustomed to seeing in airports or railway stations to indicate the whereabouts of toilets and emergency exits. Part of this is *Book from the Ground: From Point to Point*. Published in book form, this consists of 112 pages written, if that is the appropriate word, entirely in such symbols. If *Book from the Sky* was a book which nobody could read, Xu Bing claims, then *Book from the Ground* is a book which anybody can read, no matter what their native language might be. Xu Bing and his critics see it as an attempt to create a universal means of communication, independent of language as it is usually understood, and they recognise that this is an aspiration which can be traced back to earlier thinkers such as the German philosopher Gottfried Wilhelm Leibniz (1646–1716) (Xu Bing, 2013; Borysevicz, n.d.) *Book from the Ground: From Point to Point* can indeed be read as an account of a typical 24-hour period in the life of a modern office worker, something which will be very similar whether the setting is Shanghai, Paris or New York. Whether it is a satire on the banality of that existence is something which will be interpreted differently by different readers. The same is true of Xu Bing's claim that "A Universal language that surpasses the limitation of the written word has been born!" and that "this icon language is actually very effective for expressing feeling, action, and imagination" (Borysevicz, 142, 140). Those who remember how Leibnitz's contemporary Jonathan Swift satirised the idea of a universal language of signs in his account of the Academy of Lagado in *Gulliver's Travels* (1726) may wonder if we should not read *Book from the Ground: From Point to Point* as a satire of its own limitations, as well as of those of "the global village that we all inhabit with its attendant language of modern hieroglyphics" (Borysevicz, 23). The symbols will indeed for the most part be familiar to or, in the case of those Xu has devised himself, easily understood by those accustomed to international travel and life in post-industrial cities, but it has to be said that this does not include the entire human race, or at least not yet. Borysevicz compares Xu Bing's work with James Joyce's *Ulysses* and the incomprehension which greeted that text on its first appearance, but whether *Book from the Ground* suggests the future of satire, or of literature more generally, or whether it represents a return to both the potential and the limitations of the art of our cave-dwelling ancestors, are perhaps questions to which it is too early to give an answer.

9

CONCLUSION

Inevitably, this book has not been able to survey every work of satire ever produced, and has only been able to give a sketch of some major themes and developments. It is clear, nevertheless, that satire includes much more than traditional definitions which restricted it to work in a specific literary form imposed by a prevailing cultural system, whether that might have been verse in Latin hexameters or English heroic couplets. While the work of satirists who chose to adhere to such traditions has historically been of great importance, we have looked at satires in a wide range of literary styles, including, but not limited to, fables, epigrams, parodies of church hymns, plays, accounts of imaginary voyages, utopias and science fiction narratives. We have also considered proverbs and popular songs, as well as many different aspects of satire in visual form, from cave paintings to newspaper cartoons, television comedy and YouTube clips. The question then arises of whether we are any closer to a definition of satire than we were at the beginning. What, if anything, do these very different forms have in common?

One of the most obvious features of satire is that it needs to satirise something, or, in other words, it is necessary for it to have a target, for it to be directed against something, whether that be as broad as the human condition or human folly generally, or, more narrowly, particular manifestations of this, or even particular individuals. If we accept this, the next question which arises would appear to be how satire differs from other literary genres such as novels which treat of social issues, what are sometimes referred to as thesis novels. Examples of the latter might include Charles Dickens, *Hard Times* (1854), and Elizabeth Gaskell, *North and South* (1855), which both consider, among other topics, the hardships suffered by factory workers and their families during Britain's Industrial Revolution. By calling attention to social issues, these texts suggest that something ought to be done about them, rather like the way in which satirists, at least some of the time, claim to be aiming to bring about moral reform or social change. Neither of these novels are what most people would think of as satire, however, though there are revealing differences between them. Gaskell writes entirely in a style we associate with nineteenth-century realistic fiction. Dickens, on the other hand, does include some elements of fantasy, exaggeration and distortion which many readers might consider to be satirical touches, though these are only parts of the narrative as a whole. They include the repeated references to the streams of smoke coming from the factory chimneys as serpents, and to the steam engines which power the factory machinery as melancholy elephants. Dickens's frequent use of facetiously coined names for his characters is well known; in *Hard Times*, his view of the widespread obsession with educating children in a manner which would be based on verifiable and quantifiable facts to the exclusion of all else, is shown by his associating it with the characters Mr. Gradgrind and Mr. M'Choakumchild. It is further exemplified in the passage where Mr. Gradgrind expresses his indignation at discovering "Girl number twenty unable to define a horse! [...] Girl number twenty possessed of no facts, in reference to one of the commonest of animals!" While she may be "unable to define a horse," Sissy, the girl in question, belongs to the circus and knows a great deal more about horses than Mr. Gradgrind does. Dickens's characterisation is sometimes laid on with a broad brush, and in *Hard Times*, Mr. Sleary, the owner of the circus, is given an exaggerated lisp, though he also delivers an important aspect of Dickens's message in his "People must be amuthed, Thquire, thomehow" (Dickens, 2003, 11, 45). By contrast, Dickens's sympathetic treatment of the story of Stephen Blackpool, a weaver trapped in a loveless marriage to an alcoholic and fired from his factory job and ostracised because of his refusal to join a union, is carried out in a largely realistic style: the author's treatment of Stephen's Northern dialect may not be entirely convincing, but does not appear to be intended as comic or mocking.

If we see elements of satire in *Hard Times* when we do not in *North and South*, it would appear that satire is a matter of technique, of something akin to what Freud called the "joke-work" (above, Chapter 1). Something needs to be done to an idea to make it into satire. If the Earl of Rochester felt that King Charles II was an oversexed layabout, this was no more than an opinion; it was when he developed the idea into a poem of more than thirty lines in rhyming couplets that it became satire (Chapter 4). As we have seen in earlier examples, a work of satire does not have to be of great length. Rochester also seems to have felt the king was untrustworthy, an idea he turned into an epigram:

> God bless our good and gracious King,
> Whose promise none relies on,
> Who never said a foolish thing,
> Nor ever did a wise one.

(Ellis, 1994, 197).

It is more than a matter of adopting a particular literary form, however; there are plenty of well-crafted poems or novels which are not satirical by any stretch of the imagination. The example of *Hard Times*, and many of the satires we have examined earlier in this book, suggest that satire in literary forms very often makes use of elements of fantasy, exaggeration and distortion. To these we may add selection: satirists often sharpen their material by focusing only on particular aspects of a subject. In this there is a strong resemblance to caricature in the visual arts, which is itself often used for satirical ends (Chapter 8). In his preface to *The Battle of the Books* (1704), a satire on a literary controversy of the 1690s, Swift claimed that "Satire is a sort of glass, wherein beholders do generally discover everybody's face but their own; which is the chief reason for that kind of reception it meets in the world, and that so very few are offended with it" (Swift, 1999, 104). If satire is a mirror held up to society, we need to remember that the mirror image is not a direct copy of its original, since it reverses left and right. We may wonder if satire is not in fact more akin to the kind of distorting mirror traditional in fun-fairs and carnival sideshows, in that it presents a partial or warped view of reality, but at the same time we may also feel that this can sometimes reveal a sort of higher truth.

Parody and allusion, particularly incongruous allusion, are additional weapons in the satirist's armoury. One aspect of Rochester's short epigram on the king is that it is composed in a stanza form associated with the English metrical version of the Psalms by Thomas Sternhold (d. 1549) and John Hopkins (d. 1570). This was long used in the services of the Church of England, but it was regarded by Restoration wits as a choice example of bad poetry and was mocked elsewhere by Rochester (Ellis, 1994, 18, 317, 398). One effect of Rochester's use of parody here is to add the suggestion that the belief in the Divine Right of Kings, that monarchs were in some way specially endowed with God's blessing, which was still commonly accepted in Charles II's time, was as ridiculous as Sternhold and Hopkins's versification.

Does satire need to be funny? In a phrase much quoted by later writers of satire, Horace asked, "Ridentem dicere verum / quid vetat?" ("What forbids a laughing man to speak the truth?") It is clear from the context, however, that Horace thought of humour as a means to an end, since he continued, "ut pueris olim dant crustula blandi / doctores, elementa velint ut discere prima" ("as sometimes kind teachers give little pastries to boys, that they may want to learn the rudiments of grammar", *Satires*, I, i, 24–6). Humour is a means by which the satirist gently leads readers towards sharing his point of view. The view of Horace's satire as mild and gentle has often been accepted, with Byron, for example, writing in 1818 of Horace's piercing the conscience, "Awakening without wounding the touch'd heart" (*Childe Harold's Pilgrimage*, IV, 77; McGann, 2008, 170). Another phrase frequently quoted, however, was Juvenal's "facit indignatio versum" (*Satires*, I, 79), which claimed that, in view of what the poet, or the authorial persona he chose to adopt, saw around him in Roman society, his rage would oblige him to write verses in response. Any humour in a work such as Juvenal's *Sixth Satire* (Chapter 7), or Linton Kwesi Johnson's *Liesense fi Kill* (Chapter 4), is of a decidedly grim kind, but their use of other aspects of satirical technique is apparent.

In the aftermath of China's *People's Daily* taking at face value the announcement by the US satirical website The Onion that the

North Korean leader Kim Jong-un had been named as "Sexiest Man Alive for the year 2012" (see Chapter 1), an anonymous Twitter user alleged that China had "been fooled by the 'mysterious Western art of satire'" (CNN, 2012). While some particular types of satire may be specifically Western, however, and this book has largely focused on these, it is easy to find examples which demonstrate that satire can be found in different languages and cultures around the world. As well as those mentioned in earlier chapters, we may note a text such as Yan Lianke's novel *Serve the People!* which was first published in excerpts in a Chinese literary magazine in 2005. Subsequently banned in China, it has appeared in translation in several Western languages. Yan satirises China's Cultural Revolution (1966–76) in an extravagantly comic tale of official corruption and hypocrisy, in which a naïve peasant soldier is persuaded that he can best fulfil the command of Chairman Mao Zedong's revolutionary slogan, "Serve the People!", by providing sexual services for the bored wife of his commanding officer (Yan, 2007). It might be suggested that Chinese literature has been influenced by Western models since the late nineteenth century, but it is possible to cite earlier examples which show satire in Chinese developing from indigenous traditions with no discernible foreign influence. Even earlier than Li Ruzhen's *Flowers in the Mirror* (above, Chapter 1), is the novel known in English as *The Scholars*, written by Wu Jingzi (1701–54), which satirises scholars and government officials who fail to live up to the Confucian ideals to which they pay lip-service (Wu, 1957). We may also mention *xiangsheng*, usually called crosstalk in English, which is a Chinese form of stand-up comedy which relies to a significant extent on social and political satire. This is certainly an indigenous form, and can be traced back to at least the mid-nineteenth century.

There is a long tradition of verbal satire in Arabic dating back to the earliest years of Islam. Satirical newspapers and political cartoons have been a feature of life in the Arab world since the nineteenth century (Kishtainy, 1985). In more recent years, the work of cartoonists such as the Syrian Ali Farzat (علي فرزات, b. 1951) has drawn international attention (Stelfox, 2013), and the online circulation of cartoons by both well-known and anonymous artists has been an important channel for the expression of politically dissident or secularist views in the Arab world.

The Onion story does provide a useful demonstration that satire is often in the eye of the beholder. Another excellent example is the Canadian short film, *The McPassion* (2006), written by Rik Swartzwelder and directed by Benjamin Hershleder. This invites the viewer to contemplate what might happen when "The greatest story ever told, and a fast food giant, unite to deliver the tie-in of tie-ins". A mother asks her children, "Hey, kids! Who wants a McPassion meal?" The positive response leads to the following exchange against a background of appropriate quick cut visuals:

Voice-over: Every McPassion meal comes with a crown of thorns!
Mom: Non-toxic!
Voice-over: And special round fries, shaped just like the Eucharist.
Girl: Dipping the Body of Christ in ketchup is fun!
Boy: Just like real blood!
Voice-over: And the delicious vinegar sponge drink.
Girl: Mmmmm!

The quick-fire jokes continue for approximately four minutes, with repeated verbal and visual references to both the biblical narrative of the death of Jesus and to aspects of Christian practice. When the voice-over announces that "there's toys with every meal", a girl announces that these include "Rub-on tattoos" as she excitedly displays cruciform stigmata on her hands. The voice-over assures us, "Comes off with soap and water", while the girl's mother adds "Or the included Shroud of Turin moist towelette!" A small girl flogs a small boy with the "Authentic, simulated leather, cat-o'-nine-tails" which is another of the giveaway toys, as an adult male leans into shot and assures us "It's safe!" The small boy uses the "cool McPassion hammer" to pretend he is nailing the small girl to the "Kid's-size crucifix" as he announces with glee, "It clinks when you hit it!" Towards the end, the voice-over urges us to "Buy one [a McPassion meal] today – make Jesus happy!" This is followed by a choir singing "Hallelujah – God's lovin' it" in a parody of the "I'm lovin' it" slogan launched in 2003 by the international fast-food chain McDonald's, while the screen shows the McDonald's logo of the Golden Arches with a small cross added to the top of one of the arches. This adaptation of the logo appears several times in the film, and gives a degree of irony to the statement in the copyright notice and disclaimer at the very end of *The McPassion*, which assures the viewer that "Any similarity to actual persons (living or dead) or food products, is purely coincidental" (Swartzwelder and Hershleder, 2006). Many people who saw *The McPassion* soon after it was released thought it was blasphemous, and even non-believers might feel that the humour is, at the very least, in poor taste, and clearly intended to mock Christian belief. In fact, Swartzwelder identifies himself as a Christian, and has explained in an interview that he intended *The McPassion* as a satirical criticism of the way in which Mel Gibson's film *The Passion of the Christ* (2004) was being heavily marketed through endorsements from church pulpits (Moring, 2006).

The most dramatic recent example of one person's satire being another person's blasphemy is the French satirical newspaper *Charlie Hebdo*, which has continued to publish in the same manner in spite of the murder of several of its staff in 2015 (Chapter 1). *Charlie Hebdo* has repeatedly been accused of Islamophobia, but a look at a sample such as the content of the issue published to mark the anniversary of the 2015 attack (No. 1224, 6 January 2016) shows a more complex picture. The paper is part of a long-standing French tradition of militant secularism, and regards the law of 1905, which brought about the separation of church and state in France in a manner much more detailed and far-reaching than the similar constitutional separation in the United States of America, as a cornerstone of the modern French republic and its ideals of liberty, equality and fraternity. The paper claims a right to be offensive, and illustrated an article on the continuing existence of laws against blasphemy in many different countries with cartoons mocking Hinduism, Buddhism, Catholicism, Judaism and Thailand's reverence for its monarchy (No. 1224, 6 January 2016, pp. 26–7).

Terms such as "blasphemy" and "sacrilege" are generally used with reference to religious belief, and may refer to many different sorts of behaviour, from deliberate mockery and insult of beliefs dear to others, to a simple failure to share them. A 1952 opinion in a censorship case before the United States Supreme Court by Justice Felix Frankfurter noted that there were so many different definitions of the terms that no legal conclusions could be drawn from them, and his "reasoned approach to the topic, outlining the utter subjectivity of charges of blasphemy and sacrilege, helped make this one of the final court cases in the United States dealing with such issues" (Plate, 2006, 33). There is also the point that, where blasphemy laws exist in a country, they only protect that country's dominant religion. In English common law, for example, the offence of blasphemy was considered to relate solely to material or behaviour offensive to the Church of England, and not to Christian belief generally, or to non-Christian religions. After a well-publicised case in 1977, questions were raised about whether this was fair or reasonable in a British society which was increasingly composed of citizens who followed many differing religious beliefs or none at all. After the controversy which followed the publication in 1988 of Salman Rushdie's novel *The Satanic Verses*, which was viewed by many as a blasphemous attack on Islam, there were suggestions that the law should be extended to criminalise blasphemy against all religions, although this might very well have been impossible to administer in practice. In fact, the law was simply abolished in 2008 (Warburton, 2009, 42–55). Furthermore, in at least some Western countries, the concept of blasphemy has arguably been extended to cover offences to beliefs of a secular nature, such as that in the sanctity of the United States flag (Plate, 2006, 162–9).

Charlie Hebdo not only insults all religions with equal enthusiasm, but also violates what many might consider to be acceptable standards in other areas, by, for example, publishing cartoons which appear to mock the victims of plane crashes or natural disasters. The paper has been on the receiving end of law suits and strong criticism even in France, and in many other Western countries some of its material would be widely considered to be grossly offensive. To give only one example, the anniversary issue included a cartoon headlined "Et vous, que faisiez-vous le 07 janvier?" ("And you, what were you doing the 7th of January?", i.e., the date of the 2015 attack on the paper's offices). This showed a number of representatives of things the paper opposes, such as political repression, so that Kim Jong-un appeared killing those who had fallen out of favour with him, and Bashar al-Assad in the act of torturing a critic. The cartoon also included an explicit image of a priest sodomising a choirboy. While this was labelled "prêtre pédophile" ("paedophile priest"), the fact that the priest was wearing a pectoral cross and a bishop's mitre, which are traditional emblems of ecclesiastical authority, and was dressed in white robes echoing those of the image of Pope Francis in a corner of the same cartoon, makes it appear that the cartoon is suggesting that the sexual abuse of children was a crime of the Catholic Church as a whole, rather than of individual clergy. A further twist was added by the positioning next to the "priest" of an image of US President George W. Bush writing his memoirs: these are given the title "Les Memoirs d'un Âne" ("Memoirs of a Donkey") and the president is shown wearing a dunce's cap with two points instead of the usual one, so that it looks like the mitre, which in turn, appears to be being equated with the fool's cap. It is not the priest but the choirboy who is speaking, and he says ""Moi, je faisais cours pratique de caté. Thème du jour, l'Ascension du petit Jésus" ("As for me, I was doing a practical catechism course. Theme for the day, the Ascension of the Baby Jesus"). In the context, "the Ascension of the Baby Jesus" appears to refer to the priest's erection, which is unambiguously shown (*Charlie Hebdo*, No. 1224, 6 January 2016, pp. 28-9).

In the immediate aftermath of the 2015 killings, there were widespread expressions of solidarity with *Charlie Hebdo*, and the slogan "Je suis Charlie" was displayed around the world in many different contexts, including people's Facebook pages. Millions of people joined solidarity marches in Paris and other French cities, as well as in other countries. Many noted that the situation had produced some very strange bedfellows, and that some of the world leaders and official representatives who claimed to be in support of freedom of expression came from countries with dubious records in this area. Perhaps the most extreme example of this was Saudi Arabia, which in the same week that it condemned the attack on *Charlie Hebdo* as a "cowardly terrorist act" which was "incompatible with Islam", carried out the public flogging of Raif Badawi, a Saudi blogger who had ventured to criticise his country's theocratic social policies (Wright, 2015; Henningsen, 2015). In the aftermath of the marches, *Charlie Hebdo* brought out its first issue since the attack (No. 1178, 14 January 1178). This included a cartoon of figures representing Judaism, Islam, Catholicism and Orthodox Christianity, all wearing clothes with the "Je suis Charlie" slogan, and simply captioned "Nouveaux amis" ("New friends"). An article by Solène Chalvon noted various responses to the attack from around the world, including a column in the *Financial Times* by Tony Barber which had accused *Charlie Hebdo* of "editorial foolishness" and of having "just been stupid" in provoking Muslims. The conservative American website Breitbart referred to this as "victim blaming on steroids", and the comments were swiftly edited out of the version of Barber's column which remains on the *Financial Times* website (Smith, 2015). Chalvon's piece translated "editorial foolishness" as "l'irresponsabilité éditoriale", and this issue of *Charlie Hebdo* proudly added "Journal irresponsable" under its name on the front cover. This also showed a full-page cartoon of a bearded man in a turban holding up the "Je suis Charlie" slogan. This was widely interpreted as a representation of the Prophet Mohammad, and, as such, deeply offensive to many Muslims. The caption "Tout est pardonné" ("All is forgiven") left it unclear whether the paper was forgiving the Prophet, or representing the Prophet as forgiving the paper. An editorial by Gérard Biard expressly distanced the paper from its "new friends" and insisted it had no time for those who offered qualified support of the "yes, but ..." kind. "Laïcité" was an absolute value which could not be compromised. He said that what had made him and his staff laugh the most, was that the bells of the Catholic cathedral of Notre Dame de Paris had been rung in honour of them and their murdered colleagues, and he ended the editorial with what he called a message for Pope Francis. The staff of *Charlie Hebdo* would not accept the bells of Notre Dame being rung in their honour until they were being rung by the members of Femen, a controversial radical feminist group.

   Charlie Hebdo's stance is clear: that there should be no limits to freedom of expression, and that no subject should be off-limits to the satirist. If freedom of expression is completely unqualified, however, on what basis do we prevent some people from calling for the death of those they see as blasphemers? In practice, many people are prepared to concede that even in societies which consider themselves to be liberal and democratic, the right to free speech cannot be absolute, and that there ought to be restrictions on such things as libel, or hate speech, or incitements to criminal activity. Just where the boundaries should be drawn, however, and how exactly something like hate speech is to be defined, are things which are likely to provoke fierce debate (Warburton, 2009) and these are issues which are beyond the scope of this book. What the *Charlie Hebdo* case does suggest, however, is that satire often depends on norms which are shared between satirists and their expected audiences. It seems a reasonable assumption that most readers of *Charlie Hebdo* will be people who are already at least broadly sympathetic to its outlook, and who will not be particularly offended by something like the statement which appeared in large block capitals in the anniversary issue: "Dieu n'existe pas: Il ne s'est pas abonné à « Charlie »" ("God does not exist: He hasn't subscribed to *Charlie*"). Similarly, the writers in the long history of misogynistic satire could safely assume that most of their readers would share their views, particularly if literacy, or literacy in a learned language, depended on gendered educational systems which thereby ensured that their audience was predominantly male. If different types of satire in effect choose their own audiences, this would seem to be equally the case with radical as with conservative satires. A work like Linton Kwesi Johnson's *Liesense fi Kill* will have appealed mainly to those for whom the unexplained deaths of black people in police custody was already a serious issue. It is clear from the text that Johnson was not addressing police officers.

If satire is often a case of preaching to the converted, does it make a difference? As the example of *Charlie Hebdo* shows, it can certainly make a difference to the satirist if a target feels provoked to a violent response. There is a long history of this: the Roman historian Dio Cassius (c. 155–235 CE) claimed that Caracalla (Roman Emperor 198–217 CE) had had large numbers of the inhabitants of Alexandria massacred because he had heard that they had mocked him (Dio, *Roman History*, LXXVIII, 22). In modern times, satirists have often had their work banned or been subjected to violent reprisals: while the cartoonist Ali Farzat has won many international awards, he has also had his work banned in several countries and had to leave his native Syria after he was savagely beaten up in 2011 by supporters of President Bashar al-Assad, apparently as a direct result of his portrayals of the president. The example of Lycambes (Chapter 1) suggests that satire may indeed sometimes have a direct effect on its target. More often, however, satire seems to be rather like the Roman Saturnalia or the Christmas celebrations of the enslaved in the eighteenth-century Caribbean: after a few days when the world was turned upside down and servants were permitted to mock their masters, the status quo was restored in the same manner as it was at the end of the cawdies' dinner in Smollett's *Humphry Clinker* (Chapter 5). Satire, like humour more generally, can function as a safety valve, allowing dissatisfaction with an existing state of affairs to dissipate itself harmlessly. Repressive regimes are sometimes surprisingly tolerant of satire: the Russian magazine *Krokodil*, which was founded in 1922, was published regularly for the rest of the existence of the Soviet Union, and often lampooned aspects of the Soviet system.

An instructive example is the British magazine *Private Eye*, established in 1961, which, as we saw earlier, combines political and social satire with straightforward investigative journalism, often reporting on stories other periodicals are reluctant to touch. One result is that the magazine is frequently sued for libel, and, on the occasion of *Private Eye*'s fiftieth anniversary, the far-left newspaper *Socialist Worker* praised the fact that "Its mix of humour and investigation has tirelessly challenged the hypocrisy of the elite" and noted its commercial success and position as "a key institution in the media." The same article also noted that *Private Eye* had "serious weaknesses", including "a nasty streak of snobbery and prejudice", and summed up by calling it "the anti-establishment journal of the establishment" (Ward, 2011). *Private Eye* mocked itself with a fiftieth anniversary issue (No. 1300, 28 October 2011) with a front cover headlined "How Satire Makes A Difference". This showed a photograph of Harold Macmillan above the date 1961 and the caption, "Magazine pokes fun at Old Etonian Prime Minister surrounded by cronies making a hash of running the country." Next to this was a photograph of David Cameron above the date 2011. The caption to this read simply "Er ...", suggesting that very little had in fact changed in British politics, since, as readers could be expected to know, Cameron had gone to the same famous public (in British terms, private and fee-paying) school, as had several other members of his government, and his management of the country was not meeting with universal approval.

In other words, *Private Eye*'s half a century of mocking the rich and powerful had actually made little difference. In spite of the libel suits, *Private Eye* may remind us of Swift's remark about satire and how "so very few" are actually offended by it. If at some point in history radical change does occur after we can observe the presence of considerable satirical activity, we should perhaps be cautious about making a direct connection. Whether the satire has helped to effect the change, or is merely a reflection of other things such as broader social and economic developments which are the real agents of change, is likely to be always a matter for debate. Examples of satire as a conservative force, such as misogynistic satires which assume an acceptance of a patriarchy, appear to be much more common. Perhaps the last word can be left to Michael Flanders's comment in *At the Drop of Another Hat* (1963): "The purpose of satire, it has been rightly said, is to strip off the veneer of comforting illusion and cosy half-truth, and our job, as I see it, is to put it back again" (Flanders and Swan, 1991). In the early 1960s, as Harold Macmillan's "Winds of Change" speech signalled the rapid abandonment of most of what was left of the British Empire, and at a time when the satirical television programme *That Was The Week That Was* (aired on the BBC in 1962 and 1963) offered a much more provocative view of contemporary politics and events, Flanders and Swan's reinvention of satire as cosy domesticity, something which dealt with householders' concerns about tradesmen and status symbols and new fashions in garden furniture, proved enormously popular with middle-class audiences in live performances and on audio recordings. The Suez Crisis of 1956, which finally punctured Britain's illusions about still being a world power, could be ignored, and the Egyptian leader Gamal Abdul Nasser appeared only in a fleeting reference to the Aswan Dam project: in the "Hippo Encore", a reprise of their "Hippopotamus Song" from a few years earlier, Flanders and Swan told audiences that the Hippopotamus would "gambol no more on the banks of the Nile / Which Nasser is flooding next spring." While satire does sometimes "strip off the veneer of comforting illusion and cosy half-truth", there are also times when it appears to be doing its best "to put it back again". For many of us, this makes life somewhat easier to bear.

BIBLIOGRAPHY

Agard, John (2000), *Weblines*, Newcastle upon Tyne, Bloodaxe.

Anstey, Christopher (1994), *The New Bath Guide*, ed. Gavin Turner, Bristol, Broadcast Books.

Anstey, F. (1954), *Vice Versa, or, A Lesson to Fathers*, London, John Murray.

Aristophanes (2002), *Lysistrata and Other Plays*, trs. Alan H. Sommerstein, rev. ed., London, Penguin Books.

Athwal, Harmit (2002), "Black Deaths in Custody", Institute of Race Relations website, www.irr.org.uk/news/black-deaths-in-custody/, 11 November 2002, accessed 8 May 2017.

Auden, W. H., ed. (1938), *The Oxford Book of Light Verse*, Oxford, Clarendon Press.

Bahn, Paul, and Paul Pettitt (2009), *Britain's Oldest Art: The Ice Age Cave Art of Cresswell Crags*, Swindon, English Heritage.

Bakhtin, Mikhail (1984), *Rabelais and His World*, trs. Hélène Iswolsky, Bloomington, Indiana University Press.

Balch, David L. (2008), *Roman Domestic Art and Early House Churches*, Tübingen, Mohr Siebeck.

Barber, Richard, trs. (1992), *Bestiary: Being an English Translation of the Bodleian Library, Oxford M. S. Bodley 764 with All the Original Miniatures Reproduced in Facsimile*, London, Folio Society.

Bateson, F. W., ed. (1951), *Alexander Pope: Epistles to Several Persons (Moral Essays)*, London, Methuen; New Haven, Yale University Press (Twickenham Edition of the Poems of Alexander Pope, Volume III, ii).

Baumbach, Manuel (2007), "Lucian in German Nineteenth-Century Scholarship", in Christopher Ligota and Letizia Panizza, ed., *Lucian of Samosata Vivus et Redivivus*, London and Turin: Warburg Institute, Nino Aragno Editore, pp. 191–211.

BBC (2012), "China Paper Carries Onion Kim Jong-un 'heart-throb spoof'", 28 November 2012; www.bbc.co.uk/news/world-asia-20518929, accessed 26 November 2014.

Beard, Mary (2012), *All in a Don's Day*, London, Profile Books.

Bell, Steve (2002), "If only we had known back then," cartoon in *The Guardian*, 1 October, https://web.archive.org/web/20060223223113/www.guardian.co.uk/cartoons/stevebell/0%2CMFEM%2C802577%2C00.html, accessed 10 May 2017.

Bell, Steve (2011), cartoon in *The Guardian*, 21 January, www.theguardian.com/commentisfree/cartoon/2011/jan/21/steve-bell-david-cameron, accessed 25 November 2014.

Bell, Steve (2013), transcript of radio interview with Carol Hills, 31 July 2013, Public Radio International, The World, www.pri.org/stories/2013-07-31/british-cartoonist-steve-bell-draws-american-presidents, accessed 25 November 2014.

Bennett, Billy (1997), *Almost a Gentleman*, audio recordings on CD, London, Topic Records.

Benson, Larry D., ed. (1988), *The Riverside Chaucer*, 3rd ed., Oxford, Oxford University Press.

Benson, Timothy S. (2007), *The Cartoon Century: Modern Britain through the Eyes of Its Cartoonists*, London, Random House Books.

Bindman, David (2004), "Hogarth, William (1697–1764)", *Oxford Dictionary of National Biography*, 2004; online edition, May 2009, accessed 24 July 2015.

Blackman, Malorie (2001), *Noughts & Crosses*, London, Doubleday.

Blair, David (2009), "Zuma Loses His Sense of Humour Over Newspaper Cartoons", *Daily Telegraph*, 21 April.

Blank, Paula (2000), "Character' Analysis: Writing and Identity 1500–1755", *Social Semiotics*, Vol. 10, No. 3, 265–280.

Bohn, Henry G., ed. (1860), *The Epigrams of Martial, Translated Into English Prose, Each Accompanied by One or More Verse Translations, from the Works of the English Poets, and Various Other Sources*, London, Henry G. Bohn.

Borysevicz, Mathieu, ed. (n.d.), *The Book about Xu Bing's Book from the Ground*, North Adams, MA, Massachusetts Museum of Contemporary Art; Cambridge, MA, MIT Press.

Botley, Paul (2014), "Three Very Different Translators: Joseph Scaliger, Isaac Casaubon and Richard Thomson," *Canadian Review of Comparative Literature / Revue Canadienne de Littérature Comparée*, Vol. 41, No. 4 (December), 477–491.

Brodrick, Alan Houghton (1948), *Prehistoric Painting*, London, Avalon Press.

Brown, Thomas (1713), *The Fourth and Last Volume of the Works of Mr. Thomas Brown*, 2nd ed., London, Samuel Briscoe.

Bruce, Susan, ed. (1999), *Three Early Modern Utopias: Thomas More, Utopia; Francis Bacon, New Atlantis; Henry Neville, The Isle of Pines*, Oxford, Oxford University Press (Oxford World's Classics Series).

Buchanan, George (1687), *Georgii Buchanani Scoti Poemata que extant*, Amsterdam, Wetsten.

Bury, Emmanuel, ed. (1995), *La Bruyère: Les Caractères*, Paris, Livre de Poche.

Butt, John, ed. (1953, 1969), *Alexander Pope: Imitations of Horace, with An Epistle to Dr Arbuthnot and The Epilogue to the Satires*, London, Methuen; New Haven, Yale University Press (Twickenham Edition of the Poems of Alexander Pope, Volume IV).

Campbell, Miles Warren (1984), "Aelfgyva: The Mysterious Lady of the Bayeux Tapestry", *Annales de Normandie*, 34e année, no. 2, pp. 127–145.

Canby, Vincent (1970), "Movie Review: Fellini Satyricon", *New York Times*, 12 March 1970, www.nytimes.com/movie/review?res=EE05E7DF173C E765BC4A52DFB566838B669EDE, accessed 23 March 2017.

Carey, C. (1986), "Archilochus and Lycambes", *Classical Quarterly*, Vol. 36 No. 1, 60–67.

Casaubon, Isaac (1592) *Theophrasti Characteres Ethici, sive Descriptiones morum Graecè*, Lyon, François Le Preux.

Casson, Lionel, ed. and trs. (1968), *Selected Satires of Lucian*, New York, W. W. Norton and Co., Inc.

Churchill, Charles (1774), *The Works of C. Churchill*, 5th ed., 4 vols, London, John Churchill.

Cigman, Gloria, ed. (1975), *Geoffrey Chaucer: The Wife of Bath's Prologue and Tale and The Clerk's Prologue and Tale from The Canterbury Tales*, London, University of London Press.

Cissé Niang, Aliou, and Carolyn Osiek, ed. (2012), *Text, Image and Christians in the Graeco-Roman World: A Festschrift in Honor of David Lee Balch*, Eugene, Oregon, Pickwick Publications.

Clark, James M. (1947), Introduction and Notes to Hans Holbein, *The Dance of Death*, London, Phaidon Press.

Clausen, Wendell (1946), "The Beginnings of English Character-Writing in the Early Seventeenth Century", *Philological Quarterly*, Vol. 25, No. 1 (January), 32–45.

Clough, Arthur Hugh (1871), *Poems*, 3rd ed., London, Macmillan.

CNN (2012), "Onion: We Just Fooled the Chinese Government!", http://edition.cnn.com/2012/11/27/world/asia/north-korea-china-onion/, accessed 16 May 2017.

Coffey, Michael (1976), *Roman Satire*, London, Methuen.

Coin People website (2013), thread "1939 Satirical Medal Nothing Much Changes", started 3 January 2013 (with illustrations), at www.coinpeople.com/index.php/topic/33184-1939-satirical-medal-nothing-much-changes/, accessed 24 July 2015.

Considine, John (2004a), 'Healey, John (*b*. in or after 1585?, *d*. in or before 1616)', *Oxford Dictionary of National Biography*, Oxford University Press, 2004; online ed., accessed 18 August 2016.

Considine, John (2004b), 'Overbury, Sir Thomas (*bap*. 1581, *d*. 1613)', *Oxford Dictionary of National Biography*, Oxford University Press, 2004; online ed., accessed 19 August 2016.

Cornford, F. M. (1973), *Microcosmographia Academica, Being a Guide for the Young Academic Politician*, Cambridge, Bowes and Bowes.

Dabydeen, David (1985) *Hogarth's Blacks: Images of Blacks in Eighteenth Century British Art*, Mundelstrup, Denmark, Dangaroo Press.

Darmon, Jean-Charles, and Sabine Gruffat, ed. (2002), *La Fontaine: Fables*, Paris, Librairie Générale Française, Livre de Poche Classique.

Darnton, Robert (1997), *The Forbidden Best-Sellers of Pre-Revolutionary France*, London, Fontana Press.

Daunou, [Pierre-Claude-François], ed. (1825–6), *Oeuvres complètes de Boileau Despréaux*, 4 vols., Paris, P. Dupont.

Davenport, A., ed. (1949), *The Collected Poems of Joseph Hall, Bishop of Exeter and Norwich*, Liverpool, Liverpool University Press.

Davis, Natalie Zemon (1956), "Holbein's Pictures of Death and the Reformation at Lyons", *Studies in the Renaissance*, Vol. 3, 97–130.

de Leon, Rafael (1934), *Ugly Woman*. Audio recording available at https://www.youtube.com/watch?v=3DCL3zGxbnc, accessed 2 January 2016.

de Sola Pinto, Vivian, ed. (1950), *John Skelton: A Selection from His Poems*, London, Sidgwick and Jackson.

Dickens, Charles (2003), ed. Kate Flint, *Hard Times for These Times*, London, Penguin Books.

Diggle, James, ed. (2004), *Theophrastus: Characters*, Cambridge, Cambridge University Press.

Dorment, Richard (2014), "Balancing the Brilliant and the Botched", *Daily Telegraph*, 13 December, pp. R4–5.

Dryden, John, et al., trs (1693), *The Satires of Decimus Junius Juvenalis, translated into English Verse … Together with the Satires of Aulus Persius Flaccus*, London, Jacob Tonson.

Dubelaar, C. N. (1986), *South American and Caribbean Petroglyphs*, Dordrecht, Foris Publications.

DuVal, John, trs. (1990), *Tales of Trilussa*, Fayetteville and London, University of Arkansas Press.

Earle, John (1934), *Microcosmography, or A Piece of the World Discovered in Essays and Characters*, London, J. M. Dent.

Eden, P. T., ed. and trs. (1984), *Seneca: Apococolyntosis*, Cambridge, Cambridge University Press (Cambridge Greek and Latin Classics series).

Ellis, Frank H., ed. (1994), *John Wilmot, Earl of Rochester: The Complete Works*, London, Penguin Books.

Erasmus, Desiderius (1993), *Praise of Folly, and Letter to Maarten Van Dorp, 1515*, intro. and notes A. H. T. Levi, trs. Betty Radice, London, Penguin Books.

Evans, G. Blakemore, general ed. (1974), *The Riverside Shakespeare*, Boston, Houghton Mifflin.

Ezell, Margaret J. M., ed. (1993), *The Poems and Prose of Mary, Lady Chudleigh*, New York and Oxford, Oxford University Press.

Fairer, David, and Christine Gerrard, ed. (1999), *Eighteenth-Century Poetry: An Annotated Anthology*, Oxford, Blackwell.

Fava, Claudio G., and Aldo Vigan (1985), *The Films of Federico Fellini*, intro. Federico Fellini, trs. Shula Curto, Secaucus, N.J., Citadel Press.

Fitzgerald, William (2007), *Martial: The World of the Epigram*, Chicago and London, Chicago University Press.

Flanders, Michael, and Donald Swann (1991, 2009), *The Complete Flanders & Swann*, London, Parlophone Records (audio recordings on CD).

Ford, Philip J. (1982), *George Buchanan: Prince of Poets*, Aberdeen, Aberdeen University Press.

Ford, Sarah (2003), "Humor's Role in Imagining America: Ebenezer Cook's 'The Sot-Weed Factor'", *The Southern Literary Journal*, Vol. 35, No. 2 (Spring, 2003), 1–12.

Francis, Philip, trs. (1756), *A Poetical Translation of the Works of Horace*, 4 vols., 6th ed., London, A. Millar.

Francisco, Slinger (Mighty Sparrow), and Fitzroy Alexander (Lord Melody) (1957), "Picong (Duel with Insults at Six Inches)", on *Calypso Kings and Pink Gin*, various artists, recorded by Emory Cook; Stamford CT, Cook Records.

François, Claude (1963), *Si tu veux être heureux*, audio recording, available at https://www.youtube.com/watch?v=nFILAiUghAM, accessed 3 January 2016.

Freeman, Eric F. (1991), "The Identity of Aelfgyva in the Bayeux Tapestry", *Annales de Normandie*, 41e année, no. 2, 117–134.

Freud, Sigmund (2001), trs. James Strachey, *Jokes and Their Relation to the Unconscious*, London, Vintage.

Frye, Northrop (1971), *Anatomy of Criticism: Four Essays*, Princeton: Princeton University Press.

Gander, Mac (2017) "Trimalchio in the White House: The American Dream Comes True", *Vermont Views Magazine*, www.vermontviews.org/vermontviews.org/Guest_Article.html, date posted not stated, accessed 23 March 2017.

[Garth, Samuel] (1741), *The Dispensary. A Poem. In Six Canto's* [sic]. 10th ed., London, J. and R. Tonson.

Geerdink-Jesurun Pinto, N. M. (1952), *Cuentanan de Nanzi*, Curaçao (no publisher stated).

Geerdink-Jesurun Pinto, N. M. (1972), trs. Richard E. Wood, *Nanzi Stories: Curaçao Folklore*, Curaçao, Stichting Wetenschappelijke Bibliotheek.

Gilmore, John [T.] (2006), "The Nunnery Parrot: Gresset's Ver-Vert and his English Translators", in Julia Courtney and Paula James, ed., *The Role of the Parrot in Selected Texts from Ovid to Jean Rhys: Telling a Story from an Alternative Viewpoint*, Lampeter, Edwin Mellen Press, pp. 59–85, 213–215.

Green, Richard Firth(2008), " 'Allas, allas! that evere Love was Sinne!': John Bromyard v. Alice of Bath," *Chaucer Review*, Vol. 42, No. 3, 298–311.

Green, Roger Lancelyn, trs. (1957), *Two Satyr Plays: Euripides' Cyclops and Sophocles' Ichneutai*, Harmondsworth, Penguin Books.

Hall, Joseph (1608), *Characters of Vertues and Vices*, London, Printed by Melch. Bradwood for Eleazar Edgar and Samuel Macham.

Halsband, Robert, and Isobel Grundy, ed. (1993), *Lady Mary Wortley Montagu: Essays and Poems, and Simplicity, A Comedy*, Oxford, Clarendon Press.

Hampden, John, ed. (1967), *Sir Roger de Coverley, by Joseph Addison, Sir Richard Steele and Eustace Budgell*, London, Folio Society.

Harmon, A. M., trs. (1913), *Lucian*, Volume 1, London, Heinemann (Loeb Classical Library).

Hay, William (1755), *Select Epigrams of Martial*, London, R. and J. Dodsley.

Hayes, Evan, and Stephen Nimis, ed. (2015), *Lucian's Dialogues of the Gods: An Intermediate Greek Reader*, n.p., Faenum Publishing.

Healey, John, trs. (1616), *Epictetus Manuall. Cebes Table. Theophrastus Characters*, London, George Purslowe for Edward Blount.

Henderson, John (2004), *Aesop's Human Zoo: Roman Stories about Our Bodies*, Chicago, University of Chicago Press.

Henningsen, Patrick (2015), http://21stcenturywire.com/2015/01/12/je-suis-hypocrite-enemies-of-press-freedom-march-for-charlie-in-paris/, accessed 17 May 2017.

Herzog, Werner, dir. (2010) *Cave of Forgotten Dreams*. DVD, Revolver Entertainment, London, 2011.

Hodgdon, Barbara, ed. (2010), *The Taming of the Shrew* (Arden Shakespeare, Third Series), London, Bloomsbury.

Jenkinson, J. R., ed. and trs. (1980), *Persius: The Satires*, Warminster, Aris and Phillips.

Johnson, Linton Kwesi (2012), *License fi Kill*, video recording of live performance, https://www.youtube.com/watch?v=Hmtfh9vYOvg, accessed 8 May 2017.

Johnson, Samuel (1755–56), *A Dictionary of the English Language*, 2nd ed., 2 vols., London, W. Strahan for J. Knapton [and others].

Jones, Tamera (2012), "Neanderthals May Be Creators of Europe's Oldest Cave Art", Planet Earth Online, 15 June, accessed 30 April 2015.

Jones, William R. (2004), "Brown, Thomas (bap. 1663, d. 1704), writer", *Oxford Dictionary of National Biography*, online ed., accessed 10 April 2015.

Kafka, Franz (2007), *Metamorphosis and Other Stories*, trs. Michael Hofman, London, Penguin Books.

Kinsley, James, ed. (1969), *The Poems of William Dunbar*, Oxford, Clarendon Press.

Kinsman, Robert S., ed. (1969) *John Skelton: Poems*, Oxford, Clarendon Press.

Kishtainy, Khalid (1985), *Arab Political Humour*, London, Quartet.

Lafond, Jean, ed. (1976), *La Rochefoucauld: Réflexions ou Sentences et Maximes morales, suivi de Réflexions diverses et des Maximes de Madame de Sablé*, 2nd ed., Paris, Gallimard.

Lam, George (林子祥) (1984) 丫嗚婆, audio recording, available at https://www.youtube.com/watch?v=ljqP6MhmrlU, accessed 3 January 2016.

Langland, William, trs. (2000), *Piers Plowman: A New Translation of the B-Text*, ed. A. V. C. Schmidt, Oxford: Oxford University Press.

Lao She老舍(1970), *Cat Country: A Satirical Novel of China in the 1930s*, trs. William A. Lyell, Jr., [Columbus], Ohio State University Press.

Lattimore, Richmond, trs. (1951, 1961), *The Iliad of Homer*, Chicago, University of Chicago Press.

Lehrer, Tom (2000), *The Remains of Tom Lehrer*, Los Angeles, Warner Bros./ Rhino. Audio recordings on CD; book with lyrics and additional material.

Lette, Kathy (2014), "A Passion for Books", *Event* (supplement to *The Mail on Sunday*), 3 August 2014, pp. 36–7.

Li Ju-chen (Li Ruzhen, 李汝珍) (1985), *Flowers in the Mirror*, trs. Lin Tai-yi, London: Arena.

Lichtheim, Miriam, ed. and trs. (1975), *Ancient Egyptian Literature: A Book of Readings, Volume 1: The Old and Middle Kingdoms*, Berkeley, University of California Press.

Ligota, Christopher, and Letizia Panizza, ed. (2007), *Lucian of Samosata Vivus et Redivivus*, London and Turin: Warburg Institute, Nino Aragno Editore.

Lloyd-Jones, Hugh, ed. and trs. (1975), *Females of the Species: Semonides on Women*, London, Duckworth.

Low, David (1942), *British Cartoonists, Caricaturists and Comic Artists*, London, William Collins.

McCleese, James Louis (1963), *If You Wanna Be Happy*, audio recording, available at https://www.youtube.com/watch?v=gk3JbTjArUk, accessed 3 January 2016.

McGann, Jerome J., ed. (2008 [1986]), *Lord Byron: The Major Works*, Oxford: Oxford University Press.

McNulty, J. Bard (1980), "The Lady Aelfgyva in the Bayeux Tapestry," *Speculum*, Vol. 55, No. 4 (October 1980), 659–668.

Malvern, Marjorie M. (1983), " 'Who Peyntede the Leon, Tel Me Who?': Rhetorical and Didactic Roles played by an Aesopic Fable in the *Wife of Bath's Prologue*," *Studies in Philology*, Vol. 80, No. 3 (Summer 1983), 238–252.

Marlton, Andrew (2016), as First Dog on the Moon, interview with Matt Groening, "The Simpsons' Matt Groening: 'President Trump? It's Beyond Satire'", *The Guardian* website, https://www.theguardian.com/tv-and-radio/2016/oct/13/the-simpsons-matt-groening-president-trump-its-beyond-satire-first-dog, accessed 11 November 2016.

Marsh, David (1998), *Lucian and the Latins: Humor and Humanism in the Early Renaissance*, Ann Arbor, University of Michigan Press.

Mather, Victoria, "Modern Stereotypes: The Thank-You Refusenik", *Daily Telegraph*, 3 September 2016.

Mayor, A. Hyatt (1971), *Prints & People: A Social History of Printed Pictures*, New York, Metropolitan Museum of Art.

M'Cormick, W. S. (1894), "Sir Thomas Overbury", in Henry Craik, ed., *English Prose: Selections with Critical Introductions by Various Writers and General Introductions to Each Period*, Vol. II, 107–110, London, Macmillan.

Milowicki, Edward J., and Robert Rawdon Wilson (2002), "A Measure for Menippean Discourse: The Example of Shakespeare", *Poetics Today*, Vol. 23, No. 2 (Summer 2002), 291–326.

Money, D. K. (2004), "Holdsworth, Edward (1684–1746), Latin Poet", *Oxford Dictionary of National Biography*, online ed., accessed 11 April 2015.

Moring, Mark (2006), "The McPassion of the Filmmaker", www.christianitytoday.com/ct/2006/marchweb-only/rikswartzwelder.html, accessed 16 May 2017.

Navasky, Victor S. (2014), *The Art of Controversy: Political Cartoons and Their Enduring Power*, New York, Alfred A. Knopf.

Nussbaum, Felicity A. (1984), *The Brink of All We Hate: English Satires on Women 1660–1750*, Lexington, University Press of Kentucky.

Olivelle, Patrick, trs. (1997), *The Pañcatantra: The Book of India's Folk Wisdom*, Oxford, Oxford University Press.

Overbury, Sir Thomas (1614), *A Wife Now the Widdow of Sir Thomas Overburye. Being a Most Exquisite and Singular Poem of the Choice of a Wife. Whereunto Are Added Many Witty Characters and Conceited Newes, Written by Himselfe and Other Learned Gentlemen His Friends*, London, Lawrence Lisle.

Overbury, Sir Thomas (1756), *The Miscellaneous Works in Verse and Prose of Sir Thomas Overbury, Knt. with Memoirs of His Life*, "The Tenth Edition", London, Printed for W. Owen.

Owen, John (1633), *Ioann. Oweni Oxoniensis Angli Epigrammatum Editio Postrema*, Amsterdam, Blaeu.

Pares, Bernard, trs. (1942), *Russian Fables of Ivan Krylov*, Harmondsworth, Penguin Books.

Parker, Brian, ed. (1999), *Ben Jonson: Volpone, or The Fox*, rev. ed., Manchester, Manchester University Press.

Patterson, R. F. (1940, 2009), *Mein Rant: A Summary in Light Verse of "Mein Kampf"*, new ed., New Lanark, Waverley Books.

Philips, John (1720), *The Whole Works of Mr. John Philips, Late Student of Christ-Church, Oxon. [...]*, London, J. Tonson and T. Jauncy.

Pirckheimer, Willibald (1527), Θεοφραστου Χαρακτηρες: *Cum interpretatione Latina per Bilibaldum Pirckeymherum, iam recens aedita*, Nuremburg, Petreius.

Plate, S. Brent (2006), *Blasphemy: Art That Offends*, London, Black Dog Publishing.

Prior, James, ed. (1854), *The Miscellaneous Works of Oliver Goldsmith*, 4 vols., New York, G. P. Putnam and Co.

Purdie, Susan (2006), "'A byrde of Paradyse': Skelton's Speke Parot and the Parrots of its Context," in Julia Courtney and Paula James, ed., *The Role of the Parrot in Selected Texts from Ovid to Jean Rhys: Telling a Story from an Alternative Viewpoint*, Lampeter, Edwin Mellen Press, pp. 33–57, 213.

Purdom, Todd S. (2000), "When Kissinger Won the Nobel Peace Prize, Satire Died", *The Guardian*, 31 July 2000, www.theguardian.com/culture/2000/jul/31/artsfeatures1, accessed 17 November 2014.

Rattray, R. Sutherland, ed. (1916), *Ashanti Proverbs*, Oxford, Clarendon Press.

Rattray, R. S., trs. (1930), *Akan-Ashanti Folk-Tales*, Oxford, Clarendon Press.

Ricks, Christopher, ed. (1987), *The Poems of Tennyson* (Longman annotated English poets), 2nd ed., 3 vols., Harlow, Longman.

Rudd, Niall, ed. (1981), *Johnson's Juvenal: London and the Vanity of Human Wishes*, Bristol, Bristol Classical Press.

Sautel, Petrus Justus (1728), *Lusus Poetici Allegorici, sive Elegiae oblectandis animis, et moribus informandis accommodatae*, Trento, Johannes Baptista Paronius.

Schneider, David (2014), "Facebook's 'Satire' Alerts Rather Spoil The Punchline", *Daily Telegraph*, 19 August 2014.

Screech, M. A., trs. and ed. (2006), *Rabelais: Gargantua and Pantagruel*, London, Penguin Books.

[Sheridan, Thomas, trs.] (1739), *The Satires of Juvenal Translated: With Explanatory and Classical Notes, Relating to the Laws and Customs of the Greeks and Romans*, London, D. Browne.

Slattery, Jon (2010), blog entry on Steve Bell, 2 November, http://jonslattery. blogspot.co.uk/2010/11/steve-bell-why-i-put-cameron-in-condom. html, accessed 25 November 2014.

Slavs and Tatars (2012), "When Satire Conquered Iran", *NYR Daily, New York Review of Books*, online ed., 18 September, accessed 16 January 2015.

Smeed, J. W. (1985), *The Theophrastan "Character": The History of a Literary Genre*, Oxford, New York, Clarendon Press.

Smith, Sydney (2015), "Financial Times Scrubs Claim Charlie Hebdo was 'Stupid' to Publish Muhammad Cartoons", iMediaEthics, 8 January 2015, www.imediaethics.org/financial-times-scrubs-claim-charlie-hebdo-was-stupid-to-publish-muhammad-cartoons/#sthash.iYn7sNMc. dpuf, accessed 17 May 2017.

Smith, Yancy W. (2012), "Bible Translation and Ancient Visual Culture: Divine Nakedness and the 'Circumcision of Christ' in Colossians 2:11", in Aliou Cissé Niang and Carolyn Osiek, ed., *Text, Image and Christians in the Graeco-Roman World: A Festschrift in Honor of David Lee Balch*, Eugene, Oregon, Pickwick Publications, pp. 320–341.

Smollett, Tobias (1998), *The Expedition of Humphry Clinker*, ed. Lewis M. Knapp, rev. Paul-Gabriel Boucé, Oxford, Oxford University Press (Oxford World's Classics series).

Sorene, Paul (2016), "Robert Crumb Flushes 'Evil' Donald Trump down the Toilet in This 1989 Comic", posted on Flashbak [sic], 21 June, http:// flashbak.com/robert-crumb-flushes-evil-donald-trump-down-the-toilet-in-this-1989-comic-nsfw-62877/, accessed 23 March 2017.

Southey, Robert (1821), *A Vision of Judgement*, London, Longman, Hurst, Rees, Orme, and Brown.

Sowards, J. Kelley, intro. and notes, and Paul Pascal, trs. (1968), *The Julius Exclusus of Erasmus*, Bloomington, Indiana University Press.

Sparrow, John (1977), review of Reuben A. Brower, *Mirror on Mirror: Translation, Imitation, Parody* (Harvard University Press, 1974), *Classical Review*, New Series, Vol, 27, No. 1, 96–8.

Spurr, John (2004), "Earle, John (1598x1601–1665)", *Oxford Dictionary of National Biography*, Oxford University Press; online ed., accessed 19 Aug 2016.

Starr, H. W., and J. R. Hendrickson, ed. (1966, rev. 1972), *The Complete Poems of Thomas Gray, English, Latin, and Greek*, Oxford, Clarendon Press.

Stelfox, Dave (2013), "Ali Ferzat, cartoonist in exile", *The Guardian*, 19 August, https://www.theguardian.com/world/2013/aug/19/ali-ferzat-cartoonist-exile-syria, accessed 16 May 2017.

[Stronach, George] (c. 1883), *Gladstone & Co.*, Edinburgh and London, William Blackwood and Sons.

Sullivan, J. P., and A. J. Boyle (1996), *Martial in English*, London, Penguin Books.

Sutherland, James, ed. (1963), *Alexander Pope: The Dunciad*, 3rd edition, London, Methuen; New Haven, Yale University Press (Twickenham Edition of the Poems of Alexander Pope, Volume V).

Swain, Simon (2007), "The Three Faces of Lucian", in Christopher Ligota and Letizia Panizza, ed., *Lucian of Samosata Vivus et Redivivus*, London and Turin: Warburg Institute, Nino Aragno Editore, pp. 17–44.

Swartzwelder, Rik, and Benjamin Hershleder (2006), *The McPassion*, online copy of original film at http://nofatclips.com/02006/03/11/passion/The%20McPassion.mp4, accessed, 16 May 2017.

Swift, Jonathan (1999), *A Tale of a Tub and Other Works*, ed. Angus Ross and David Woolley, Oxford, Oxford University Press (Oxford World's Classics series).

Swift, Jonathan (2005), *Gulliver's Travels*, ed. and intro. Claude Rawson, notes Ian Higgins, Oxford, Oxford University Press (Oxford World's Classics series).

Taylor, David Francis (2012), "The Disenchanted Island: A Political History of *The Tempest*, 1760–1830," *Shakespeare Quarterly*, Vol. 63, No. 4 (Winter 2012), 487–517.

Temple, Olivia, and Robert Temple, trs. (1998), *Aesop: The Complete Fables*, London, Penguin Books.

Thion, Edmond, trs. (1875), *Julius: Dialogue entre Saint Pierre et le Pape Jules II à la porte du Paradis (1513), Attribué à Érasme, à Fausto Andrelini et plus communément à Ulrich de Hutten*, Paris, Isidore Liseux.

Thompson, C. R. (1939–40), "The Translations of Lucian by Erasmus and St Thomas More," *Revue belge de philologie et d'histoire*, tome 18, fasc. 4, 855–881; tome 19, 5–35.

Thompson, E. P., and Marian Sugden, eds. (1989), *"The Thresher's Labour" by Stephen Duck, "The Woman's Labour" by Mary Collier: Two Eighteenth Century Poems*, London, Merlin Press.

Thorpe, Lewis, ed. (1973), *The Bayeux Tapestry and the Norman Invasion*, London, Folio Society.

Thurman, Judith (2008), "First Impressions: What Does the World's Oldest Art Say about Us?" *The New Yorker*, 23 June, www.newyorker.com/magazine/2008/06/23/first-impressions, accessed 29 April 2015.

Tillotson, Geoffrey, ed. (1962, 1972), *Alexander Pope: The Rape of the Lock and Other Poems*, 3rd ed., London, Methuen; New Haven, Yale University Press (Twickenham Edition of the Poems of Alexander Pope, Volume II).

Ton-That, Thanh-Vân, ed. (2007), *Molière: Les Femmes Savantes*, Petits Classiques Larousse, Paris, Larousse.

Turner, Margaret (1953), "The Influence of La Bruyère on the *Tatler* and the *Spectator*", *Modern Language Review*, Vol. 48, No 1 (January), 10–16.

Vissac [J. A.] (1862), *De la Poésie Latine en France au Siècle de Louis XIV*, Paris: Aug. Durand.

Walsh, P. G., ed. (1997a) *Thirty Poems from the Carmina Burana*, London, Bristol Classical Press (first published 1976).

Walsh, P. G., trs. (1997b, 1999), *Petronius: The Satyricon*, Oxford, Oxford University Press (Oxford World's Classics series).

Warburton, Nigel (2009), *Free Speech: A Very Short Introduction*, Oxford, Oxford University Press.

Ward, Patrick (2011), "Private Eye: The First 50 Years", *Socialist Worker*, 1 November, https://socialistworker.co.uk/art/26069/Private+Eye%3A+The+First+50+Years, accessed 17 May 2015.

Warmington, E. H., ed. and trs. (1967), *Remains of Old Latin*, rev. ed., 4 vols., Cambridge, MA, Harvard University Press; London, William Heinemann (Loeb Classical Library series.)

Watling, E. F., trs. (1965), *Plautus: The Pot of Gold and Other plays*, Harmondsworth, Penguin.

Watson, David, and Samuel Patrick, ed. and trs. (1760), *The Works of Horace, Translated into English Prose, as Near as the Propriety of the Two Languages Will Admit*, 4th ed., London, C. Hitch and L. Hawes (et al.).

Watson, Lindsay, and Patricia Watson, ed. (2014), *Juvenal: Satire 6*, Cambridge, Cambridge University Press.

Weinbrot, Howard D. (1988), *Eighteenth-Century Satire: Essays on Text and Context from Dryden to Peter Pindar*, Cambridge, Cambridge University Press.

Weisman, Ze'ev (1998), *Political Satire in the Bible*, Atlanta, Georgia, Scholars Press.

Wender, Dorothea, trs. (1973), *Hesiod: Theogony, Works and Days; Theognis: Elegies*, Harmondsworth, Penguin Books.

Woiski, Max, Jr. (1963) *Want je bent nog niet gelukkig met een mooie vrouw*, audio recording, available at https://www.youtube.com/watch?v=pt2klX6JQDg, accessed 3 January 2016.

Wood, H. Harvey, ed., (1958), *The Poems and Fables of Robert Henrsyson, Schoolmaster of Dunfermline*, 2nd ed., Edinburgh, Oliver and Boyd.

Wright, Robin (2015), "A Saudi Whipping", *The New Yorker*, 9 January, www.newyorker.com/news/news-desk/saudi-whipping; accessed 17 May 2017.

Wright, Thomas (1839), *The Political Songs of England, from the Reign of John to That of Edward II*, London, Camden Society.

Wu Ching-Tzu (Wu Jingzi吴敬梓) (1957), trs. Yang Hsien-Yi and Gladys Yang, *The Scholars*, Peking (Beijing), Foreign Languages Press.

Xu Bing徐冰 (2013), *Book from the Ground: From Point to Point*, North Adams, MA, Massachusetts Museum of Contemporary Art, and Cambridge, MA, MIT Press.

Yan Lianke阎连科(2007), *Serve the People!* trs. Julia Lovell, London, Constable.

Yarbrough, Oliver Larry (2012), "The Shadow of an Ass: On Reading the Alexamenos Graffito," in Aliou Cissé Niang and Carolyn Osiek, ed., *Text, Image and Christians in the Graeco-Roman World: A Festschrift in Honor of David Lee Balch*, Eugene, Oregon, Pickwick Publications, pp. 239–254.

Ynetnews (2006), "ADL: Concerned over Borat's Depiction of anti-Semitism", 30 September, www.ynetnews.com/articles/0,7340,L-3309866,00.html, accessed 31 July 2017.

Yunck, John A. (1988), "Satire", in John A. Alford, ed., *A Companion to Piers Plowman*, Berkeley, University of California Press, pp. 135–154.

Index